T0301272

Carbon Pricing

CRITICAL ISSUES IN ENVIRONMENTAL TAXATION

Series Editors: Larry Kreiser, *Cleveland State University, USA*, Hope Ashiabor, *Macquarie University, Australia* and Janet E. Milne, *Vermont Law School, USA*

The *Critical Issues in Environmental Taxation* series provides insights and analysis on environmental taxation issues on an international basis and explores detailed theories for achieving environmental goals through fiscal policy. Each book in the series contains pioneering and thought-provoking contributions by the world's leading environmental tax scholars who respond to the diverse challenges posed by environmental sustainability.

Previous volumes in the series:

Original book published by CCH Incorporated

Volumes I–IV published by Richmond Law Publishers

Volumes V–VIII published by Oxford University Press

Titles in the series include:

Carbon Pricing

Design, Experiences and Issues

Edited by

Larry Kreiser

Professor Emeritus of Accounting, Cleveland State University, USA

Mikael Skou Andersen

Professor of Environmental Policy Analysis, Aarhus University, Denmark

Birgitte Egelund Olsen

Professor of Law, Aarhus University, Denmark

Stefan Speck

Project Manager, European Environment Agency (EEA), Denmark

Janet E. Milne

Professor of Law, Vermont Law School, USA

Hope Ashiabor

Associate Professor of Law, Macquarie University, Australia

CRITICAL ISSUES IN ENVIRONMENTAL TAXATION, VOLUME XV

 Edward Elgar
PUBLISHING

Cheltenham, UK • Northampton, MA, USA

Published by
Edward Elgar Publishing Limited
The Lypiatts
15 Lansdown Road
Cheltenham
Glos GL50 2JA
UK

Edward Elgar Publishing, Inc.
William Pratt House
9 Dewey Court
Northampton
Massachusetts 01060
USA

A catalogue record for this book
is available from the British Library

Library of Congress Control Number: 2015935905

This book is available electronically in the **Elgar**online
Law subject collection
DOI 10.4337/9781785360237

ISBN 978 1 78536 022 0 (cased)
ISBN 978 1 78536 023 7 (eBook)

Typeset by Servis Filmsetting Ltd, Stockport, Cheshire
Printed and bound in Great Britain by T.J. International Ltd, Padstow

Contents

Figures

Tables

Editorial review board

The 14 chapters in this book have been brought to publication with the help of an editorial review board dedicated to peer review. The 19 members of the board are committed to the field of environmental taxation and are active participants in environmental taxation events around the world.

Birgitte Egelund Olsen
Aarhus University, Denmark

Sven Rudolph
Kyoto University, Japan

Stefan Speck
European Environment Agency (EEA), Denmark

Natalie Stoianoff
University of Technology, Sydney, Australia

Rahmat Tavallali
Walsh University, USA

Walter Wang
University of San Diego, USA

Stefan E. Weishaar
University of Groningen, the Netherlands

Yan Xu
The Chinese University of Hong Kong, Hong Kong

Contributors

Bahn-Walkowiak, Bettina, Wuppertal Institute for Climate, Environment and Energy, Germany

Brůha, Jan, Kolin Institute of Technology, Czech Republic

Brůhová-Foltýnová, Hana, Kolin Institute of Technology, Czech Republic

Butcher, Bill, The University of New South Wales, Australia

Calaf Forn, Maria, ENT Environment and Management, Spain

Chalifour, Nathalie, University of Ottawa, Canada

Cheng, Selina, The University of New South Wales, Australia

Croci, Edoardo, IEFE – Bocconi University, Italy

Elgie, Stewart, University of Ottawa, Canada

Guglyuvatyy, Evgeny, Southern Cross University, Australia

Jofra Sora, Marta, ENT Environment and Management, Spain

Kettner, Claudia, Austrian Institute of Economic Research (WIFO), Austria

Kratena, Kurt, Austrian Institute of Economic Research (WIFO), Austria

Meyer, Eike, GIZ, Germany

Meyer, Ina, Austrian Institute of Economic Research (WIFO), Austria

Onoda, Shinji, Hosei University, Japan, Japan Center for a Sustainable Environment and Society (JACSES), Japan

Papy, Jacques, Université du Québec à Montréal (UQAM), Canada

Pedersen, Thomas F., University of Victoria, Canada

Píša, Vítězslav, Kolin Institute of Technology, Czech Republic

Puig Ventosa, Ignasi, ENT Environment and Management, Spain

Ravazzi Douvan, Aldo, Italian Ministry of Environment, Italy

Sargl, Manfred, Bundeswehr University Munich, Germany

Schlegelmilch, Kai, Green Budget Europe (GBE), Belgium

Sommer, Mark Wolfgang, Austrian Institute of Economic Research (WIFO), Austria

Stoianoff, Natalie P., University of Technology, Sydney, Australia

ten Brink, Patrick, Institute for European Environmental Policy (IEEP), Belgium

Weishaar, Stefan E., University of Groningen, the Netherlands

Wilts, Henning, Wuppertal Institute for Climate, Environment and Energy, Germany

Withana, Sirini, Institute for European Environmental Policy (IEEP), Belgium

Wittmann, Günter, Public Servant, Regensburg, Germany

Wolfsteiner, Andreas, Public Servant, Regensburg, Germany

Foreword

'The market is a splendid servant, but a terrible master' chuckled our former colleague at Aarhus University, Svend Auken, who was Denmark's longest-serving Minister of Environment and Energy and the instigator of significant environmental tax reforms in the 1990s.

His quote comes to mind as we enter the seventh year of the global financial crisis, where governments around the world continue to grapple with economic imbalances, banking mismanagement and severe unemployment challenges. While the 'boom and bust' business cycles we are suffering from are not exactly mastering the economy, they have again proven their ability to influence negatively the conditions for human life and well-being, as well as the capacity for sustainable management of our natural environment.

There can be different interpretations as to whether it was the absence of regulation or just badly conceived interventions that allowed the market collapses that have taken place but, in looking forward, new and better ways must be found to get the horse in front of the carriage and hedge damaging market forces.

In this context, it is promising that the call for pricing of carbon to help contain climate change and provide a way to steer away from the use of fossil fuels has been winning wider recognition. Lawrence Summers, a former United States Secretary of the Treasury, who was influential in deregulating the banking system, is now counted among those who publicly is expressing 'no doubt that starting from the current zero tax rate on carbon, increased taxation would be desirable' (*Financial Times* 4 January 2015).

Volume XV of *Critical Issues in Environmental Taxation* reflects on and further develops this ongoing and worthwhile global debate on how to design carbon pricing and use the financial proceeds in the best possible way for society.

We gratefully acknowledge support for the presentation of these studies from the European Cooperation in Science and Technology (COST) action 'Innovations in Climate Governance' (INOGOV).

Mikael Skou Andersen
Professor of Environmental Policy Analysis
Aarhus University, Denmark

Preface

Over the past year, the world has witnessed a significant downward adjustment in fossil fuel prices. This downward adjustment will have negative implications for the environment. Lower fossil fuel prices will mean less attention is paid to energy efficiency and less interest being displayed by investors in making investments in renewable energy projects. With these negative developments, it is more important than ever to promote the benefits of environmental sustainability through well-documented research studies. This is the mission of *Critical Issues in Environmental Taxation*.

Volume XV of *Critical Issues* contains 14 chapters on environmental issues involving carbon pricing: design and experiences. These chapters have been prepared by environmental experts and are worthy of serious consideration by policymakers around the world.

Larry Kreiser, Lead Editor
Mikael Skou Andersen, Co-Editor
Birgitte Egelund Olsen, Co-Editor
Stefan Speck, Co-Editor
Janet E. Milne, Co-Editor
Hope Ashiabor, Co-Editor
August 2015

Abbreviations

ACPRS	Australian Carbon Pollution Reduction Scheme
ATPA	Andean Trade Preference Act
BAM	border adjustment measure
BC	British Columbia
BC-CT	British Columbia Carbon Tax
CAL-ETS	California Cap-and-Trade Program
CARB	Californian's Air Resource Board
CBERA	Caribbean Basin Economic Recovery Act
CDM	Clean Development Mechanism
CER	Certified Emission Reductions
CHP	combined heat and power plants
CITSS	Compliance Instrument Tracking Service System
CO_2	carbon dioxide
DPJ	Democratic Party of Japan
EEA	European Environment Agency
EFR	Environmental Fiscal Reform
EMU	European Monetary Union
EP	European Parliament
ERC	Early Reduction Credits
ERF	Emissions Reduction Fund
ERU	Emission Reduction Unit
ETD	energy taxation directive
ETR	ecological/environmental tax reform
ETS	emissions trading system
EU	European Union
EUA	European Allowance
EUAA	European Aviation Allowance
EU ETS	European Union Emissions Trading System
FIT	Feed-in-Tariff
FY	fiscal year
GATS	General Agreement on Trade in Services
GATT	General Agreement on Tariffs and Trade
GDP	gross domestic product
GHG	greenhouse gas

GNI	gross national income
GSP	Generalized System of Preferences
IEEP	Institute for European Environmental Policy
IenM	Ministry of Infrastructure and the Environment of the Netherlands
INDC	intended nationally determined contributions
IPCC	Intergovernmental Panel on Climate Change
JI	Joint Implementation
LDC	least developed countries
LDP	Liberal Democratic Party
MAFF	Ministry of Agriculture, Forestry and Fisheries
METI	Ministry of Economy, Trade and Industry
MIAC	Ministry of Internal Affairs and Communications
MOE	Ministry of the Environment
NAP	National Allocation Plan
NGO	nongovernmental organization
NREAP	national renewable energy action plan
OECD	Organisation for Economic Co-operation and Development
PPM	production and processing method
QC-ETS	Québec Commission Emissions Trading System
RGGI	Regional Greenhouse Gas Initiative
RoC	rest of Canada
SDP	Social Democratic Party
UNEP	United Nations Environment Programme
UNFCCC	United Nations Framework Convention on Climate Change
VAT	value added tax
WCI	Western Climate Initiative

PART I

Carbon taxes and emissions trading

1.   A template for the world: British Columbia's carbon tax shift

Thomas F. Pedersen and Stewart Elgie

INTRODUCTION

Throughout the nineteenth and most of the twentieth centuries, the Mountain Pine Bark Beetle, a relatively innocuous five millimetre-long member of the weevil family, was known to attack and kill a limited number of mature pine trees annually in the forests of British Columbia (BC). That changed in the late 1990s when the beetle launched an assault on British Columbia's pine forests that by the mid-2000s had become 'the most severe bark beetle infestation in recorded North American history.'[1]

By 2012, approximately one-third of British Columbia's 55 million hectares of forest had been afflicted by the pine bark beetle. Over 50 per cent of the stock of commercially valuable pine was dead, representing some 710 million m^3 of wood. The harvest and processing of a cubic metre of timber in BC yields some \$110–\$130 to provincial GDP;[2] hence, even though it was possible to harvest some of the dead pine trees, the net economic impact of the pine bark beetle has been severe.

As concern about the economic, social and environmental implications of the beetle epidemic grew, the Government of BC accepted that the beetle outbreak had been facilitated by warming associated with greenhouse gas emissions. The strong-willed Premier of the day, Gordon Campbell, decided that BC had to take steps to contribute to climate change mitigation by reducing fossil fuel use. He heeded economists who advised that by assigning a slowly rising cost to emissions demand for fossil fuels would decline and the economy would have time to adjust without serious dislocation. Campbell and his government wasted no time; BC's Finance Minister announced in her February 2008 budget that a carbon tax was to be put in place, and five months later it took effect: on 1 July 2008, British Columbia became the first jurisdiction in North America to impose a legislated, progressively increasing, broad-spectrum, revenue-neutral carbon emissions tax, thanks in part to the activities of a half-centimetre-long bark beetle that was busily carving a swath of destruction through the pine forests of BC's interior.

This chapter describes the structure of the tax, its apparent positive impact on reducing the consumption of fossil fuels in BC, and implications for emissions mitigations policy that we believe warrant serious consideration by other national and sub-national jurisdictions.

STRUCTURE AND APPLICATION OF THE TAX

Seven key elements define the structure and application of the tax:

1. The tax is comprehensive. It is applied to all greenhouse gas emissions generated by combustion of fossil fuels purchased in the Province, with the exceptions of aviation fuel used for out-of-province flights and fuel used in interjurisdictional cruise ships, since most of the combustion of such fuels would occur outside BC's borders.
2. Tax rates were scheduled for five years. The initial rate established in 2008 was relatively modest at $10 (CAD) per tonne of CO_2 equivalent (CO_2e) emitted. Importantly, the schedule required the tax to increase by $5 per tonne on 1 July of each of the next four years, to $30/t CO_2e/year on 1 July 2012. It has been fixed at that rate since. The rationale for the slow upward ramp in the tariff was that it would encourage gradual adjustment in fossil fuel use both by industry and private consumers while minimizing economic dislocation. $5/t/year equates to a 1.1 cent annual increase in the cost of a litre of regular gasoline, a rate of increase that was judged to be acceptable to average consumers.
3. Higher carbon fuels are taxed at a higher rate, as shown in Table 1.1. This design feature ensures that relative externality costs of each fuel are fairly assessed.
4. The tax was mandated to be revenue neutral. Every penny of revenue was required by law to be returned to the residents of British Columbia through reductions in personal, small business and corporate income taxes and some direct fiscal transfers. Thus, the carbon tax in reality represented a tax shift, not new revenue. This design element: (a) strongly encouraged conservation – those individuals or companies that reduced fossil fuel consumption benefitted with a lower overall tax burden, since income taxes were reduced regardless; (b) erased any opportunity to describe the initiative as a 'tax grab'; and (c) minimized or avoided an overall adverse effect on the economy, by lowering other taxes.

Table 1.1 *British Columbia carbon tax rates for selected fuels as of 1 July 2008 and as of 1 July 2012, following four years of successive increases*[3]

Fuel	Units	2008 Tax Rate	2012 Tax Rate
Gasoline	¢/litre	2.41	6.67
Diesel[4]	¢/litre	2.76	7.67
Natural gas	¢/cubic metre	1.90	5.70
Propane	¢/litre	1.53	4.62
Coal, high heat value	$/tonne	20.79	62.31
Coal, low heat value	$/tonne	17.72	53.31

Note: The 2008 and 2012 rates are calculated on the basis of $10 and $30 (CAD) per tonne of CO_2 equivalent released via combustion, respectively.

5. Social equity was accommodated via two provisions: (a) on 1 January 2008, six months before the carbon tax took effect, personal income tax rates in BC were reduced by 5 per cent on each of the lowest two tiers of BC's progressive income tax rate schedule. As a result, BC now has the lowest personal income taxes in Canada for anyone earning up to $122,000 in net taxable income; (b) a 'Low Income Climate Action Tax Credit'[5] was established to offset the impact of the carbon tax. The credit is non-taxable and paid quarterly, with the current annual maximum being $115.50 per adult and $34.50 per child ($115.50 for the first child in a single parent family). The credit diminishes by 2 per cent of net annual family income over a current threshold of $37,589. The threshold is adjusted upward annually to allow for inflation.
6. General corporate income tax rates were reduced from 12 per cent to 11 per cent on 1 July 2008, to 10.5 per cent on 1 January 2010, and to 10 per cent on 1 January 2011[6] taking them to a level amongst the lowest in the OECD countries. The Small Business Corporate Tax rate, which applied to companies with annual business income up to $400,000 was reduced from 3.5 to 2.5 per cent on 1 December 2008, a net reduction of nearly 29 per cent.
7. Bureaucratic requirements were minimized. On all fossil fuels other than natural gas, the carbon tax built upon existing fuel tax collection mechanisms that require tax to be collected and remitted at the wholesale level.[7] For natural gas, the retailer collects and remits the tax.[8] This approach greatly minimizes administrative and compliance costs.

APPARENT IMPACT OF THE CARBON TAX ON EMISSIONS

Methods

Changes in fossil fuel use since 1 July 2008 were assessed using fuel volume data from Statistics Canada through December 2013. Annual results are computed for the period 1 July to 30 June, to isolate better the effects of annual increases in the carbon tax rate that took effect on 1 July of each year. The data are thus reported for hybrid years (for example, 2008–2009). BC consumption patterns are compared with the rest of Canada, which helps to factor out any effects resulting from GDP changes or other common impacts like the recession of 2008–2009. Population change influences are removed by reporting the data on a per capita basis.

Volumetric fuel use figures were taken from Statistics Canada's dataset 'Supply and Disposition of Refined Petroleum Products (CANSIM 134-004)'. Population data came from CANSIM 051-0001 and GDP figures from CANSIM 379-0030. Note that GDP results are given by calendar year, rather than 1 July to 30 June year, due to constraints in data availability.

Inclusion of natural gas in the analysis required combining two Statistics Canada datasets (Petroleum Products, and Sales of Natural Gas / CANSIM 129-0003), and converting all fuel figures from volume to energy (terajoules) to enable comparability (since natural gas has very high volumes per unit of energy compared with other fuels).

A few values were missing for certain petroleum products for select months from March to June 2013, due to recent changes in data sharing agreements between Statistics Canada and particular companies. To fill the gaps, values for the missing months were estimated using standard methods in consultation with Statistics Canada, and total fuel sales for 2012–2013 were estimated using a Kalman filter algorithm.[9] Given that data were missing for only a few months of one year, we have confidence that the final results are accurate within a very small margin of error. All data are available from Dr Elgie upon request.

Results

Since the midpoint of 2008 when the carbon tax was first imposed, per capita consumption of fossil fuels in British Columbia has fallen by just over 16 per cent (Table 1.2) in absolute terms, and by just over 19 per cent relative to the rest of Canada (RoC). The contrast between BC and the

Table 1.2   *Per cent changes in per capita consumption of petroleum*
products (gasoline, diesel, fuel oil and propane) in British
Columbia and the rest of Canada between 1 July 2007 and
30 June 2013

	2007/08–2008/09	2008/09–2009/10	2009/10–2010/11	2010/11–2011/12	2011/12–2012/13	2007/08–2012/13
British Columbia	−3.5	−6.7	−1.3	−6.2	0.2	−16.1
Rest of Canada	−2.5	−1.5	6.8	−1.7	1.7	3.0
Difference	−1.0	−5.2	−8.1	−4.5	−1.5	−19.1

Note: With the exception of the final column, the data are reported as year-to-year
differences between 12-month July through June averages.

RoC is stark. BC outperformed the RoC every year since the carbon tax
came in, in terms of changes in per capita fuel use, including between
2011/12 and 2012/13, which includes the 12 months after the carbon tax
was frozen.

   This analysis begs the key question: can the clear decline in both absolute
and relative fossil fuel consumption in BC since mid-2008 be unequivocally
attributed to the carbon tax? The simple answer is no, attribution is not
unequivocal. But a closer examination of the data and of other plausible
drivers suggests strongly that the tax is indeed responsible for at least a
large portion of BC's gains.

   The tax was introduced just as the severe global recession of 2008–2009
struck the world economy. British Columbia was hit hard by the recession:
provincial GDP fell from an average annual growth rate of 3.49 per cent
over the 2002–2007 period to 0.97 per cent in 2008 and −2.58 per cent
in 2009, before recovering in 2010 to +3.3 per cent.[10] Undoubtedly, the
decline in industrial production and demand for the Province's raw materials had a negative impact on fuel use during the depth of the recession.
But other provinces went through a similar downturn and comparing their
fuel consumption data with those in BC helps to normalize out the impact
of the recession while casting the spotlight on the possible influence of
the carbon tax. The difference data in Table 1.2 compare the change in
annual per capita consumption of fossil fuel products in British Columbia
since 2007/08 with the same variable aggregated over the RoC. In two of
the three post-recession years, per capita fuel consumption increased in
the RoC while it declined in BC. Over the course of the five years of data
tabulated in Table 1.2, per capita fossil fuel use in BC fell by just over
19 per cent relative to the rest of the country. The contrast is dramatic, and

signals clearly that the recession cannot be blamed for the decline in fuel consumption in BC relative to the rest of Canada in the years following the introduction of the tax.

Perhaps other influences exclusive of the carbon tax can explain the declining fuel use in British Columbia. Two such candidates are: (a) access to cheaper gas in Washington State, recognizing that a significant proportion of BC residents live within 50 km of the border; and (b) continuation of an independent downward trend that began before the carbon tax was introduced. We consider these in turn.

It is a fact that traffic between BC and Washington has increased substantially since 2008, a cross-border response that most likely reflects the very high value of the Canadian dollar from 2009 to 2013 and the lower cost of most consumer goods in the United States. And while shopping south of the border, it is quite likely that many BC residents filled up the gas tanks in their cars. Two independent researchers,[11] one in Canada and one in the US, have recently estimated that this could account for only a 1 to 2 per cent drop in fuel purchases in BC, a small fraction of the ~16 per cent overall decline witnessed since 2008 (Table 1.2). Moreover there has been a decline in use in recent years of every type of fuel covered by BC's tax policy, relative to the rest of Canada (Figure 1.1), and with the exceptions of gasoline and diesel, these fuels are not subject to cross-border shopping. We conclude that cross-border purchases can explain only a small fraction of BC's dramatic drop in fuel use since the advent of the carbon tax.

A second possible explanation for BC's declining fossil-fuel consumption could be that it is the continuation of a pre-existing trend, which if true, would suggest that the carbon tax was less effective or even ineffective. To test this, we looked at the sales data for all fuels subject to the tax back to 2000 (Figure 1.2). British Columbians did use less fuel per capita relative to the rest of Canada prior to 1 July 2008, in part because BC enjoys an abundance of carbon-free hydropower. But as Figure 1.2 illustrates, per capita fuel use in BC was actually rising slightly (by ~1 per cent per year) compared with the rest of Canada between 2000 and 2008. Following imposition of the carbon tax on 1 July 2008, fuel use in BC fell by ~4 per cent per year compared with the rest of Canada. This before-and-after shift in the data is clear, and argues against the possibility that the decline in fuel consumption post-tax was simply a continuation of a pre-existing trend.

Behavioural Implications

Although the data clearly show that per capita fossil-fuel consumption has declined in recent years as the carbon tax escalated, we cannot

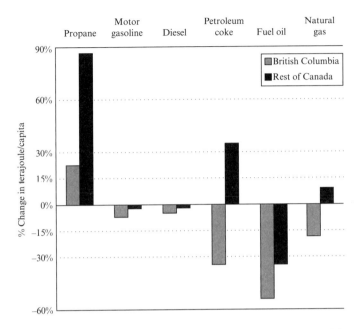

Note: The steep decline in sales of fuel oil is attributed to refineries in BC switching production from 'heavy fuel oil' to ultra-low sulfur diesel in response to new marine shipping and domestic transportation regulations on sulfur content of fuels.

Source: Figure produced by Sustainable Prosperity, University of Ottawa.

Figure 1.1   *Percentage change in sales of specific fuels in British Columbia, reported as terajoules per capita over the six years beginning 1 July 2007*

conclude with 100 per cent confidence that the tax on its own is the reason. Correlation is not enough. BC introduced other initiatives in 2008 designed to reduce emissions, including for example the introduction of a Renewable and Low Carbon Fuel Standard (RLCFS).[12] But while the RLCFS can contribute to an *emissions* decline, given that it purposely reduces the fossil carbon content of fuels, it does not send a price signal that would reduce fuel-*volume* demand. The carbon tax does send such a signal, however, and its impact is borne out by fuel sales data. Statistics Canada data show that per capita sales of motor gasoline in British Columbia fell from an average of 1.121 m³ in the 2000–2007 time span to 1.037 m³ over the 2008–2013 period, a decline of 7.5 per cent. Over the same two time periods, the rest of Canada witnessed an increase in sales of motor gasoline from 1.294 to 1.316 m³/per capita (+1.7 per cent). We suggest that the carbon tax

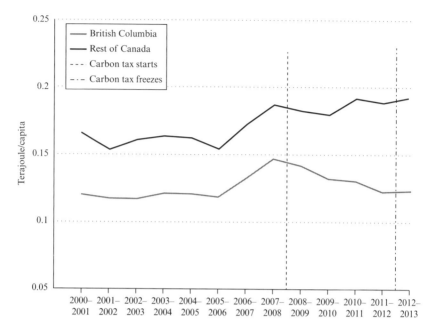

Note: The vertical dashed line indicates the date of imposition of the carbon tax while the vertical dashed/dotted line marks the beginning of the tax freeze plateau (the tax has been fixed at $30/tonne CO_2e since 1 July 2012).

Source: Figure produced by Sustainable Prosperity, University of Ottawa.

Figure 1.2   *Aggregate annual per capita fuel sales in BC (grey) and the rest of Canada (black) from 1 July 2000 to 30 June 2013*

contributed to this contrast. BC also introduced in 2008 a requirement for all provincial government institutions to become carbon neutral by 2012. That requirement was met in 2011, in small part through energy conservation measures and in large part with the purchase of offsets.[13] Thus, while it may have attuned the population to the need to take climate action, it had little actual impact on fossil fuel sales.

While we can reasonably assume that the carbon tax played a significant role in encouraging lower fuel use, quantifying such an impact is difficult. The tax may, for example, have stimulated an adoption rate for hybrid-electric vehicles that is more than twice the average for Canada – between 2007 and 2010, hybrid sales in BC grew by 31 per cent per year, faster than elsewhere in the country.[14] But hybrid vehicles sales still comprise less than 2 per cent of all vehicles sold in BC so their aggregate impact on fuel economy is judged to be small.[15] Public transit ridership in BC grew by nearly 12 per cent between 2007/08 and 2011/12[16] and while it is tempting to point to an influence of the carbon tax in promoting such growth, transit service was also expanded during this period and that confounds attribution of increased ridership to the tax. Moreover improvements to building codes, including better insulation standards, and building retrofits supported with provincial government rebates have also reduced consumption of fossil fuels used for space heating in BC. The presence of a carbon tax makes such improvements more attractive but it is not possible to quantify its proportionate impact relative to other policies like retrofit rebates.

Better quantification is possible, however, using an econometric approach to explore the supposition that tax-driven price changes generate distinct responses in demand when compared with equivalent market-based price movements. Nicholas Rivers and Brandon Schaufele at the University of Ottawa recently conducted detailed econometric analyses in examining this hypothesis, and noted that, 'the BC carbon tax generated demand response that is 4.9 times larger than is attributable to an equivalent change in the carbon tax-exclusive price'.[17] This differential behavioural response is judged by these authors to be causal and is attributed to the high visibility of the tax, the 'relief of guilt' associated with paying an 'environmental tax', and possibly to resentment of free-ridership, wherein since every fuel consumer pays the carbon tax, environmental responsibility practiced by one, for example by driving less, cannot be subverted by another who cares less and drives more when congestion eases. Of these options, the high visibility of the tax is assumed here to have been of critical importance.

The media in British Columbia played a direct role in reinforcing that visibility. The imposition of the tax on 1 July 2008 coincided with a record high world price for oil, which peaked at about US $132 per barrel[18] at almost exactly the same time. The quantum of the carbon tax added to the gasoline price was tiny, just 2.4 ¢/L for regular gasoline in British Columbia. In Victoria, BC, for example, the price rose from $1.469/L on 30 June to $1.494/L at 00:00 hours on 1 July, after having risen substantially and progressively by about 40 ¢/L over the previous six months. That half-year history did not faze the headline writer in the local *Times Colonist* newspaper, who wrote in bold print on the front page of the 2 July 2008 edition[19]: 'Gas prices push $1.50 as carbon tax kicks in'. Similar headlines appeared repeatedly in subsequent years, near or on the anniversary date. On 1 July 2010, the CBC posted,[20] 'BC carbon tax jumps more than 1 cent'. (That headline, of course, was inaccurate – the tax actually rose $5/t/$CO_2$e, which translates to a little over 1 ¢/L on gasoline, but regardless, it strengthened the public message.) On 1 July 2011, the Canadian Press echoed the theme[21] with a story entitled, 'Carbon tax bumps up BC fuels prices', and exactly one year later Canada's 'national newspaper', the *Globe and Mail*, added yet another reinforcing headline:[22] 'BC to raise carbon tax, price of gasoline on July 1'. Over the course of five years, the British Columbia public repeatedly heard at the end of June or beginning of July that the price of fuels went up, and they were repeatedly signalled that this trend was to continue, thanks to the carbon tax. That message sunk in, and we believe – but cannot prove with absolute confidence – that it was instrumental in shifting behaviour at the individual level towards lowering fossil fuel consumption.

THE REVENUE NEUTRALITY ISSUE

The evident success of the tax has introduced an unanticipated irony: revenue neutrality was never reached. Personal and corporate income tax cuts have exceeded carbon tax revenue in every year since the introduction of the tariff in 2008. In 2012–2013 for example, the tax generated an estimated $1120 million in revenue while the personal and corporate income tax cuts accounted for an estimated decline in revenue to the treasury of $1380 million, a shortfall of $260 million relative to neutrality. Rather than the tax being a net imposition on the taxpayers of British Columbia, it has instead put nearly $800 million net into their pockets since 2008. The reason for this disparity is simple: the decline in the consumption of fossil fuels since the tax was introduced exceeded that anticipated by the economic models used in 2007 to forecast revenue from the tax. Those forecasts were used to determine the scale of income tax reductions put in place in 2008. From the revenue neutrality perspective, therefore, the tax appears to have been too successful.

RELATIVE ECONOMIC PERFORMANCE IN BRITISH COLUMBIA

Some commentators have suggested that carbon taxes harm economic growth. While this must be true at some taxation level, there is no indication that BC's tax has had any overall negative economic impact since inception in 2008. Indeed, British Columbia's GDP growth has kept pace with or slightly exceeded that of Canada as a whole since 2006/07 despite constraints including lagging demand for BC lumber by the sluggish US housing market.[23] The carbon tax is only a tiny component of the overall economy, so one would not expect it to have a significant effect, especially given its revenue neutrality.

The lack of negative economic impact extends to the sectoral level. Rivers and Schaufele (2014) have recently shown for example that BC's carbon tax has had no discernible impact, positive or negative, on the export of agricultural products from BC.[24] When considered collectively, the data now available at both the macro (pan-Canadian) and provincial sectoral levels confirm that, as designed and applied, British Columbia's now permanent carbon-emissions taxation program has not produced economic harm. In fact, the carbon tax may well have been a factor in stimulating significant growth in recent years in the energy-related high technology sector in the Province. Between 2009 and 2011, for example, revenue generated by the clean technology sector in BC grew 17 per cent[25] and the sector remains a locus of significant expansion.

CONCLUSION

By all yardsticks, BC's carbon tax has been a success. Its primary objective has been achieved: fossil fuel consumption on a per capita basis has fallen substantially, and interim emissions reductions targets set by legislation have been met,[26,27] albeit in part through the purchase of offsets. Some 70 per cent of British Columbians now support the tax, and a majority would like to see it increase[28,29] but with the new revenue being directed towards green initiatives like home–energy–efficiency retrofits rather than further corporate tax reductions. And there has been little negative political backlash to the tax; indeed the centre-right BC Liberal Party that introduced the tax in 2008 was re-elected in 2009 to a third successive term in part because the carbon tax attracted the environmental vote.[30]

BC's experience shows that a carefully thought-through tax shift that penalizes pollution while rewarding conservation and improving environmental outcomes can be a winner. Indeed, the tax has received much attention on the international stage. Professor Paul Ekins, head of the Green Fiscal Commission of the United Kingdom, for example, has praised the BC carbon tax as being 'among the best designed measures of its kind in the world'.[31] The evidence presented here fully supports his observation.

NOTES

1. BC Ministry of Forests, Lands and Natural Resource Operations (2012), 'A History of the Battle Against the Mountain Pine Beetle: 2000 to 2012', www.for.gov.bc.ca/hfp/mountain_pine_beetle/Pine%20Beetle%20Response%20Brief%20History%20May%2023%202012.pdf, accessed 26 July 2014.
2. BC Ministry of Forests, Mines and Lands (2010), 'The State of British Columbia's

Forests, 3rd edn', www.for.gov.bc.ca/hfp/sof/index.htm#2010_report, accessed 28 July 2014.

3. BC Ministry of Finance (2014), 'Tax Rates on Fuels', www.sbr.gov.bc.ca/documents_library/bulletins/mft-ct_005.pdf, accessed 25 July 2014.

4. The carbon tax rate for gasoline and diesel is lower than would be expected for pure gasoline and diesel because the fuels contain some ethanol and biodiesel as required by renewable fuels legislation. These non-fossil components are factored into the rate charged per litre.

5. Government of BC (2014), 'Low Income Climate Action Tax Credit', www2.gov.bc.ca/gov/topic.page?id=E9258ADE1AE3423080A1B2674F4EAABD, accessed 22 July 2014.

6. Government of BC (2014), 'Tax Rates and Business Limits', www2.gov.bc.ca/gov/topic.page?id=68E5DBC15D4F458CB2783F35CFABB19C, accessed 22 July 2014.

7. BC Ministry of Finance (2014), 'Fuel Sellers', www.sbr.gov.bc.ca/documents_library/bulletins/mft-ct_001.pdf, accessed 22 July 2014.

8. BC Ministry of Finance (2014), 'Natural Gas and Biomethane Sellers', www.sbr.gov.bc.ca/documents_library/bulletins/ct_001.pdf, accessed 22 July 2014.

9. McLeod, A.I., H. Yu and E. Mahdi (2011), 'Time Series Analysis with R', *Handbook of Statistics*, 30, Elsevier.

10. BC Stats (2014), '1997–2013 Chained 2007$', www.bcstats.gov.bc.ca/StatisticsBySubject/Economy/EconomicAccounts.aspx, accessed 23 July 2014.

11. Skuce, Andy (2014), http://critical-angle.net/2013/08/18/the-effect-of-cross-border-shopping-on-bc-fuel-consumption-estimates/, and Bauman, Yoram (2014), http://daily.sightline.org/2014/05/21/the-canadians-are-coming/, both accessed 24 July 2014.

12. Government of BC (2008), 'Bill 16 – Greenhouse Gas Reduction Act', www.leg.bc.ca/38th4th/3rd_read/gov16-3.htm, accessed 24 July 2014.

13. Government of BC (2012), www.livesmartbc.ca/attachments/carbon_neutral_action_reports/CarbonNeutralBC-transformingBCpublicsector.pdf, accessed 24 July 2014.

14. Littlejohn, Dale (2012), 'A Primer on the Transition to Electric Vehicles in Vancouver', www.communityenergy.bc.ca/sites/default/files/Road%20to%20Zero-Metro%20Vancouver%20EV%20Primer%202012-02-09.pdf, accessed 24 July 2014.

15. Chandra, A., S. Gulati and M. Kandlikar (2010), 'Green Drivers or Free Riders? An Analysis of Tax Rebates for Hybrid Vehicles', *Journal of Environmental Economics and Management*, **60**(2), 78–93.

16. Office of the Auditor General of BC, Summary Report 8 (2012), www.OAGBC%20Dec%20Summary%20Report2012.pdf, accessed 24 July 2014.

17. Rivers, N. and B. Schaufele (2013), 'Salience of Carbon Taxes in the Gasoline Market', http:/dx.doi.org/10.2139/ssrn.2131468, accessed 25 July 2014.

18. Index Mundi (2014), www.indexmundi.com/commodities/?commodity=crude-oil&months=240, accessed 26 July 2014.

19. *Victoria Times Colonist* (2008), www.canada.com/victoriatimescolonist/story.html?id=9d7dfec8-9174-48c9-a766-1af4274a64cd, accessed 28 July 2014.

20. CBC News (2010), www.cbc.ca/news/canada/british-columbia/b-c-carbon-tax-jumps-more-than-1-cent-1.915792, accessed 28 July 2014.

21. CBC News (2011), www.cbc.ca/news/canada/british-columbia/carbon-tax-bumps-up-b-c-fuels-prices-1.1009204, accessed 28 July 2014.

22. *Globe and Mail* (2012), www.theglobeandmail.com/report-on-business/industry-news/energy-and-resources/bc-to-raise-carbon-tax-price-of-gasoline-july-1/article4374532/#dashboard/follows/, accessed 28 July 2014.

23. Service Canada (2013), 'Environmental Scan, British Columbia', www.esdc.gc.ca/eng/jobs/lmi/publications/e-scan/bc/bc-e-scan-201303.pdf, accessed 28 July 2014.

24. Rivers, N. and B. Schaufele (2014), 'The Effect of British Columbia's Carbon Tax on Agricultural Trade', www.pics.uvic.ca/sites/default/files/uploads/publications/Carbon%20Tax%20on%20Agricultural%20Trade.pdf, accessed 28 July 2014.

25. Bennett, N. (2012), http://www.biv.com/article/2012/11/bc-companies-finding-the-green-in-clean/, accessed 12 November 2014.
26. Government of BC (2012), www.env.gov.bc.ca/cas/pdfs/2012-Progress-to-Targets.pdf, accessed 28 July 2014.
27. Government of BC (2014), www.env.gov.bc.ca/cas/pdfs/2014-Progress-to-Targets.pdf, accessed 28 July 2014.
28. Pembina Institute (2012), 'British Columbians Willing to Pay More Carbon Tax: Poll', www.pembina.org/media-release/2377, accessed 28 July 2014.
29. Pembina Institute (2012), www.pembina.org/reports/carbon-tax-polling-results.pdf, accessed 28 July 2014.
30. Coyne, A. (2009), www.macleans.ca/news/canada/a-new-coalition-a-different-politics/, accessed 28 July 2014.
31. Ekins, Paul (2012), Submission to the British Columbia Government's Carbon Tax Review, August 2012.

2. The cost of enforcing carbon pricing mechanisms: a comparison of the British Columbia carbon tax and the Québec emissions trading system[1]

Nathalie Chalifour[2] and Jacques Papy[3]

INTRODUCTION

There is widespread agreement within economics that carbon pricing is an efficient means of reducing the greenhouse gas (GHG) emissions contributing to climate change.[4] The two most common carbon pricing instruments are carbon taxes and emissions trading (cap and trade) systems.[5] There has been a vibrant ongoing debate, supported by an abundance of research, about the relative merits of taxes versus trading systems for achieving cost-effective, lasting GHG reductions.[6] Increasingly, scholarship shows that the instrument choice question is not an either/or proposition, since policies can be combined in various ways, such as using regulations to set an allowable level of emissions (a 'cap'), allocating permits for some economic actors to trade their allowances within the cap, and imposing carbon taxes on actors not covered by the emissions trading system, or even throughout the entire economy.[7] Ultimately, many factors will determine which instrument or combination of instruments is (or is not) applied in a given jurisdiction, many of which have to do with the relevant legal, socio-economic and public policy context, not to mention the political ideologies of the decision-makers in power.

Comparative analyses of carbon taxes and emissions trading systems consider many different variables in evaluating which instrument is optimal in a given set of circumstances. These include, inter alia, environmental effectiveness, economic efficiency, administration/implementation, distributional impacts, political feasibility and price certainty/volatility.[8] This chapter focuses on the enforcement mechanisms that underpin a carbon price instrument. This issue has received considerably less attention than many of the other factors considered in analyses of policy options, even though the rate of compliance with a policy instrument has important implications for its ultimate effectiveness and the costs of its administration. Economic analyses show that market-based instruments are more efficient than regulations, but the studies often do not taken into account the costs associated with monitoring and enforcement.[9] As Heyes aptly states, '[i]t risks banality to say that implementation is an important part of policy-making, yet in many fields economists pay scant attention to issues of enforcement and compliance.'[10]

In this chapter we explore the issue of compliance and enforcement in the context of British Columbia's carbon tax and Québec's emissions trading system. Our goal is to offer early observations about the surveillance burden to the British Columbia (BC) and Québec governments with respect to these mechanisms, with an emphasis on the costs of enforcement. We explain the surveillance and enforcement mechanisms used for each measure (Part II). Part III discusses what is known about the costs of enforcement. We begin, however, in Part I with a brief description of the BC carbon tax and Québec emissions trading system.

PART I – AN INTRODUCTION TO THE BRITISH COLUMBIA CARBON TAX (BC-CT) AND QUÉBEC EMISSIONS TRADING SYSTEM (QC-ETS)

Overview of the BC-CT[11]

British Columbia introduced a carbon tax effective July 2008 as part of the government's plan to reduce GHG emissions by 33 percent below 2007 levels by 2020.[12] The tax applies to purchasers and importers of the affected fuels and combustibles, which include gasoline, diesel, natural gas, and coal.[13] This means that the tax covers most emissions from fossil fuel combustion in BC, which accounts for 70 percent of total emissions in the province.[14] The tax was introduced at a rate equal to $10/ton of CO_2e, and increased annually by $5 until it reached its current level of $30/ton on July 1, 2012.[15]

The carbon tax generates considerable revenue ($1.2 billion in 2013, for instance).[16] The Carbon Tax Act requires that this revenue be used to reduce other taxes, making the tax revenue-neutral.[17] The province has achieved this goal by lowering personal and corporate income taxes rates, and providing specific tax credits (such as a low-income refundable tax credit).[18] The province has enforced its commitment to revenue-neutrality by providing that should the Minister fail to introduce the legislation required to implement the tax reductions, the Minister's salary will be reduced by 15 percent.[19] In practice to date, the province has returned approximately $300M more than it has collected from the tax, making the tax revenue negative.[20]

Has the tax been effective? One paper reports that between 2008 and 2012, fuel consumption per person in the province declined by 17.4 percent.[21] During the same period, BC's gross domestic product (GDP) has increased at a slightly higher rate than the national average, suggesting that the tax has not had a negative impact on economic growth.[22] While it is still early to draw causal conclusions, Rivers and Schaufele concluded that the carbon tax generated a reduction in fuel consumption 4.9 times greater than would have happened without the tax.[23]

While it has been subject to controversy within the province, the carbon tax survived two provincial elections where the continuation of the tax was made a political issue. In terms of its design as a policy tool to reduce GHG emissions, the BC-CT is widely viewed as a successful example of carbon pricing. In fact, the Secretary-General to the Organisation for Economic Co-operation and Development (OECD) referred to the BC-CT as a leading example of carbon pricing globally.[24]

Overview of the QC-ETS

Québec introduced an emissions trading scheme (QC-ETS) effective January 2013 as the primary tool of the government's plan to reduce GHG emissions by 20 percent below 1990 levels by 2020.[25] The scheme's features are based on design recommendations developed by the Western Climate Initiative.[26] As of January 2014, a bilateral agreement links the QC-ETS with California's Cap-and-Trade Program (CAL-ETS) and provides for a common carbon market between the two territories.[27]

The QC-ETS, which replaces an upstream carbon tax introduced in 2007,[28] covers seven greenhouse gases from emitters of targeted sectors whose emissions are greater than or equal to 25,000 metric tons of equivalent CO_2.[29] Covered sectors are industry and electricity generators, as well as, effective January 2015, fuel and combustible distributors (about 94 establishments).[30] Participation in the scheme can also be voluntary. Overall the QC-ETS covers directly or indirectly about 85 percent of total emissions in the province.[31]

The trading scheme is structured around three compliance periods and several categories of compliance instruments.[32] These categories include emission units, offset credits and early reduction credits, each being equal to one metric ton of equivalent CO_2. Early Reduction Credits (ERC) were issued in January 2014, for eligible reductions made by covered emitters between January 1, 2008 and December 31, 2011. This part of the program has now ended.[33] Offset credits are delivered for eligible emission reduction projects and can be used to satisfy up to 8 percent of an emitter's coverage obligation for a compliance period.[34] Emission units are allocated for free to emitters exposed to international competition.[35] They can also be bought directly from the Minister's reserve at a set price, as a price containment measure.[36] Finally, emissions units can be bought through auctions conducted jointly with the CAL-ETS.[37] Auctions have a joint floor price of CA \$10 (base year of 2012) increasing annually by 5 percent plus inflation until 2020.[38] The estimated auction revenue to 2020 for the QC-ETS is \$3 billion CA.[39]

The scheme is too recent to draw conclusions about its environmental effectiveness or economic efficiency. However, it possesses two notable features. First the QC-ETS enjoys wide political support as it was adopted by a unanimous vote of the Province's legislature in 2009 and never contested in the two subsequent provincial elections. Second, being too small to exist on its own, the scheme is entirely dependent on its link with the CAL-ETS. This second aspect will be more broadly discussed in the second part of this chapter.

PART II – SURVEILLANCE AND ENFORCEMENT MECHANISMS IN THE BC-CT AND QC-ETS

The raison d'être of carbon pricing is to stimulate changes in behavior that lead to reductions in GHG emissions. The mechanisms through which such policies influence behavior are varied (for instance, the mere fact of instituting a carbon price can send an important signal that may create shifts in decision-making). However, one of the key determinants of a carbon price's effectiveness is its ability to impose additional costs on carbon via the tax or requirement for a permit. If an economic actor can avoid paying the tax or purchasing a permit, the measure's effectiveness will be undermined. As such, an important design feature of any carbon pricing mechanism is the system established to ensure compliance.[40] The enforcement system will vary depending on the type of instrument. In this section, we examine the systems established by the BC and Québec governments to ensure compliance with their carbon pricing policies.

Description of Enforcement System for the BC-CT[41]

It is commonly stated that carbon taxes are administratively simple to implement since countries can use existing systems for collecting fuel taxes.[42] This was indeed the case in BC, which benefited from an existing administrative structure for motor fuel taxation in the province. With the exception of natural gas, the carbon tax is applied and collected in essentially the same way as the motor fuel tax, with the enabling legislation for the carbon tax[43] largely mirroring that of the motor fuel tax.[44]

The carbon tax collection method is very straightforward. First, any entity that manufactures or imports fuel into the province and plans to sell that fuel for the first time in the province, must be appointed as a collector. Second, the collector must remit security to the province equal to the tax that will eventually be collected from the end purchaser at the retail level. The collector is then reimbursed by charging the deputy collector or wholesaler, or by collecting from the end purchaser, depending on the length of the security chain. The collectors must report and remit the taxes monthly, quarterly or annually depending on the amount of tax collected.

Thus, although the tax is characterized as a downstream tax that is ultimately paid by the consumer at the point of retail sale, the producer or importer serves as the point of collection. This design feature of the tax greatly simplifies its administration. The security chain provides a simple administrative structure for the province in that it can focus surveillance efforts on the relatively small number of collectors. There were 185 registered collectors in BC as of September 2014.[45]

To ensure compliance with the tax, the legislation provides for auditing and inspection powers which empower the Ministry of Finance to assess collectors for tax or security owed, to assess monetary penalties equal to the tax owed, and impose additional penalties of up to 25 percent of the tax owed in cases of evasion (rather than administrative error or ignorance).[46] The legislation also includes criminal offences, which allows additional fines of $10,000 plus the amount of tax unpaid, plus imprisonment of up to two years. There are also provisions for director liability in cases of insolvency.

Description of Enforcement Mechanism for the QC-ETS

The implementation and monitoring of an emissions trading scheme is less straightforward than a carbon tax, first because this kind of pricing instrument implies a double monitoring dynamic. In this context, double monitoring means on one hand, monitoring the environmental part of the system (for example, emissions declaration and verification, delivery of the right amount of emission rights once the compliance period is up) and on the other hand, monitoring the carbon trading part of the system (trading in the primary, secondary and derivatives markets). Both aspects of monitoring are relevant to a comprehensive discussion of governmental administrative costs. However, because it has been less frequently discussed, this chapter focuses on the trading part of the system.

In addition, this kind of pricing instrument entails a new administrative structure. This was indeed the case for Québec which created the *Direction du marché du carbone* within the Ministère du Développement durable, de l'Environnement et de la Lutte contre les Changements Climatiques (MDDELCC).[47] Linking with the CAL-ETS with the aim of creating the WCI common carbon market also led to the creation of Western Climate Initiative Inc. (WCI Inc.).[48]

WCI Inc. provides three main infrastructure and administrative services to the WCI common carbon market on behalf of the Québec and Californian authorities. These services are provided through private, for-profit contractors based in the US. The first service is to manage the Compliance Instrument Tracking Service System (CITSS). CITSS is the WCI central registry and as such, plays a critical role in market operations.[49] The second service is to conduct and monitor the central auctioning process of Québec and California allowances.[50] The third service is to monitor ownership transfers of emission rights.[51]

Although the carbon market administrative infrastructure is primarily structured around WCI Inc., a significant portion of emission rights transactions lies outside its monitoring jurisdiction. In the primary market, free allocation of allowances and initial issuance of offsets are not monitored by WCI Inc., but respectively by the Québec MDDELCC and the California Air Resources Board.[52] In the secondary market, spot trades are monitored by WCI Inc., but carbon forwards trading is not routinely monitored by anyone.[53] The WCI carbon derivatives market is regulated in the same way as other commodity derivatives by financial market authorities in the US and Canada.[54] As a consequence, there is no institutional monitoring arrangement that covers all aspects of the carbon market in an integrated way.

PART III – DISCUSSION

In this section, we examine what is known (and not known) about the administrative costs of enforcement. The costs of enforcing a policy are generally not included in empirical evaluations of alternative environmental policy options. Yet, they can be important since a calculation of net benefits is incomplete if it does not take transaction costs into account.[55] While the question of enforcement warrants a broader discussion than just that of cost (such as a comparative assessment of the relative points of vulnerability to evasion and fraud in each system), our focus in this chapter is on enforcement costs. Our main objective is to offer some analysis of this common (but almost always unsubstantiated) claim that carbon taxes are less costly to administer than emissions trading systems. We plan to address other aspects of the enforcement of carbon pricing instrument in later work.

We begin, though, with some points of clarification about terminology and the various stages of the policy process during which costs arise. Confusion can arise because similar terms are used in research that focuses on the perspective of the government (the emphasis in this chapter), the perspective of private entities subject to the policy, or both, and may relate to different stages in the policy process. With respect to the policy process, McCann's analytical framework, elaborated upon by Coggan, identifies several stages of the policy process during which costs arise for both the public entity implementing the policy and the actors subject to the policy. These are:

1. Research, information and analysis of policy design
2. Enactment
3. Establishment
4. Implementation (including contracting)
5. Administration and support
6. Monitoring
7. Enforcement.[56]

Our analysis of costs focuses on the last three stages.

When referring to costs, the literature (which spans several disciplines) refers to transaction costs, operating costs, administrative costs and compliance costs. Administration costs are typically those incurred by the government actor in order to assess and collect a tax/issue permits, monitor compliance, and impose penalties for non-observance (the costs incurred by dispute settlement bodies, such as courts and tribunals, could be captured here too). Compliance costs, on the other hand, is the term generally used to describe the costs incurred by the entities subject to the policy (in the case of carbon taxes, the costs taxpayers incur for calculating and remitting the tax, or in the case of emissions trading, the costs market participants incur for participating in the market).[57] Administration and compliance costs are both types of transaction costs.[58] In the tax literature, administration and compliance costs are sometimes referred to jointly as tax operating costs.[59] In this chapter, we are concerned only with administration costs.

Administration Costs in the BC-CT

The costs associated with administering a carbon tax depend upon a number of factors, including the number of sources to be assessed and monitored.[60] An upstream tax, for instance, will involve far fewer sources than a downstream tax.[61] However, as the BC example illustrates, a downstream tax can be designed in such a way that offers the same administrative advantage of an upstream tax (for example, by imposing a requirement for the remittance of security on taxes owed). This security chain is an important feature of the carbon tax's enforcement system, since it enables the Ministry of Finance to focus its efforts on a small number of entities.[62]

It is impossible to identify the precise costs of administering and enforcing the carbon tax because the tax's administration is embedded within that of other taxes collected by the province, including the motor fuel tax and the provincial sales tax, and the costs associated with the carbon tax are not disaggregated.[63] The Ministry of Finance, Revenue Division is responsible for auditing businesses for compliance with all taxes payable, not only the carbon tax. However, we can reasonably make certain assumptions. The total annual operating expenses for the Ministry of Finance, Revenue Division, responsible for the assessment of all taxes, was CA \$66 million in 2013–2014.[64] While we cannot know what proportion of this is assignable to carbon taxes, we can safely assume it is a small proportion given the number of programs (such as audit, refunds and rulings) and taxes (such as provincial sales, provincial income, tobacco, and motor fuel) administered by the Division, and the economies of scale created by the fact that carbon tax administration mirrors that of the motor fuel tax.[65] If we assumed that carbon taxes accounted for one-tenth of the administration costs of the Revenue Division, the carbon tax administration costs would be CA \$6.6 million. With carbon tax revenues forecast to be CA \$1.2 billion in 2013–14,[66] this puts administration costs at approximately 0.01 percent of revenue generated.

We can compare this estimate to the administration costs of other taxes in Canada. Estimates of the costs of tax administration in Canada range from 0.8 percent of revenues for federal sales and excise taxes and 0.6 percent for Ontario retail sales tax,[67] to 1 percent of revenue for income and payroll taxes.[68] Our findings regarding the BC-CT are broadly consistent with findings in other jurisdictions, where administrative costs varied from 0.12 percent of revenues raised for a petroleum revenue tax to 1.53 percent of revenues raised for income tax.[69] Internationally, several empirical analyses have demonstrated that the administration costs of environmental taxes are a small proportion of revenues: Germany = 0.13 percent;[70] Czech = 0.7 percent to 2.7 percent;[71] Poland = 0.8 percent to 4.5 percent;[72]

and the UK $= 0.21$ percent to 0.34 percent.[73] For our purposes, the main point to emerge from these comparisons is that the administration costs of the carbon tax are very low, relative to other taxes and as a proportion of revenue generated. This supports the common claim that carbon taxes have low administration costs.

Administration Costs in the QC-ETS

Like with a carbon tax, the costs associated with administering a trading scheme depend upon a number of factors such as an upstream or down-stream point of obligation. In addition, as previously mentioned a trading scheme also involves the creation and maintenance of a specialized administrative structure to monitor emissions and trading. This is the reason why emissions trading is usually associated with higher costs of administration.[74] The QC-ETS has been designed with a mainly upstream point of obligation, which greatly reduces the number of covered entities.[75] It was also designed to share some of the administrative costs with the CAL-ETS through the services provided by WCI Inc.

It is, however, difficult to assess precisely the costs of monitoring the QC-ETS because some of these costs are embedded within the broader administrative costs of the ETS but also of other agencies responsible for monitoring part of the market, including the Autorité des marchés financiers. Some preliminary numbers might nevertheless be good indica-tors of their magnitude. For example, the *Direction du marché du carbone* had an operating budget of CA $1.46 million for the year 2013–2014.[76] In contrast, the costs of monitoring through WCI Inc. are clearer because the service contracts of third party providers as well as budget documents are posted on the WCI Inc. website. The documents reveal that the planned operating budget of WCI Inc. including trading services, operations and personnel for the years 2014 and 2015 is respectively US $3,924,548 and US $2,957,796.[77] Québec's global contribution to WCI Inc. is US $1,937,024 for the two year period of 2014 and 2015.[78] For the same period, California's contribution is US $4 million.[79] It appears that the two jurisdictions have adjusted cost-sharing according to differences in their respective size and share of revenues. Based on these numbers and taking into account currency exchange, the QC-ETS administrative costs were roughly CA $2.5 million in 2014.[80]

The four separate auctions held through WCI Inc. by the QC-ETS in 2013 and 2014 have yielded CA $106.7 million. The amount generated through auctioning should increase sharply beginning in 2015 after cov-erage of the QC-ETS is extended to fuel and combustible distributors, reaching an estimated total of CA $3 billion over the period of 2013 to

2020.[81] While we could generate a percentage of administrative costs per revenue generated based on these projections, we have resisted doing so given the early stage of the QC-ETS at the time of writing. However, we can reasonably conclude that administrative costs are a minimal proportion of revenue.

CONCLUSION

Our conclusions with respect to the carbon tax are that while the enforcement costs are not known, we can reliably make several assumptions. First, because the administrative structures for monitoring the tax were already established when the carbon tax was created, it is fair to conclude that the 'set-up' costs would have been very modest. Relatedly, including the carbon tax – a straightforward tax with clear rates on a small number of fuels – into an existing auditing system likely required only a modest increase in auditing responsibilities. Second, the security chain design of carbon tax collection is a cost-effective way of simplifying the number of entities that require oversight. As such, our research suggests that the common claim that carbon taxes are relatively simple to administer and involve modest costs to monitor, are justifiable in the case of the BC carbon tax. Our preliminary findings with respect to the administration costs of the QC-ETS show that although the exact amount might be difficult to obtain, it is possible to establish an order of their magnitude. They also show that the main strategy used by the QC-ETS to enhance cost-effectiveness is cost-sharing with the CAL-ETS through WCI Inc. This strategy has been identified as an opportunity to improve administrative efficiency by other jurisdictions in the United States.[82]

It is often stated in scholarship comparing carbon pricing policies that the costs of administering carbon taxes, including costs associated with ensuring compliance, are considerably less than an emissions trading system, largely because the institutional infrastructure for tax collection, administration and enforcement is usually pre-existing. The experience with the BC carbon tax and Québec carbon market is consistent with this general comment. The QC-ETS was indeed more complex to set up and administer than the BC-CT, since it involved new institutional arrangements, specialization and expertise. However, even if the collected data is incomplete, it tends to indicate that this higher degree of complexity is not automatically translated into high administration costs (although still likely higher than a carbon tax when compared with the revenue generated). It will be interesting to see whether this preliminary finding continues to hold true when the QC-ETS matures and more data is available.

Regardless of whether the international community agrees on a set of binding global targets for GHG emissions reductions at COP 21 in 2015, carbon pricing policies at the regional, national and sub-national level will continue to emerge. Having a sound, cost-effective enforcement system for ensuring compliance with the carbon price is important, and our research suggests that the administrative costs of both BC's carbon tax and the QC-ETS are a modest proportion of revenue. As experience with the QC-ETS grows, it will be possible to offer a more robust comparison of the two systems' administrative costs.

NOTES

1. The authors wish to acknowledge the research assistance received by Mark James, JD 2014 (University of Ottawa), LLM 2016 (Vermont Law School); Sophine Johnsson, LLB 2014 (Université Laval), JD 2015 (University of Ottawa) and Cédric Livet, MSc 2016 (Université du Québec à Montréal).
2. Associate Professor, Faculty of Law, University of Ottawa (natchali@uottawa.ca).
3. Professeur agrégé, Département des sciences juridiques, Faculté de science politique et de droit, Université du Québec à Montréal (papy.jacques@uqam.ca).
4. See, for example, Aldy, J.E. and R.N. Stavins (2012), 'The Promise and Problems of Pricing Carbon: Theory and Experience', *Journal of Environment and Development*, **21** (2), 152–180; Jaccard, M. and N. Rivers (2007), 'Canadian Policies for Deep Greenhouse Gas Reductions', irpp.org/research-studies/jaccard-rivers-2007-10-29, accessed January 9, 2015.
5. For a comprehensive discussion of a carbon tax in Canada, see Rivers, Nicholas (2014), 'The Case for a Carbon Tax in Canada', canada2020.ca/canada-carbon-tax, accessed January 9, 2015.
   For an in-depth discussion about emissions trading as a pricing instrument, see OECD (2004), *Tradeable Permits: Policy Evaluation, Design and Reform*, Paris: OECD Publishing.
6. See, for example, OECD (2007), *Instrument Mixes for Environmental Policy*, Paris: OECD Publishing; OECD (1997), *Evaluating the Efficiency and Effectiveness of Economic Instruments in Environmental Policy*, Paris: OECD Publishing; Cavaliere, Alberto et al. (eds) (2006), 'Part IV: Choice of Instrument', in *Critical Issues in Environmental Taxation*, vol. III, Oxford: Oxford University Press (containing several articles on instrument choice); Nordhaus, William D. (2001), 'After Kyoto: Alternative Mechanisms to Control Global Warming', www.angelfire.com/co4/macroeconomics302/c.pdf, accessed January 9, 2015; Goulder, L.H. and A.R. Schein (2013), 'Carbon Taxes vs. Cap and Trade: A Critical Review', *Climate Change Economics*, **4** (3), 1–28. See also Weitzman, Martin L. (1974), 'Price vs. Quantities', *Review of Economic Studies*, **41** (4), 477–491 (a seminal piece of research concluding that there is no basic or universal rationale for concluding that either price or quantity instruments are advantageous).
7. Research from the former National Round Table on the Environment and the Economy concluded that an economy-wide carbon tax, an upstream cap-and-trade system, or a downstream cap-and-trade system combined with a tax, would all yield similar GHG emissions reductions. See National Round Table on the Environment and Economy (2009), *Achieving 2050: A Carbon Pricing Policy for Canada*, Ottawa: Government of Canada Collections, 26. The NRTEE reminds readers that the design of these instruments would be critical to ensuring their effectiveness (ibid. at 27).

8. Other factors include flexibility, impacts upon international competitiveness, the incentive effect, coverage, interaction with other climate policies and potential for linkages across jurisdictions. See for example, L.R. Goulder and A. R. Schein, *supra* note 6.
9. Rousseau, S. and S. Proost (2005), 'Comparing Environmental Policy Instruments in the Presence of Imperfect Compliance', *Environmental and Resource Economics*, **32**, 337.
10. Heyes, Anthony (2000), 'Implementing Environmental Regulation: Enforcement and Compliance', *Journal of Regulatory Economics*, **17** (2), 123. Economists generally assume that fines for non-compliance are treated as a cost of doing business and that regulated entities act to minimize the compliance costs plus expected penalties. Although the enforcement dimension of regulations, including taxation, has been extensively studied both theoretically and empirically, there remain many unanswered questions. See generally Becker, Gary S. (1968), 'Crime and Punishment: An Economic Approach', *Journal of Political Economy*, **76** (2), 169–217 (who established the basic approach to modeling compliance with regulations); Allingham, M. and A. Sandmo (1972), 'Income Tax Evasion: A Theoretical Analysis', *Journal of Public Economics*, **1** (6), 323–338 (considering tax compliance); Graetz, M. et al. (1986), 'The Tax Compliance Game: Toward an Interactive Theory of Law Enforcement', *Journal of Law, Economics and Organization*, **2** (1), 1–32 (taking into account the influence of the regulator).
11. For discussion of various elements of the BC carbon tax, see Harrison, Kathryn (2013), 'The Political Economy of British Columbia's Carbon Tax', *OECD Environment Working Papers*, No. 63, Paris: OECD Publishing; Rivers, N. and B. Schaufele (2012), 'Carbon Tax Salience and Gasoline Demand', *Working Papers 1211E*, University of Ottawa: Department of Economics; Elgie, S. and J. McClay (2013), 'BC's Carbon Tax Shift is Working Well After Four Years (Attention Ottawa)', *Canadian Public Policy*, **39**, S1–S10; Hsu, S. and R. Elliot (2009), 'Regulating Greenhouse Gases in Canada: Constitutional and Policy Dimensions', *McGill Law Journal*, **54**, 463–516; Duff, David G. (2008), 'Carbon Taxation in British Columbia', *Vermont Journal of Environmental Law*, **10** (1), 87–107; Chalifour, Nathalie J. (2008), 'Making Federalism Work for Climate Change – Canada's Division of Powers Over Carbon Taxes', *National Journal of Constitutional Law*, **22**, 119–214.
12. British Columbia Ministry of Finance (2013), 'Carbon Tax Review', www.fin.gov.bc.ca/tbs/tp/climate/Carbon_Tax_Review_Topic_Box.pdf, accessed January 9, 2015.
13. Carbon Tax Act, S.B.C. 2008, c. 40.
14. British Columbia Ministry of Finance (2014), 'Myths and Facts about the Carbon Tax', www.fin.gov.bc.ca/tbs/tp/climate/A6.htm, accessed January 9, 2015.
15. This represents approximately $0.07 at the gasoline pump. In comparison, the federal fuel excise tax is 10 cents per liter for gasoline and 4 cents for diesel. Ibid. at Schedule II. The act creates an administrative system for the collection of the taxes that mirrors that of the province's existing fuel taxes (ibid. at ss. 3, 17, 13(2)). Gasoline prices in British Columbia have varied by roughly 70 cents over the last three years.
16. In comparison, the federal fuel excise tax raised $5.1 billion in 2006–2007. Mintz, J. and N. Olewiler (2008), 'A Simple Approach for Bettering the Environment and the Economy: Restructuring the Federal Fuel Excise Tax', *Sustainable Prosperity*, Ottawa: Institute of the Environment. See also Parry, Ian W.H. et al. (2014), *Getting Energy Prices Right – From Principle to Practice*, IMF Publications at 149 (recommending that Canada raise fuel tax rates to 55 cents for gasoline and 64 cents for diesel).
17. Ibid. at s. 3–4. The Act requires the Minister of Finance to prepare a carbon tax plan that estimates how much revenue will be raised by the tax and identifies how the revenues will be used to reduce other taxes. While there have been recommendations to invest the revenue into environmental programs, the province decided in 2013 to maintain the current approach. See British Columbia Ministry of Finance (2013), *supra* note 12.
18. The revenue generated by the tax has been used to reduce the general and small business corporate income tax rates and the two lowest provincial personal income tax brackets

by 5 percent. Revenue is also used to fund a variety of tax credits, such as the low-income tax credit, a northern and rural homeowners property tax benefit and exceptions for the greenhouse industry. See British Columbia Ministry of Finance (2014), 'Tax Reductions, Funded by a Revenue Neutral Carbon Tax', www.fin.gov.bc.ca/tbs/tp/climate/tax_cuts.htm, accessed January 9, 2015.

19. Ibid. at s. 5.
20. British Columbia Ministry of Finance (2010), 'Budget and Fiscal Plan 2010/11–2012/13', www.bcbudget.gov.bc.ca/2010/bfp/2010_Budget_Fiscal_Plan.pdf#tax, accessed January 9, 2015, at 105–106.
21. Elgie, S. and J. McClay (2013), *supra* note 11.
22. However, the province's own review of the Tax as part of the Budget 2013 process concluded that the tax has had, and will continue to have, a small negative impact on GDP in the province. See British Columbia Ministry of Finance (2013), *supra* note 12.
23. Rivers, N. and B. Schaufele, *supra* note 11, at 2. See also Bernard, Jean-Thomas et al. (Working Paper, October 2014), 'Price and Carbon Tax Effects on Gasoline and Diesel Demand'.
24. Gurria, Angel (2013), 'The Climate Challenge: Achieving Zero Emissions', Lecture by the OECD Secretary-General, http://www.oecd.org/about/secretary-general/The-climate-challenge-achieving-zero-emissions.htm, accessed January 9, 2015.
25. Québec Ministry of Sustainable Development, Environment and the Fight against Climate Change (MDDELCC) (2012), '2013–2020 Climate Change Action Plan', www.mddelcc.gouv.qc.ca/changements/plan_action/pacc2020-en.pdf, accessed January 9, 2015.
26. For a complete list of design recommendations, see Western Climate Initiative (2013), 'Program Design', www.westernclimateinitiative.org/designing-the-program, accessed January 9, 2015.
27. Government of Québec (2013), 'Order in Council 1181-2013: Agreement between the Gouvernement du Québec and the California Air Resources Board concerning the harmonization and integration of cap-and-trade programs for reducing greenhouse gas emissions – Ratification', *Gazette Officielle du Québec*, Partie 2, **145** (49), 3389–3390.
28. The carbon tax, known as the redevance annuelle au Fonds vert was phased out in December 2014. The tax targeted fuel and combustible distributors and yielded $200 million per year.
29. Carbon dioxide, methane, nitrous oxide, hydrofluorocarbons, perfluorocarbons, sulphur hexafluoride and nitrogen trifluoride.
30. Québec Ministry of Sustainable Development, Environment and the Fight against Climate Change (MDDELCC) (2013), 'Regulation Respecting a Cap-and-Trade System for Greenhouse Gas Emission Allowances – Technical Overview', www.mddelcc.gouv.qc.ca/changements/carbone/ventes-encheres/SPEDE-description-technique.pdf, accessed January 9, 2015.
31. Québec Ministry of Sustainable Development, Environment and the Fight against Climate Change (MDDELCC) (2013), *supra* note 30.
32. The first compliance period (January 1, 2013 to December 31, 2014) targeted only the industrial and electricity generation sectors. The second and third compliance periods (including the fuel and combustible distributors) will run respectively from January 1, 2015 to December 31, 2017 and from January 1, 2018 to December 31, 2020. Banking of emission units is allowed between compliance periods.
33. Québec Ministry of Sustainable Development, Environment and the Fight against Climate Change (MDDELCC) (2013), 'The Québec Cap-and-Trade System for Greenhouse Gas Emission Allowances-Frequently Asked Questions', www.mddelcc.gouv.qc.ca/changements/carbone/ventes-encheres/faq-spede-en.pdf, accessed January 9, 2015.
34. Three offset protocols have been approved (manure storage facilities, landfill sites, destruction of ODS) and more are currently being developed. Ibid. at 6.
35. Free allocation benefits mostly emitters from the industrial sector. Ibid. at 8.

36. Sales by mutual agreement are carried with a predetermined price of CA $40, $45 and $50 plus an annual increase of 5 percent plus inflation until 2020, for each of the reserve categories. Ibid. at 10.

37. The first joint auction has taken place on November 25, 2014. Before that date the QC-ETS has held four separate auctions in 2013 and 2014. Québec Ministry of Sustainable Development, Environment and the Fight against Climate Change (MDDELCC) (2014), 'The Carbon Market Auction Notices and Results', www.mddelcc.gouv.qc.ca/changements/carbone/avis-resultats-en.htm, accessed January 9, 2015.

38. Québec Ministry of Sustainable Development, Environment and the Fight against Climate Change (MDDELCC) (2013), *supra* note 30.

39. Québec Ministry of Sustainable Development, Environment and the Fight against Climate Change (MDDELCC) (2014), 'Communiqué de Presse: Troisième vente aux enchères du marché du carbone du Québec – La demande a dépassé l'offre', www.mddelcc.gouv.qc.ca/infuseur/communique.asp?no=2869, accessed January 9, 2015; for a detailed presentation of projected revenue see Purdon, M., D. Houle and E. Lachapelle (2014), 'The Political Economy of California and Québec's Cap-and-Trade Systems', *Sustainable Prosperity*, Ottawa: Institute of the Environment.

40. There is an interesting discussion in the theoretical economics literature about the effect administrative costs can have on the optimal design of emissions prices. See, for example, Stranlund, J.K. and C.A. Chavez (2013), 'Who Should Bear the Administrative Costs of an Emissions Tax', *Journal of Regulatory Economics*, **44**, 53–79.

41. See Section XX of the Carbon Tax Act, S.B.C. 2008, c. 40.

42. See, for example, Aldy, J.E. and R.N. Stavins (2012), *supra* note 4, at 155. They note that the molecular properties of fossil fuels lend themselves to accurate estimates of CO_2 emissions from their combustion.

43. Carbon Tax Act, S.B.C. 2008, c. 40.

44. Motor Fuel Tax Act, R.S.B.C. 1996, c. 317.

45. Personal Communication, Ministry of Finance, Revenue Division, Tuesday, September 23, 2014.

46. The legislation also provides a mechanism of appeal if a collector contests the assessment or penalty.

47. The *Direction du marché du carbone* forms part of the Bureau des changements climatiques and in 2014 employed 12 people. Personal communication with a representative of the *Direction du marché du carbone*, Tuesday, November 11, 2014.

48. This institutional arrangement was inspired by the example of the Regional Greenhouse Gas Initiative, another regional initiative made of nine north-eastern US states and which began operating in 2009, see Regional Greenhouse Gas Initiative (2014) 'An initiative of the Northeast and Mid-Atlantic States of the US', www.rggi.org, accessed January 9, 2015; WCI Inc. is a Delaware incorporated non-profit corporation with an office in Sacramento (California), Western Climate Initiative (2013), *supra* note 26.

49. CITSS tracks all accounts and all categories of emission rights in the QC-ETS and the CAL-ETS from creation to retirement. It is essentially managed by ICF Incorporated, LLC and SRA International, Inc.; see Western Climate Initiative (2015) 'WCI Inc. Documents', www.wci-inc.org/documents.php, accessed January 9, 2015.

50. A few separate auctions have been conducted through WCI Inc. by the QC-ETS and the CAL-ETS. The first joint auction has been conducted on November 25, 2014 with a floor price of US $11.34. Auctioning services are provided by Deutsche Bank National Trust Company and Markit Group Limited and include vetting potential bidders, checking bids, collecting escrow funds and auction proceeds, processing the bids and establishing the final price for the auction, ibid.

51. This service is provided by Monitoring Analytics, LLC, ibid.

52. The primary market is where the initial distribution of emission rights takes place and includes free allocation and auction of allowances as well as the initial issuance of offsets.

53. The secondary market is the resale market for emissions rights. Although carbon forwards are not routinely monitored, financial regulation authorities responsible for overseeing the commodities market may step in if they suspect price manipulation. However, terms of intervention are still unclear as financial regulation in Canada and the US is still being overhauled in response to the 2008 financial crisis. For a discussion on regulation from a Canadian perspective see Fluker, S. and S. Janmohamed (2014), 'Who Regulates Trading in the Carbon Market', *Journal of Environmental Law and Practice*, **26** (2), 83–119.

54. At the moment, there is no exchange traded derivatives contract for QC-ETS emission rights. Several futures and options contracts for CAL-ETS emission rights are being traded by the CME Group (CME Group (2014) 'California Carbon Allowance (CCA) Futures Contract Specs', www.cmegroup.com/trading/energy/emissions/california-carbon-allowance-cca-futures_contract_specifications.html, accessed January 9, 2015) and Intercontinental Exchange, Inc. (Intercontinental Exchange (2015) 'California Carbon Allowance Vintage 2014 Future', www.theice.com/products/6747557/California-Carbon-Allowance-Vintage-2014-Future, accessed January 9, 2015).

55. McCann, L. et al. (2005), 'Transaction Cost Measurement for Evaluating Environmental Policies', *Ecological Economics*, **52**, 527–542; Coggan, A. et al. (2010), 'Influences of Transaction Costs in Environmental Policy', *Ecological Economics*, **69**, 1777–1784. See also Pavel, J. and L. Vitek (2012), 'Transaction Costs of Environmental Taxation: The Administrative Burden', in J. Milne and M. Skou-Andersen (eds), *Handbook of Environmental Taxation*, Aldershot, UK and Brookfield, VT, USA: Edward Elgar Publishing, pp. 273–282, noting at p. 277 that the size of transaction costs significantly influence the impact of a given tool on economic effectiveness.

56. Rousseau and Proost offer a simpler, three-stage framework that includes rule-making (loosely corresponding to Coggan's stages 1–3), implementation (which corresponds to 4 and 5) and enforcement (corresponding to 6 and 7). Rousseau, S. and S. Proost (2005), *supra* note 9, at 339.

57. See Smulders, S. and H.R.J. Vollergergh (2001), 'Green Taxes and Administrative Costs: The Case of Carbon Taxation' in C. Carraro and G.E. Metcalf (eds), *Behavioural and Distributional Effects of Environmental Policy*, Chicago: University of Chicago Press, p. 94. See, for example, Pope, Jeff (2014), 'Estimating the Compliance Costs of Australia's Carbon Pricing Scheme', *Australia Tax Forum*, **29** (1), 109–137 (a paper that focuses on the costs of carbon pricing for private actors).

58. See Pavel, J. and L. Vitek (2012), *supra* note 55. Relying on McCann, Coggan defines transaction costs as the cost of resources used to define, establish, maintain and transfer property rights. See Coggan, A. et al. (2010), *supra* note 55 at 2.

59. See Evans, Chris (2003), 'Studying the Studies: An Overview of Recent Research into Taxation Operating Costs', *eJournal of Tax Research*, **1** (1), 64.

60. Goulder, L.H. and A.R. Schein (2013), *supra* note 6, at 11. See also Field, B.C. and N.D. Olewiler (2011), 'Emissions Taxes and Subsidies', in *Environmental Economics 3rd Canadian Edition*, Toronto, Ontario: McGraw-Hill Ryerson.

61. Goulder and Schein point out that a cap-and-trade system can also be implemented upstream, suggesting that the claim that carbon taxes are easier to administer (which assumes carbon taxes are administered upstream and cap-and-trade implemented downstream) should be evaluated more closely.

62. This was 185 in 2014. See Motor Fuel Tax Act, *supra* note 45.

63. The lack of empirical analysis about the costs of implementation is not unique to the carbon tax – there is little empirical data on the costs of implementing environmental policies in general. Smulders, S. and H.R.J. Vollergergh (2001), *supra* note 57, at 115.

64. British Columbia Ministry of Finance (2014), 'Supplement to the Estimates, Fiscal Year Ending March 31, 2015', http://bcbudget.gov.bc.ca/2014/cstimates/2014_Supplement_to_the_Estimates.pdf, accessed January 9, 2015, at 34.

65. This estimate, which is the authors', was derived following exchanges with staff at the

British Columbia Ministry of Finance, Revenue Division, between November 2014 and January 2015. Smulders and Vollergergh are in agreement, noting that to the extent that carbon taxes are linked with existing energy excise taxes, it is safe to assume that there will only be a small rise in administrative costs. Smulders, S. and H.R.J. Vollergergh (2001), *supra* note 57, at 121.
66. British Columbia Ministry of Finance (2010), *supra* note 20 (Carbon Tax Report and Plan at 64).
67. Andersen, A. et al. (1985), 'The Administrative and Compliance Costs for the Federal Sales Tax System with a Brief Comparison to the Retail Sales Tax System of Ontario', for the Department of Finance, Ottawa, cited in Evans (2003), *supra* note 59, at 80.
68. F. Vaillancourt, 'The Administrative and Compliance Costs of the Personal Income Tax and Payroll Tax System in Canada (1986) Canadian Tax Foundation, Toronto (1989)', cited in Evans (2003), *supra* note 60, at 81. Administration costs of income taxes are generally higher than excise taxes.
69. Sanford, C. et al. (1989), *Administrative and Compliance Costs of Taxation*, Bath, UK: Fiscal Publications. These results were consistent with: OECD (1988), *Taxing Consumption*, Paris: OECD Publishing. On average, compliance costs (to the private sector actor) are three times higher than administrative costs, with compliance costs of income tax the highest and those for excise duties the lowest. Sanford, ibid.
70. Deutscher Bundestag, 2002.
71. Pavel, J. and L. Vitek (2012), *supra* note 55, at 279.
72. OECD (2007), *Instrument Mixes for Environmental Policy*, Paris: OECD Publishing.
73. Pavel, J. and L. Vitek (2012), *supra* note 55, at 279.
74. Goulder, L.H. and A.R. Schein (2013), *supra* note 6, at 12.
75. Over 100 in 2015. Québec Ministry of Sustainable Development, Environment and the Fight against Climate Change (MDDELCC) (2013), 'The Carbon Market', www.mddelcc.gouv.qc.ca/changements/carbone/index-en.htm, accessed January 9, 2015.
76. The *Direction du marché du carbone* is responsible for the establishment, implementation and administration of the QC-ETS. Personal communication with a representative of the *Direction du marché du carbone*, Tuesday, November 11, 2014.
77. Western Climate Initiative (2013), *supra* note 26, at 2.
78. Ibid.
79. Air Resources Board (2014–2015), 'Jurisdiction Agreement', www.wci-inc.org/docs/13-407%20Final%20STD%20%20213.pdf, accessed January 9, 2015.
80. CA $1.46 million (*Direction du marché du carbone*) plus US $968,512 (QC share of WCI Inc. budget for 2014).
81. Québec Ministry of Sustainable Development, Environment and the Fight against Climate Change (MDDELCC) (2014), *supra* note 39.
82. For example by partners of the Regional Greenhouse Gas Initiative, through RGGI Inc. (Regional Greenhouse Gas Initiative (2014), supra note 49). See also Emissions Reduction Taskforce (2014) 'Report to the Washington State Governor's Office', www.governor.wa.gov/issues/climate/documents/CERT_Final_Report.pdf, accessed January 9, 2015.

3. Fault lines between fees and taxes: legal obstacles for linking

Stefan E. Weishaar[1,2]

INTRODUCTION

Over the last decades concerns about climate change have been intensifying[3] yet international agreements on a global solution in the form of a second Kyoto Protocol are not forthcoming. In the absence of such a global solution, an increasing number of national and regional greenhouse gas emissions trading schemes address climate change. Currently such schemes are operating in the European Union, in Switzerland, in North America (the Regional Greenhouse Gas Initiative (RGGI) and the Western Climate Initiative (WCI)), New Zealand, Australia, Japan, Kazakhstan and China.

Because least cost abatement options are spread all over the world, linking of emissions trading schemes reduces overall abatement costs and leads to a convergence of international emission allowances prices: consequently the same amount of global warming protection can be attained at lower costs.[4] Moreover, linking by enlarging emissions trading markets and creating more opportunities for trading would lead to more market liquidity with a more stable price signal.[5] Allowance prices that are the same across different emissions trading systems would also eliminate competitive distortions that might arise from differences in pre-link allowance prices. Without having to wait for a global solution to climate change, creating a link between existing and emerging emissions trading systems (ETSs) can help to reduce carbon emissions at low costs and thereby help to foster political acceptance for greenhouse gas reductions and perhaps even lead to further proliferation of ETSs that could help to overcome the current political stalemate.[6]

The various emissions trading systems have different designs that can obstruct 'linking'.[7] The US schemes for example use reserve price auctions where the reserve price is set in accordance with a predetermined price-trajectory. These schemes thus have a price support element inherent in their design. The European Union (EU) ETS by contrast does not use any reserve price nor any price-based support scheme. Linking, for example, the Californian ETS with the EU ETS would endanger the attainment of the Californian policy objectives and hence be unattractive unless the EU would introduce reserve price auctioning.

Yet from Commission documents related to the structural reform review to address oversupply in the EU ETS, it is apparent that the Commission has an aversion against reserve price auctioning. When the Commission invited a response to its report on the state of the European carbon market in which it proposed structural reform options, it subsumed reserve price auctions under the heading of 'discretionary price instruments'.[8] Moreover, in the following stakeholder meetings (March and April 2013) on the structural options to strengthen the EU ETS, none of the invited stakeholders in the session on discretionary price instruments was actually talking about such instruments. As long as the Commission is not transparent, it can only be speculated why it is so disposed against this instrument. This could be on economic grounds (setting the right price trajectory is difficult and subject to controversy), on institutional grounds (the Commission's earlier experience when it favoured a carbon tax) or on legal grounds. Regarding the legal dimension giving the EU ETS a more price-based character by introducing reserve price auctioning could necessitate its qualification as a 'primarily fiscal measure' under Article 192(2) TFEU that would entail unanimity voting in the Council and thus potentially endanger current EU climate policy.

Differences in ETS design can constitute an obstacle to linking. While the economic and institutional dimensions are not considered here, this chapter focuses on the question whether the tax law qualification of reserve price auctioning constitutes a legal bar preventing the EU ETS from being linked to a scheme that employs reserve price auctioning.

This chapter commences by describing various instances in which an ETS was described and criticized to constitute a tax scheme and describes the importance of distinguishing taxes from fees. The next section examines how reserve price auctions would be treated under EU law, and then reserve price auctions are approached from a law making perspective to examine if its introduction could indeed put an end to EU climate policy. The final section presents concluding remarks.

TAX CHALLENGES IN OTHER ETSs

Emissions trading for environmental pollution was introduced by J.H. Dales[9] in the 1960s. It was soon recognized that market-based instruments such as emissions trading or environmental taxation have superior efficiency properties if compared with command and control type regulation.[10] Bearing in mind the political discussions concerning the introduction of carbon taxes or emissions trading systems to counter climate change in the 1990s and beyond, it may not be surprising that in the climate change literature both taxes and emissions trading are generally contrasted with each other.

From an economic perspective both instruments are fundamentally different. A carbon tax can best be described as a pricing mechanism that sets a price incentive for the internalization of negative externalities, in other words, for greenhouse gas emissions. In its generic form an emissions trading system by contrast restricts the overall quantity of greenhouse gas emissions and thereby sets incentives for abatement. In the presence of scientific uncertainty both instruments thus offer policymakers a choice either to set a price or to set a quantity to address climate change. Even though in practice several emissions trading systems combine both quantity-setting with price-setting, such systems are still described as emission trading systems. Examples where there is a strong price-setting element in the emissions trading system include RGGI, WCI and Korea.

It may therefore strike some readers as curious and strange that emission trading schemes have been criticized and challenged as constituting a 'tax' measure.

The Australian Carbon Pricing Mechanism that was an emissions trading scheme with an initial fixed price period was quickly and widely discredited as a 'carbon tax'. Even before the flexible price period could actually start it was dismantled following a change in the government in 2014.

Also in the US where Environmental Protection Agencies in various states have been charged with the task to establish ETSs, the systems have been legally challenged as constituting an illegal tax measure. The American discussion is interesting since it suggests that the relationship between auctioning and environmental taxation or environmental fees is indeed richer than what is commonly recognized in the climate law literature thus far where auctioning is generally seen as a particular form of allocation of allowances.

More specifically in the arising US court cases plaintiffs challenged the legality of introducing auctioning of greenhouse gas emission allowance auctions.[11] The Environmental Protection Agencies do not have the authority to establish taxes but are only permitted to levy environmental fees.

In Thrun et al.[12] it was alleged that the New York RGGI program was ultra vires, that administrative bodies acted ultra vires in promulgating the RGGI regulations, that RGGI rules were arbitrary and capricious and that

RGGI created an unlawful tax. The court held that the plaintiffs lacked standing and that the claims were barred by the doctrine of laches so the court unfortunately did not discuss the substance of the claims.

In California Chamber of Commerce[13] plaintiffs challenged the Californian's Air Resource Board's (CARB) right to sell allowances at auction. In particular the court examined if AB32 authorized CARB to sell allowances and whether the auction provisions constitute a tax that would result to be unconstitutional since it was not passed with the necessary voting procedures. While the first part of the judgement is not of interest for this chapter, the court's line of argumentation regarding the question if reserve price auctions constitute a tax or a fee is presented in detail.

The court commences by clarifying that a tax is a forced contribution levied by the authority of the state for the general governmental purposes[14] and that a 'tax' can mean different things in different contexts.[15] The court then examined if the reserve price auction scheme could be subsumed under one of the general categories of compulsory fees or charges that have been distinguished from taxes in earlier cases[16] and would thus not require a particular voting procedure.

Although reserve price auctions do have attributes of some of these categories, auctions do 'not fit squarely' within any. Yet the court is of the opinion that auctions are more like traditional regulatory fees than taxes albeit it concedes 'that it is a close question'. It then examines properties of auctions in light of its tax properties and fee properties.

With regard to the tax properties it finds the following. First, auctions are not entirely voluntary in the sense that covered entities are forbidden from emitting greenhouse gases without acquiring allowances and will find it difficult to avoid having to acquire them. Second, there is no 'benefit' associated with the purchase of allowances in the sense that such benefits are only existing vis-à-vis other covered entities but absent vis-à-vis non-covered entities. Third, the auction price is at least partly determined by the government through its setting of the 'reserve floor', by decisions to sell off the 'containment reserve' and by setting the 'allowance cap'. Fourthly, although the auction revenues are earmarked for furthering AB32's regulatory goal of reducing GHG emissions, in practice many regulatory activities can be construed to have a link with these objectives so that auction proceeds could be used in the form of 'general government purposes'.

On the other hand auction reserve prices have also attributes of a regulatory 'mitigation' fee or charge that the court identifies as follows. First, purchasers of allowances receive a scarce public resource to pollute the environment: this right has a market value and is tradable. Second, purchasing allowances at auction is not mandatory in the sense that entities receive significant quantities of allowances for free and can either abate emission or purchase on the secondary market. Third, the price of allowances is partially determined by market forces and the charges are used (ostensibly, at least) for regulatory purposes.

For a mitigation fee to constitute a regulatory fee rather than a tax several requirements must be satisfied: (1) the primary purpose of the fee must be regulatory rather than revenue generation; (2) the total amount of fees collected cannot exceed the costs of the activities they support; (3) there must be a reasonable relationship between the amount of the fees and the burden imposed by the fee payers pollution.

The purpose of a measure is ascertained by the intended result, the effect of the legislation,[17] its incidents, and the natural and legal effect of the language employed[18] rather than by its legislative designation.[19] Since every regulatory fee is aimed at revenue raising and every tax is in some ways regulatory[20] courts must proceed carefully in determining the purpose.

That the primary purpose of auctioning is regulatory rather than revenue raising is evidenced in the way auctioning helps CARB to realize its regulatory goals: (1) auctions increases compliance costs and thus incentivizes abatement; (2) auctions are an effective allocation mechanism; (3) they create a reliable price signal; and (4) they moderate price shocks. In addition the court recognizes that auction revenues must be used for regulatory purposes of AB32.

Regarding the requirement that total amount of fees collected cannot exceed the costs of the activities they support the court takes a pragmatic approach. It concedes that since the legislator limits the use of revenues only to the regulatory purpose of AB32, by definition, the total amount of revenues collected cannot exceed the costs of the associated regulatory programs they support.

The last step to determine if auction revenues constitute a fee is to analyze if there is a 'reasonable relationship' between the amount of the fees and the burden imposed by the fee payers' pollution. The court distinguishes the present case from other cases previously decided and concludes that the amount paid at auction must not be closely linked to the payers' burdens on the regulatory programs they fund, but that a 'reasonable relationship' between the monies and the covered entities' (collective) responsibility for the harmful effects of GHG emissions is present. Given that AB32 covers large amounts of California's GHG emissions, the court deems this link to be present and dismisses the application.

In California the reserve price auctions thus constitute a 'fee' rather than a tax. An appeal case was logged in February 2014 before the 3rd Appellate District Court.[21]

EU ETS AND TAXES AND FEES

The previous section presented how reserve price auctions are qualified in other jurisdictions as 'fees'. This section examines how they are treated in the EU. It first examines whether they could be qualified as taxes or fees and subsequently examines their legal qualification under the environmental law provisions of Article 192(1) and (2) TFEU.

Reserve Price Auctions: 'Fees' or 'Taxes'?

Determining if reserve price auctions constitute a fee or a tax under EU law is a non-trivial question. There is no general definition of a 'tax' in the EU; a more functional concept of a tax is preferred,[22] possibly because every national tax law system has its own peculiarities and consequently there is no 'one hat fits all' definition.[23] The European Commission introduced the term 'environmental levies' to describe environmental taxes and environmental charges. The Commission describes them as covering all compulsory, unrequited payments, whether the revenue accrues directly to the government budget or is destined for particular purposes (for example, earmarking).[24] Yet taxes and charges or fees are not the same from a tax law perspective.

Examining various tax definitions it appears that taxes are characterized as compulsory and unrequited payments to the general government.[25] Despite also having regulatory and redistributive tasks, taxes are predominantly instruments to raise revenue. By contrast fees 'are compulsory, requited payments to either general government or to bodies outside general government',[26] thus emphasizing that amounts paid should be for services rendered and consequently also be in proportion with the costs incurred.

In order to examine if reserve price auctioning constitutes a fee in the EU, a doctrinal approach is chosen for want of a clear cut EU definition. From a theoretic perspective taxes and fees differ in determining the price for pollution. Pigouvian taxes would determine the value of externalities, Baumol-Oates taxes would set prices so as to achieve environmental standards, environmental fees would relate the price to the benefit provided.[27] This suggests that 'benefits' for services rendered are an important element.

Under a benefit approach to fees, the economic rationale for an environmental fee must be rationalized on the basis of benefits to the purchasers of allowances. Such benefits could stem from covered installations purchasing the right to pollute from a government which is entrusted with the management and protection of public assets (public trust doctrine) and the right to pollute would thus constitute a benefit.[28]

Given that the EU ETS extends to 31 states, it may not be easily proven that all states officially entrusted the Commission with the management of public assets while implicitly this is the case because the 28 EU Member States are barred from taking action under EU law in an area of shared competence to the extent that the field is occupied by the Union.

In a more regulatory vein, one could argue that covered entities do not have an inherent right to pollute and that the government grants the benefit to use the environment which it could otherwise restrict unless a fee would be paid in return for the usage right.

It could thus be arguable that under an EU ETS with a reserve price auction there would be a transfer of benefits (the right to emit) in return for the amount paid at auction and thus satisfy the 'requiting criterion' of a fee.

Other elements that – in light of the Californian court case presented in the previous section – could be examined are the regulatory purpose, the proportionality of the levied amount and costs and the reasonable relationship between the fee and the burden imposed by polluting.

These elements are difficult to assess in the absence of a concrete auction reserve price proposal by the Commission, but it appears to be clear that auctions fulfil similar functions under AB32 as they would in the EU ETS. Consequently the first criterion of regulatory purpose is deemed to be met.

Regarding the second criterion of proportionality between the fee and the costs of the service, it bears mentioning that also in the EU the majority of the auction revenues are to be spent for environmental purposes even if some money is collected for the purpose of industry support measures for Energy Intensive Trade Exposed industries. Since the budgetary use of these funds is determined at Member State level, this criterion is not easily resolved. From a law making history point of view, it bears mentioning, however, that the present Auction Regulation 1031/2010 has been decided upon by delegation of Directive 2003/87/EC that has Article 192(1) TFEU as a legal basis and should therefore not contain fiscal measures.

The third criterion concerning the reasonable relationship between the amount of fees and the burden imposed by the fee payers' pollution is difficult to assess in the abstract. If the value of an allowance could be based on public perception of the value of the asset or on the cost of any mitigation measure, a link between the fee and the damage could be established. As is the case under AB32, also the EU ETS covers large amounts (40 per cent) of EU's GHG emissions so that a 'reasonable relationship' between the amounts paid and the covered entities' (collective) responsibility could be present.

The above examination is not conclusive given that the level of reserve prices are unknown, that there are no clear definitions of what a fee or a tax is under EU law and that various different Member States currently use their auction proceeds in different ways. Some elements of a fee seem satisfied while others are questionable. In this light it should be observed that the ECJ ruled in Case C-366/10[29] that Directive 2008/101 (extending the EU ETS to aviation) does not involve a form of obligatory levy in favour of public authorities that could be regarded as a customs duty, tax, fee or charge on fuel held or consumed by aircraft operators and thus concluded that the EU ETS constitutes a market-based instrument and not a duty, tax, fee or charge on fuel load. While this finding can be criticized from an economic perspective because also taxes are 'market-based instruments',[30] it also raises questions from a US law perspective since the differentiation between taxes and fees is motivated by the quest to determine the competences of actors such as the California Air Resources Board or Environmental Protection Agencies. In the context of EU law, it might, however, suggest that the EU ETS does not contain any fiscal measures.[31]

Tax or a Fee under Article 192(2) TFEU

After examining if reserve price auctions could constitute a tax or a fee, this section examines how they would be treated under the environmental law provisions of Article 192(1) and (2) TFEU.

Article 192(1) is the general legal basis for environmental measures and is decided by qualified majority voting. By way of derogation from Article 192(1), Article 192(2) requires unanimity in the Council to adopt (inter alia) 'provisions primarily of a fiscal nature'. Cases clarifying this provision are rare yet the Court will consider the content and the aim of the proposed measure to discern whether to use Article 192(1) or 192(2)[32] and measures such as clean energy or environmental taxes are believed to fall under 192(2).[33] Also the Commission as well seems to avoid Article 192(2) TFEU. In the context of the proposed carbon tax in 1992 the Commission relied upon ex Article 130s EC Treaty (now Article 192 TFEU). At that time, however, this environmental provision did not yet distinguish between fiscal and non-fiscal measures and required unanimity; due to different interests of Member States the carbon tax was unsuccessful.

There is uncertainty about the meaning of 'primarily' and the meaning of 'fiscal measures'. Each is considered in turn.

In the literature it has been suggested that 'primarily of fiscal nature' would mean that the fiscal aspect of the measure is predominant. This interpretation would prevent fiscal measures to be passed under Article 192(1). The effectiveness of Article 192(2) would however be undermined if the legislator could reduce the importance of the fiscal element so as to circumvent the provision. The main focus of interpreting 'primarily' should thus extend to tax revenue implications to safeguard sovereignty concerns of Member States.[34]

Examining the interpretation of the meaning of 'fiscal measure' in EU law is complicated by the various equally authentic language versions of the Treaty and the differences in national tax laws and legal traditions. At times attempts to interpret 'fiscal measure' are arguing on the basis of national tax law which may not always be very helpful. In any event one can generally distinguish between a narrow interpretation of 'fiscal measures' that only refers to taxes but not to fees and a broad interpretation that encompasses both taxes and fees.

Proponents of a narrow interpretation (only taxes) point towards Article 192(2) constituting a derogation to the ordinary legislative procedure under Article 192(1)[35] and argue that this narrow interpretation safeguards the 'effet utile' (Article 19 TEU) of EU law.[36]

Some authors point out that an inconsistency between environmental fees and fees in other policy areas would arise if the concept of 'fiscal nature' would include regulatory fees since then such measures could be adopted under other treaty provisions with qualified majority but in the area of environment unanimity would be required.[37] Others suggest that non-tax fiscal charges would in their nature be more selective and hence be less intrusive for the Member States sovereignty than tax measures.[38]

There are also proponents of a broad interpretation that subsume both taxes and fees under Article 192(2). Freytag (2001) for example argues that the object and purpose of this provision is the safeguarding of the financial autonomy of Member States. The budgetary impact of the measure must thus be considered and consequently a differentiation between different types of measures is not expedient. A broad interpretation of Article 192(2) may, however, be obstructed by its function as a derogation to Article 192(1) TFEU.[39]

The above can be summarized as follows. It is unclear how reserve price auctioning would be qualified under EU tax law. There are some pointers towards a 'fee' but also a court ruling that indicates that the EU ETS is a market-based instrument not akin to neither a tax nor a fee. Also the examination of the environmental legal base is inconclusive if a qualification of an auction reserve price as a fee would allow the use of Article 192(1) as a legal base and thus circumvent unanimity voting in the Council. In order to determine if the tax law qualification of reserve price auctioning constitutes a legal bar preventing the EU ETS from being linked to a scheme that employs reserve price auctioning without endangering the current EU climate change policy, the law making process must be examined. This will be done in the following section.

A LAW MAKING APPROACH TO RESERVE PRICE AUCTIONING IN THE EU

A legal obstacle that might prevent linking the EU ETS with an emissions trading system that uses reserve price auctioning stems from the threat that the introduction of a reserve price auction in the EU would require unanimity voting in the Council[40] and thereby endanger the current EU ETS. While the above tax law examination could not dispel concerns that reserve price auctioning in the EU would not be falling under 192(1) TFEU, a law making perspective is taken in this section.

Law making in the EU is to a large extent a 'treaty based game' in which the centre of gravity (in other words, the legal bases) of legislative proposals needs to be assessed.[41] Legislators enjoy a margin of discretion in framing the aim and purpose of a legal measure in such a way that a suitable legal basis can be found. Legal bases differ in terms of their involvement of actors and consultative bodies and with regard to their voting requirements. Some legal bases require simple majority, others qualified majority voting while a few require unanimity. In case of reserve price auctioning the possible legal bases are Article 192(1) TFEU which requires qualified majority and Article 192(2) TFEU which requires unanimity voting in the Council.

To introduce reserve price auctioning into the existing framework of the EU ETS there are essentially two possibilities: either the current Emissions Trading Directive (2003/87/EC) has to be amended (scenario I) or a new Directive has to be adopted (scenario II).

The qualification of the legislative proposal that introduces reserve price auctioning as being of a non-fiscal nature would allow the use of Article 192(1) TFEU as a legal basis in both scenarios. On the other side, the qualification of the measure as having a fiscal nature would not automatically require the use of Article 192(2) TFEU as a legal basis. The EU legislator has still the possibility to avoid the unanimity requirement of Article 192(2) if the centre of gravity of the measure would be considered as not to fall on its fiscal nature.

In case the introduction of reserve price auctioning qualifies as a measure of primarily fiscal nature than Article 192(2) TFEU is to be used as a legal basis. In scenario I, amending Directive 2003/87/EC would require that the legal basis of Article 192(2) TFEU has to be assessed jointly with the first paragraph of Article 192 TFEU. For not undermining the rights of the European Parliament under the first paragraph of the Article, the requirement for unanimity voting in the Council has to be combined with the ordinary legislative procedure.[42] In the second scenario, Article 192(2) TFEU can be used alone for adopting a new directive under a special legislative procedure requiring unanimity.[43]

However, not reaching the unanimity requirement in the Council in both scenarios would not lead to the collapse of the EU ETS. Directive 2003/87/EC would remain in force in its current form and regulate the operation of the EU ETS. Consequently concerns that the introduction of auction reserve pricing into the legal framework of the EU ETS would dismantle the current EU climate change policy are unfounded.

CONCLUSION

Differences in emissions trading designs can obstruct possibilities for linking. Linking between ETS that have a reserve price auction system, such as the Californian ETS, for example, and the EU ETS that does not have such a reserve price would endanger the attainment of the Californian policy objectives and hence be unattractive unless the EU would introduce reserve price auctioning as well. In analysing if there is a legal obstacle for the EU to introduce reserve price auctioning into the EU ETS, this chapter has drawn upon various legal fields including climate law, tax law and European law.

Despite the encountered difficulties in qualifying reserve price auctions under EU law as a fiscal measure (either as a tax or a fee), it was possible to answer the research question by relying on a law making approach. Current EU climate policy would not be threatened if the Commission were to decide to propose the introduction of a reserve price auction scheme. If the Commission chooses not to do so the motivation must be found in realms other than law.

Besides this finding this research has generated a number of interesting insights. First, it has shown that the emissions trading systems can be assessed from a tax law perspective in ways that are very different from traditional climate change policy or environmental economics where emissions trading systems tend to be contrasted to taxation rather than to be subsumed under it.

Second, one could have been expecting that in the EU there would be more clarity as to the powers conferred upon the Commission to propose measures that affect the fiscal sovereignty of Member States. The lack of clarity as to what is a 'primarily fiscal measure' appears to be in striking contrast to the strongly developed differences between fiscal instruments in, for example, the US where regulatory authorities seem to push the boundaries of the powers conferred upon them by introducing 'fees' that in their language and attributes appear to be 'taxes'.[44]

NOTES

1. Dr S.E. Weishaar, MSc, LLM is Associate Professor of Law and Economics at Groningen University and is Leader of the LETS Link Emissions Trading Systems research project.
2. Financial support by the Gratama Foundation to visit Vermont Law School to conduct research for this chapter is gratefully acknowledged. I am very grateful for valuable discussion with Janet Milne, Rainer Prokisch and Irene Burgers. All remaining errors are of course my own.
3. IPCC (2014).
4. Flachsland et al. (2009a), Grull and Taschini (2012).
5. Jaffe and Stavins (2007), Tuerk et al. (2009).
6. Aldy and Stavins (2011).
7. Weishaar (2014).
8. COM (2012) 652 final of 14 November 2012.
9. Dales (1968).
10. Faure and Weishaar (2012).
11. California Chamber of Commerce et al. *v.* California Air Resources Board et al., Sacramento Superior Court, Case No. 34-2012-80001313; Morning Star Packing Co. et al. *v.* California Air Resources Board et al., Sacramento Superior Court, Case No. 34-2013-80001464, Thrun et al. Index No.: 4358-11; RJI No.: 01-11-104776.
12. Thrun et al. Index No.: 4358-11; RJI No.: 01-11-104776.
13. California Chamber of Commerce et al. *v.* California Air Resources Board et al., Sacramento Superior Court, Case No. 34-2012-80001313; Morning Star Packing Co. et al. *v.* California Air Resources Board et al., Sacramento Superior Court, Case No. 34-2013-80001464.
14. McHenry *v.* Downer (1897) 116 Cal. 20, 24.
15. Sinclair Paint Co. *v.* State Bd. Of Equalization (1997) 15 Cal. 4th 866, 874.
16. These categories are special assessments and related business charges, development fees, user fees, and regulatory fees.
17. Davis *v.* San Diego (1939) 33 Cal.App.2d 190, 193.
18. Ingels *v.* Riley (1936) 5 Cal.2d 154, 159.
19. Weekes *v.* City of Oakland (1978) 21 Cal.3d 386, 392.
20. Sinclair Paint, 15 Cal.4th at 880.
21. Morning Star Packing Company et al. *v.* California Air Resources Board et al., C075954 and California Chamber of Commerce et al. v. California Air Resources Board et al., C075930.
22. Barker (2005), p. 23.
23. At times the use of the fiscal measure will be entirely up to the discretion of the Member State. See the former Directive 2006/12/EC of the European Parliament and the Council of 5 April 2006 on Waste and Case C-254/08 *Futura Immobiliare* [2009] ERC I-06995.
24. COM (97) 9 final, 26 March 1997, pp. 3–4.
25. SNA (2008) p. 143, conceptualizes taxes as 'compulsory, unrequited payments, in cash or kind, made by institutional units to government units'. Similarly the OECD (2014) p. 318 conceptualizes 'taxes' as being 'confined to compulsory unrequited payments to general government. Taxes are unrequited in the sense that benefits provided by government to taxpayers are not normally in proportion to their payments'.
26. OECD (1999), p. 9.
27. Milne (2014), p. 13.
28. Blumm and Guthrie (2012).
29. C-366/10 *Air Transport Association of America and Others* [20011] ECR I-13755.
30. See in general Horn (2013).
31. Also in the third trading phase 2013–2020 allowances for aviation continue to be largely allocated on the basis of benchmarks, thus for free.

32. C-36/98 Spain *v.* Council [2001] ERC I-00779.
33. Advocate General Léger on C-36/98 Spain *v.* Council, ECLI:EU:C:2000:246.
34. See Kreibohm (2003).
35. Calliess and Ruffert (2011), EGV/EUV, Rn 28-32.
36. Calliess and Ruffert (2011), EGV/EUV, Rn 28-32.
37. Mueller (1994), p. 83.
38. Epiney (1997), p. 57.
39. Freytag (2001) p. 80 ff.
40. One has to keep in mind that the Council, according to Article 16(2) TFEU consists of a representative of each Member State at ministerial level.
41. C-376/98 Federal Republic of Germany *v.* European Parliament and Council of the European Union [2000] ECR I-08419, para. 32.
42. The way the ordinary legislative procedure operates is regulated in Article 294 TFEU and according to this Article, the Parliament co-decides with the Council.
43. The special legislative procedure prescribed for this case requires the consultation of the European Parliament as well as of the Economic and Social Committee and of the Committee of Regions.
44. For enlightening work on this issue the interested reader is referred to the work by Milne (2014).

BIBLIOGRAPHY

Aldy, J.E. and Stavins R.N. (2011), 'The promise and problems of pricing carbon: Theory and experience', Harvard Institute of Economic Research Discussion Paper, retrieved from: http://papers.ssrn.com/sol3/papers.cfm?abstract_id=1950693, last viewed 11 March 2015.
Barker, W.B. (2005), 'The relevance of a concept of tax', in B. Peeters (ed.), *The Concept of Tax*, EATLP Congress, Naples, 27–29 May 2005.
Baron, R. and Philibert, C. (2005), 'Act locally, trade globally: Emissions trading for climate policy', International Energy Agency, retrieved from: http://www.iea.org/publications/freepublications/publication/act_locally.pdf, last viewed 11 March 2015.
Blumm, M.C. and Guthrie, R.D. (2012), 'Internalizing the public trust doctrine: Natural law and constitutional and statutory approaches to fulfilling the Saxion version', *UC Dacis Law Review*, 45, 741–808.
Calliess, C. and Ruffert, M. (2011), EGV/EUV AEUV, Art. 192, 4th edn, Beck.
COM (1997) 9 final, Environmental Taxes and Charges in the Single Market, 26 March 1997.
COM (2012) 652 final, Report from the Commission to the European Parliament and the Council: The state of the European carbon market in 2012, Brussels, 14 November 2012.
Dales, J. (1968), *Pollution, Property and Prices: An Essay in Policy*, Toronto: University of Toronto Press.
Epiney, A. (1997), *Umweltrecht in der Europaeischen Union*, Koeln Berlin, Bonn, Muenchen.
Faure, M. and Weishaar S.E. (2012), 'The role of environmental taxation: economics and the law', in J. Milne and M.S. Andersen (eds), *Handbook of Research on Environmental Taxation*, Cheltenham, UK and Northampton, MA, USA: Edward Elgar Publishing, pp. 399–421.
Flachsland, C., Marschinski, R. and Edenhofer O. (2009a), 'To link or not to link:

Benefits and disbenefits of linking cap-and-trade systems', *Climate Policy*, 9 (4) Special Issue Linking GHG Trading Systems, 358–372.

Flachsland, C., Marschinski, R. and Edenhofer O. (2009b), 'Global trading versus linking: Architectures for international emissions trading', *Energy Policy*, 37 (5), 1637–1647.

Freytag, G. (2001), Europaeische Anforderungen an Umweltabgaben, dargestellt am Beispiel von Abgaben zur Reduzierung der Umweltbelastung durch den Strassenverkehr, Baden-Baden.

Grull, G. and Taschini, L. (2012), 'Linking emissions trading schemes: A short note', *Economics of Energy and Environmental Policy*, 1 (3), 31–38.

Horn, H. (2013), 'The ECJ Judgment on the Extensions of the ETS to Aviation: An Economist's Discontent', IFN Working Paper No. 980, Research Institute for Industrial Economics, pp. 36.

IPCC (2014), Climate Change 2014: Synthesis Report, Fifth Assessment Synthesis Report, retrieved from: http://www.ipcc.ch/report/ar5/syr/, last viewed 11 March 2015.

Jaffe, J. and Stavins, R.N. (2007), 'Linking tradable permit systems for greenhouse gas emissions: Opportunities, implications and challenges', International Emissions Trading Association, Geneva, retrieved from: http://belfercenter.ksg.harvard.edu/files/IETA_Linking_Report.pdf, last viewed 11 March 2015.

Kreibohm, P. (2003), Der Begriff der Steuer im Europaeischen Gemeinschaftsrecht, Carl Heymanns Verlag KG, Koen, Berlin, Muenchen.

Milne, J.E. (2014), 'Environmental taxes and fees: Wrestling with theory', in Kreiser, L., Lee, S., Ueta, K., Milne, J.E. and Ashiabor, H. (eds), *Environmental Taxation and Green Fiscal Reform, Theory and Impact*, Cheltenham, UK and Northampton, MA, USA: Edward Elgar Publishing, pp. 5–23.

Mueller, C. (1994), Möglichkeiten und Grenzen der indirekten Verhaltenssteuerung durch Abgaben im Umweltrecht, Heymanns Verlag KG, Koen, Berlin, Muenchen.

OECD (1999), 'Economic instruments for pollution control and natural resources management in OECD Countries: A survey', Paris: OECD, p. 9.

OECD (2014), The OECD Interpretative Guide, Annex A, retrieved from: http://www.oecd.org/ctp/tax-policy/OECD-Revenue-Statistics-2014-Interpretative-Guide.pdf, last viewed 11 March 2015.

SNA (2008), The Inter-Secretariat Working Group on National Accounts, System of National Accounts 2008, New York, retrieved from: http://unstats.un.org/unsd/nationalaccount/docs/SNA2008.pdf, last viewed 11 March 2015.

Tuerk, A., Sterk, W., Haites, E., Mehling, M., Flachsland, C., Kimura, H., Betz, R. and Jotzo, F. (2009), 'Linking of emissions trading schemes: Synthesis report', Climate Strategies, 20 May 2009, retrieved from: https://www.mcc-berlin.net/fileadmin/data/pdf/Publikationen/Tuerk_Sterk_Haites_Mehling_Flachsland_Kimura_Betz_Jotzo_2009_Linking_Emissions_Trading_Schemes.pdf, last viewed 11 March 2015.

Weishaar, S.E. (2014), *Emissions Trading Design: A Critical Overview*, Cheltenham, UK and Northampton, MA, USA: Edward Elgar Publishing, p. 272.

4. Policy changes on Ecological Tax Reform/carbon tax in Germany and Japan

Shinji Onoda and Kai Schlegelmilch

INTRODUCTION

After about 20 years of discussion, Germany and Japan introduced an Ecological Tax Reform (ETR)/carbon tax[1] (BMF, 2003; MOE, 2012). The two countries share common aspects in their economic and political systems, yet the contents of the two tax systems are quite different. The reasons can be traced to the economic and social situation in each country. However, only part of the answer can be found there because the situation itself cannot answer questions about how the tax rates or taxed objects were determined. Here, analysis of the policymaking process is one way to understand how policy was shaped by the combination of varying interests and ideas. Therefore, by investigating and comparing the policymaking processes of the ETR/carbon tax in Germany and Japan, we aim to reveal reasons behind the tax systems in each country, roles of related actors, and eventually factors which promote but also hinder or limit policy changes.

ANALYTICAL VIEWPOINT

Policymaking means a change of policy. To analyze a policymaking process, it is necessary to comprehend at what level and how a policy change occurred. Peter Hall identified three distinct levels of policy change (Hall, 1993). A first-order change is a change to instrument settings, such as a budget adjustment, which features incrementalism. A second-order change is a change to policy instruments and their settings, such as the introduction of a new system of monetary control. A third-order change is a change in policy instruments, instrument settings and overall goals behind policy, such as a change in overall economic policy from Keynesian to monetarism. In this chapter, we pay more attention to whether or not

46

a policy change could overcome incrementalism, because, by reflecting vested interests, an incremental decision may obstruct flexible responses to a social problem. In addition, (1) higher policy change is not always right or better, and (2) changing instruments or their settings can bring a change of overall goals. Therefore we will carefully look at policymaking processes and policy contents to determine the level of policy change.

Three 'I's are often referred to how policy change occurs: 'Idea', 'Interest' and 'Institution'.[2] Because 'Idea' can be divided into different levels, we use the term 'belief' as a deeper idea that relates to a sense of value such as justice and ideology,[3] and 'policy idea' for a technical/instrumental idea. 'Interest' mainly refers to economic and organizational interest. 'Institution' provides incentives and constraints to actors' thoughts and behaviours and defines relationships among actors. It includes official and unofficial rules and procedures, practice, past decisions and statements by politicians. Actors decide their policy ideas and preferences based on their belief and interest as internal factors as well as objective situations and institutional conditions as external factors. In addition we divide the policymaking process into three stages, namely the knowledge accumulation and direction-setting stage, the pillar design stage and the detail design stage, in order to grasp the three 'I's appropriately, yet as far as of relevance we look at other later stages too.

POLICYMAKING PROCESS ON ETR IN GERMANY

Knowledge Accumulation and Direction-setting Stage

The concept of an ETR was invented by Hans-Christoph Binswanger and his colleagues in 1983 to simultaneously cope with unemployment and the environmental problem (Binswanger et al., 1983; Schlegelmilch, 2005). The first major debate on ETR occurred in Germany triggered by the Heidelberg-based Environment and Prognosis Institute (UPI) in the late 1980s (UPI, 1988). Political parties also came to propose different types of environmental taxes and levies. For example, the Social Democratic Party (SPD) outlined tax reform centered on the environmental taxes in *Fortschritt 90* (Progress 90) in 1989 (SPD, 1989). Proposals on environmental tax in this period can be divided into two types: (1) spending all tax revenue for environmental protection measures, for example, a proposal by the Greens, (2) utilizing tax revenue neutrally to reduce other taxes, coinciding with Binswanger's ETR idea. The first type lost its popularity because of the perceived increase in tax burdens on the people, which had been already high, and for bringing inflexibility in the national budget.

Although debate on the environmental tax stalled because of stagnation in the economy brought by German reunification, the second major debate occurred after the report confirming the double dividend by the German Institute for Economic Research (DIW) in 1994 (DIW, 1994). A veritable competition for the best concept of an ETR which could also be implemented nationally ensued, and stimulated fruitful debates and insights. In this period the Greens changed their proposal to an ETR. However, energy-intensive companies discovered that DIW, for simplicity reasons, did not include any reduced tax rates for energy-intensive sectors, which made some sectors losers. The fear of skipping the entire ETR concept simply because of such potential impacts of only a few sectors gave birth to a new platform in favour of the implementation of an ETR. On 8 November 1994 scientists, entrepreneurs and engaged citizens formed the '*Förderverein Ökologische Steuerreform*' (FÖS, in English: Green Budget Germany/GBG, www.foes.de). They thus launched a slightly more business-friendly concept of an ETR, compared with the DIW, to offer industry to be more receptive. German Industry Association (BDI) asked then Chancellor Helmut Kohl not to introduce such an ETR, and he promised that off the record (Krebs and Reiche, 1997). Ex post this explained very well why the debate had become so silent after the intensive debates in the years 1994–1995.

Pillar Design Stage

SPD won in the federal election on 27 September 1998 and formed a new government with the Greens on 27 October. In this election, ETR was considered one of the key issues. The Greens' election promises in April outlined raising the Mineral Oil Tax on motor fuel by 50 pfennig (0.26€) per litre in the first year and thereafter by 30 pfennig (0.15€) annually so that the tax rate will reach 5DM (2.56€) in 10 years (Bündnis 90/Die Grünen, 1998a). However facing strong criticism, the Greens removed those numbers except for the 5DM goal in July (Bündnis 90/Die Grünen, 1998b). In SPD's promises, there were no specific numbers for the ETR. However the candidate Chancellor, Gerhard Schröder, declared before the election that gasoline prices must not rise more than 6 pfennig (0.0307€ = 3.07Ct) per litre because commuters were concerned. He also previously served on the Volkswagen board (Reiche and Krebs, 1999). Coalition negotiations between the two parties were conducted from 7 October through 17 October 1998, and a 50-page coalition agreement was signed on 20 October.

On 8 October both parties agreed to reduce social security contributions from 42.3 per cent to less than 40 per cent by acquiring the revenues from energy taxes (Reiche and Krebs, 1999). Particular concern was how to secure enough money after Schröder's 6 pfennig declaration. The Environment Minister Jürgen Trittin pointed out that 6 pfennig contributes only 0.43 billion DM even though 1.5 billion DM is necessary to reduce social security contributions by 1 per cent. Because Oskar Lafontaine, the SPD leader, was also concerned about Schröder's declaration, there was a lack of consistency within the SPD. In addition, Reiche and Krebs (1999) raised three more areas of conflict: (1) SPD wanted to avoid imposing tax on lignite and hard coal while the Greens demanded tax rates according to with environmental impact; (2) SPD demanded a large exception for the energy-intensive sector from a certain threshold regarding the indicator energy consumption/value added on, while the Greens preferred much more differentiation in the tax rates; and (3) the parties had different opinions on how to design measures for people who do not benefit from the reduction in social security contributions, for example, students, unemployed people and welfare recipients. The two parties finally agreed on an ETR system for the first year as follows:

- The Mineral Oil Tax on motor fuel would increase by 6 pfennig per litre, on heating oil by 4 pfennig per litre and on natural gas for heating by 0.32 pfennig per cubic metre.
- The Electricity Tax would be introduced at a rate of 2 pfennig per kWh.
- The above two tax increases will begin on 1 January 1999 as the first phase of the ETR.
- Tax exemption is applied for energy-intensive industries, and electricity generated from renewable sources.
- The second phase of the ETR will be decided in the latter half of 1999 when Germany finishes its EU Council Presidency and it begins efforts toward European harmonization of energy taxation.
- By implementing subsequent steps, the social security contributions will decline from 42.3 per cent to less than 40.0 per cent.

Describing exact tax rates in a coalition agreement is said to be rare in Germany (Interview, 24 April 2014). According to an official from the Federal Ministry of Finance (BMF), the reason why SPD and the Greens agreed on tax rates and not a tax based on carbon content was to secure revenues for social security contributions as soon as possible. In that sense, the Mineral Oil Tax was a good item because it existed and was consistent with European rules (Interview, 21 June 2014). Therefore, it is possible to interpret that the pillar design was conducted with more practical reasons than theoretical ones.

Detail Design Stage

After the coalition agreement, the details of the tax system and the drafting of a bill remained to be done. The arena for this work transferred from the politicians to the ministries. A central part of it was taken by BMF's unit for mineral oil taxation, and they coordinated with other units from related ministries in a timely manner (Interview, 21 June 2014). If we call this an informal working group, politicians and interest groups are excluded from the discussion. However, this is the normal process for preparing details in Germany. In the informal working group, 90 per cent of the work was about tax reduction and exemption which involved various interests, and many issues could not be solved by the working group alone. Therefore they often consulted ministers and state secretaries, stating something to the effect of, 'We have this problem, so please make a decision on the political level'. If some documents from BMF were sent to BMU, they were brought to the attention of Minister Jürgen Trittin from the Greens, so that a mutual understanding between BMU and the Greens was closely maintained. Other ministries including the Federal Ministry of Economics and Technology (BMWi) did the same with SPD. By doing so, the draft bill was prepared, reflecting political intentions (Interview, 24 April 2014).

One of the biggest issues was how to deal with energy intensive industries. It is said the Greens insisted on responding with tax reduction but not tax elimination, whereas the Minister of BMWi, Werner Müller, demanded complete exemption for the entire industrial sector. The Greens were willing to accept exemptions for 27 energy-intensive industries in exchange for introducing, in particular, a promotion fund measure for renewable energy. Including this point, the draft bill was agreed on by the government in the middle of November. The following schedule was then decided: hold the first reading at the Bundestag on 20 November, hold an open public hearing on 30 November, and adopt the bill in the first week of December. However one day before the first reading, in response to a delay in the implementation of the law which stipulates a reduction in the pension contribution for 630 mark-jobs on 1 April 1999, the introduction of '*Gesetz zum Einstieg in die ökologische Steuerreform* (the Law on the Introduction of the Ecological Tax Reform)' was also postponed to 1 April 1999. The Greens simply did not want to be blamed for raising taxes immediately on 1 January 1999 while not reducing social security contributions until April.

Despite the change of the introduction date, the draft bill was presented to Bundestag on 20 November as planned and then was sent to the European competition authority on 16 December. However the tax exemption for 27 industrial sectors was considered 'ineligible state aid' in the European law (Interview, 21 June 2014). Having this assignment, the bill was modified over the New Year holiday and a change in direction was agreed upon before the first public hearing on 20 January. Approximately 80 experts including individual researchers, research institutions, economic associations, environmental groups, trade unions and the European Commission were invited to the hearing of the Finance Committee of the Bundestag. Participants were asked to comment generally, but also on the tax rates and tax exemption/reduction of the ETR draft. While industries and agricultural sectors expected to benefit from the exemptions and reductions criticized the small scope of those exemptions and reductions, and they showed strong concern for their businesses, environmental non-governmental organizations (NGOs) criticized the low tax rates (Reiche and Krebs, 1999).

Based on opinions gained at the public hearing, further modifications were made. The informal working group reached final agreement for the bill on 10 February 1999. The scope of the reductions and exemptions was broadly extended. Reiche and Krebs (1999) interpreted that postponement of the ETR to 1 April 1999 as a greater influence by interest groups. Finally the detail design was decided as follows:

- Manufacturing, agricultural and forestry sectors will receive a 20 per cent reduction in the Electricity Tax and no more than a 20 per cent tax increase from the mineral oil duty on heating oil and gas for heating purposes.
- Manufacturing industry will receive a 95 per cent tax refund if the burden from increased tax rates is 1.2 times greater than the tax relief from the reduction in pension contributions.
- Electricity produced from renewable sources will receive an exemption from the Electricity Tax if a direct line between the point of generation and the point of consumption exists with no other sources of electricity.
- Tax reduction and exemption measures will be applied for public transport, combined heat and power plants (CHP) and night-storage heating systems, and so on.

The bill was then commented on again at the second public hearing on 18 February, given second and third readings in the Bundestag on 24 February, adopted in the Bundestag on 3 March, adopted in the Bundesrat on 19 March, and then finally became effective 1 April 1999, which is now, in 2015, more than 16 years ago. During this process, there was no further significant change to the bill.

Later Stages of the ETR

At the time of the introduction of the ETR, the world oil prices, together with a stronger US$-exchange rate, increased sharply (from US$9 in 1998 to US$35 in mid-2000). Opposition and tabloid newspapers used that opportunity to blame the entire price increase on the ETR while only 25 per cent of the 60 pfennig price increase in gasoline was caused by the first two steps of the ETR. Forced by some protests on the streets by farmers and lorry drivers, support was forming in the Parliament for a formal vote on a draft law for abolishing the ETR, which was not adopted. Chancellor Gerhard Schröder had thus to decide whether or not to continue with the next steps of the ETR. Parliament and government had wisely put into the law back in 1999 that on 1 January of each year the next step of the ETR would commence. Hence, an additional decision would have been necessary to prevent the further steps from entering into force.

Although the Chancellor did not like the protests, endangering his popularity, he then made the somewhat courageous decision to continue the ETR because he wanted to lower unemployment, the nation's top priority. And otherwise, labour costs would have to increase again, endangering this overall objective.

Together with the last step of the ETR in 2003, light oil heating fuel taxes were increased to about the same level as the ones for natural gas for heating purposes, thus creating a level playing field. However, the Finance Minister claimed almost all the revenue for his budget while the Greens could at least succeed to launch a program for supporting ambitious house renovations. The laws and ETR tax rates from 1999 to 2003 were as follows:

- Introduction of laws
  - 1.Apr.1999: *Gesetz zum Einstieg in die ökologische Steuerreform* (Law on the Introduction of the Ecological Tax Reform)
  - 1.Jan.2000: *Gesetz zur Fortführung der ökologischen Steuerreform* (Law on the Continue of the Ecological Tax Reform)
  - 1.Jan.2003: *Gesetz zur Fortentwicklung der ökologischen Steuerreform* (Law on the Further Development of the Ecological Tax Reform)
- Steady increases in 1999–2003:
  - Electricity Tax 1.02Ct/kWh in 1999 (+0.26Ct/kWh p.a. between 2000–2003)
  - Mineral Oil Tax on transport fuels (+3.07Ct/litre p.a. between 1999–2003)
- Single increase in 1999 (+2003):

- Tax on Natural Gas +0.16Ct/kWh (+0.2Ct/l in 2003)
- Tax on Light Heating Oil: +2.05Ct/litre.

The ETR was then also extended to an Environmental Fiscal Reform (EFR) now also comprising the reduction and abolition of environmentally harmful subsidies, such as the commuters' tax allowance, which had favoured cars. From 2001 on, all modes of commuting received the same tax allowance.

In 2011 the conservative–liberal government introduced further elements of an ETR. Kerosene was hard to tax because of international agreements in the Chicago Treaty, therefore a route was followed which other countries such as the United Kingdom, France and the Netherlands had already taken: an air ticket tax was introduced. In order to gain revenues, but also to support Germany's decision to definitely phase out nuclear power, a nuclear fuel tax was introduced. Here Germany followed the examples of Japan, Sweden and the Netherlands. This no longer left nuclear power, with so many risks and problems, untaxed.

However after these final steps, the political will, even amongst the Greens, to take further steps of an EFR has faded substantially, and it is not clear if further steps will be taken. The protests in 2000 are still bad memories for many politicians and something they don't want to see repeated.

POLICYMAKING PROCESS ON CARBON TAX IN JAPAN

Annual Tax Reform Procedure

In Japan, tax reform is performed annually using a particular procedure. Around August, each ministry submits their requests for tax reform for the next fiscal year (FY).[4] Examining those requests, the Government Tax Commission presents the Outline of a Tax Reform Plan in December. Then the cabinet approves and sends it to the Parliament. Within this official procedure, unofficial procedure by the ruling party, which has veto power, is incorporated. The main ruling party (Liberal Democratic Party (LDP): June 1994 to September 2009, Democratic Party of Japan (DPJ): September 2009 to December 2012) has different divisions, such as environment, under the Policy Research Council, which corresponds to the Standing Committees of the Parliament. Having inputs from related ministries, each division makes their own requests and submits them to the LDP's Research Commission or DPJ's Project Team on the Tax

System. The commission or project team adjusts requests received from the divisions, interest groups and ministries, and produces the Tax Reform Proposal. Without any change, the proposal is incorporated in the government's Outline of a Tax Reform Plan.

Knowledge Accumulation and Direction-setting Stage

In Japan, consideration of an environmental/carbon tax, started in the early 1990s led by the Ministry of the Environment (MOE). The MOE formed a study group which still exists today, but under a different name and has accumulated knowledge and considered possible tax systems. Other ministries also formed similar study groups according to their needs. Individual researchers and research institutions able to perform complicated analyses participated in these study groups or did so in the academic field. For economic reasons, the Ministry of Economy, Trade and Industry (METI) showed opposition to an environmental/ carbon tax in the beginning but later changed their attitude. In 2003, the MOE and the METI decided to transform and strengthen the Petroleum Tax, renaming it the Petroleum and Coal Tax. At the same time, they reduced the tax rate on electricity (the Promotion of Power-Resources Development Tax) so that total revenue would not change (MOE, 2003). For METI, this tax reform was aimed at enhancing the competitiveness of nuclear power as well as securing financial resources for acquiring Kyoto credits. The MOE also had an advantage in that they became able to use tax revenues for reducing greenhouse gases (GHGs) from energy-oriented CO_2.[5] Both ministries agreed not to call this reform an introduction of environmental/carbon tax although it increased the tax burden on fossil fuels. The tax rates gradually changed as follows:

	Coal	LPG	LNG	Electricity
Before	JPY0/t	JPY670/t	JPY720/t	JPY0.445/kWh
From 1 Oct 2003	JPY230/t	JPY800/t	JPY840/t	JPY0.425/kWh
From 1 Apr 2005	JPY460/t	JPY940/t	JPY960t	JPY0.400/kWh
From 1 Apr 2007	JPY700/t	JPY1080/t		JPY0.375/kWh

Note: Tax rate on petroleum remained JPY2040/kl throughout this period.

Every year after 2004, the MOE, sometimes together with the Ministry of Agriculture, Forestry and Fisheries (MAFF), requested an introduction of a carbon tax with relatively low tax rates, expecting to use the revenues for GHG reduction including forest carbon-sink. At the political level, the environmental division and agricultural division of the LDP presented a carbon tax proposal in 2004 which very much resembled the one by MOE. The MOE created this strategy to gain support from influential politicians in the agricultural division for LDP's Research Commission on the Tax System by providing tax revenue for foresters. However, all those proposals were declined by the METI and LDP politicians in the economy divisions because of their impacts on the economy and the increasing Petroleum and Coal Tax through 2007, reflecting intentions of industries (Interview, 28 August 2013). During this period, a carbon tax was set with a low tax rate, using revenue for GHG reduction. Because of that, an ETR proposal presented in 2001, later revised several times, by the Carbon Tax Study Group which consisted of several NGOs, was barely heard (Interview, 25 August 2014).

Pillar and Detail Design Stage

On 16 September 2009, the DPJ president Yukio Hatoyama was elected as Prime Minister. He formed a three-party coalition government centered on DPJ with the People's New Party and the Social Democratic Party of Japan. Unlike the German case, measures to address global warming were mentioned in a vague tone in the coalition agreement, for example, the establishment of basic laws concerning global warming measures (DPJ et al., 2009). DPJ's campaign pledges outlined slightly more detailed promises. While presenting a tasty menu to the public, including a child allowance, individual income-based subsidies for farmers, abolition of the provisional tax rate of the Gasoline Tax and the Diesel Oil Delivery Tax,[6] they emphasized that financial resources would be gained by eliminating budget waste. Regarding global warming measures, they promised a 25 per cent GHG reduction by 2020 compared with 1990 levels, the establishment of an Emissions Trading Scheme (ETS) and a Feed-in Tariff (FIT), and consideration of a global warming/carbon tax (DPJ, 2009). Moreover they criticized the dual-power structure between political parties and government practiced during the LDP government. Aiming at transparent administrative policymaking, Hatoyama abolished the Policy Research Council of DPJ including the party's tax project team.

The tax reform discussion for FY2010 took place under such an environment. On 11 November 2009, the MOE proposed a two-tiered carbon tax system, assuming a 2.5 trillion yen reduction from the abolishment of the provisional tax rate of the Gasoline Tax and the Diesel Oil Delivery Tax. One is the taxation of all fossil fuels for 1 trillion yen in tax revenue, and the other is the taxation of gasoline for an additional 1 trillion yen (Government Tax Commission of Japan, 2009).[7] Because this proposal was created without any consultation with the party and other ministries, discussions between the Hatoyama administration and the DPJ did not progress smoothly. Furthermore finding budget waste did not go as well as intended. In the end the government decided to change the name of but maintain the level of the provisional tax rate while postponing the decision to introduce a carbon tax the following year.

On 15 March 2010, the Hatoyama Cabinet approved a bill, the Basic Laws Concerning Global Warming Measures, which included a 25 per cent GHG reduction by 2020 compared with 1990 levels and the consideration of a carbon tax, ETS and FIT. After that Hatoyama resigned as a result of failure in national security issues. Naoto Kan then took over as Prime Minister and DPJ President in June 2010. He revived the Policy Research Council of DPJ because of the regret and dissatisfaction over the tax reform in the previous year among party members related to their inability in decision-making. The annual procedure for tax reform including the unofficial process changed back to normal.

Ministries submitted requests for the FY2011 tax system reforms by early September. Reflecting their political intentions, the MOE and the METI both demanded the introduction of a carbon tax (Government Tax Commission of Japan, 2010). The MOE proposed a two-tier system again, asking for taxation of all fossil fuels and a tax on gasoline. The METI did not demand taxation on gasoline but otherwise demanded the same.

On 28 September, under the Project Team on Tax Reform of DPJ, the Subcommittee for Global Warming Tax Consideration was launched. The subcommittee chairman, Ikko Nakatsuka, selected members from among DPJ politicians who are familiar with tax issues and belonged to related divisions of the party's Policy Research Council. This subcommittee assumed the role of coordinating between the divisions and related ministries. The significance of establishing this subcommittee was that whatever happens, the government would introduce a carbon tax (Interview, 30 October 2013).

With support from the Ministry of Finance, the subcommittee closely and intensively held meetings. In the beginning interviews with not only relevant ministries but also interests groups were conducted. Then, to build a pillar of tax system, which entailed taxation targets, tax rates and the use of tax revenue, the MOE and the METI were asked to consider a theoretical story that could gain understanding from the public and industries (Interview, 30 October 2013).

The MOE was considering carbon tax through the ministry's Committee for Mid- to Long-term Road Map, which had been established in April following cabinet approval for the global warming bill (Interview, 27 August 2013). In the scenarios of carbon tax presented at the 9th meeting, the

MOE put more emphasis on the price effect than the budget effect. Following the global warming bill, METI also established the Policy Measures Working Group in June, whose purpose was to evaluate policy measures for global warming. The interim report was released in September and outlined that Japan's marginal abatement costs of GHGs was much higher than those of the USA or European countries. It continued that, 'there is a limit to the effect that could be gained by using carbon prices to reduce emissions' through ETS or a high-rate carbon tax. They concluded that using the revenue from a low-rate carbon tax for a combination of support measures for technology development and dissemination would be effective (METI, 2010b). Furthermore METI conducted a second revision of the Basic Energy Plan in June. This plan outlined improvements to the energy supply and demand structure, including 14 new nuclear power plants, which eventually reduced energy-related CO_2 by 30 per cent by 2030 (METI, 2010a).

The result of considering the price effect and budget effect of a carbon tax at the DPJ's subcommittee was that no significant price effect would be expected. They evaluated the effects of abolishing the provisional tax rate on the Gasoline Tax, which would bring 25 yen per litre less, and found it would contribute only 1 per cent increase in GHG emissions. On the other hand, they concluded that a budget effect could be expected because 'the government would contribute to the reduction of GHGs by conducting projects aimed at enhancing energy supply and demand structure' (Nakatsuka, 2010). For these reasons, having METI's story at hand, the subcommittee decided to require an annual public budget in the Basic Energy Plan as the basis for taxation. In this decision, the policy idea that clear use for tax revenue can obtain more understanding from tax payers was incorporated (Interview, 30 October 2013).

Of course the subcommittee made numerous adjustments, including reductions and exemptions, as well as tax revenue utilization. In addition to inputs to the subcommittee, interest groups and related ministries directly lobbied subcommittee members. The MAFF requested tax revenue is used for forest carbon-sinks, and the Ministry of Internal Affairs and Communications (MIAC) requested measures be taken by local governments. In response to these requests, the METI was in strong opposition because the purpose of the carbon tax was to enhance energy supply and demand structure, that is, energy-oriented CO_2 reduction measures, therefore taxes collected from industries should be returned to the industries. Because Chairman Nakatsuka had the same opinion, those requests by MAFF and MIAC were declined (Interview, 30 October 2013). Eventually tax and relief measures were decided (MOE, 2012; MOF, 2012):

- Add the above tax rates to the Petroleum and Coal Tax.
- Adjust the tax rate to correspond to the amount of CO_2 emissions for all fossil fuels (JPY 289/t-CO_2).
- Gradually increasing the tax rates as follows:

	Coal	LPG&LNG	Petroleum
From 1 Oct 2012	JPY920/t	JPY1340/t	JPY2290/kl
From 1 Apr 2014	JPY1140/t	JPY1600/t	JPY2540/kl
From 1 Apr 2016	JPY1370/t	JPY2540/t	JPY2800/kl

- Tax revenue was estimated to be 39.1 billion yen for FY2012 and 262.3 billion yen for each normal year after FY2016.
- Tax revenue will be allotted to energy-oriented CO_2 emissions restraint measures.
- Exemptions and reimbursement measures will be made for the transport industry, including marine transport, railways, buses, trucks and airlines.
- Support was given for covering the reduction of fuel production and distribution costs and supply stabilization.
- Support was given for depopulating regions and cold climate regions, and so on.

Later Stages of the Carbon Tax

After the great earthquake in March 2011, based on the outcome of DPJ's subcommittee, the law was eventually enacted in 2012. Because of the nuclear disaster and subsequent increase of fossil fuel use, tax revenue was increased much more than estimated, now giving industries a strong reason to stop tax rate increases. The government needs to explain how the budget is effectively used to respond those voices.

COMPARATIVE ANALYSIS OF THE TWO CASES

Levels of Policy Change

Seeing the contents and intentions of a tax system, the German ETR was at least a second-order policy change because it brought a new instrument to send the price signal and intended a tax shift from labour to environment. The Japanese carbon tax was an incremental policy change because it was intended to increase only subsidies. Here we compare and analyze how policymaking proceeded in each stage.

Knowledge Accumulation and Direction-setting Stage

In Germany two major debates in which various actors participated were triggered and supported by analyses of research institutions and expert groups. Political parties participated as well and presented their own ETR/ environment tax proposals. As the Greens changed their proposal from a revenue increase type to revenue-neutral ETR, the parties learnt and refined their policy ideas through communication in society. In Japan, knowledge was accumulated within the ministries. Policy ideas for the carbon tax were narrowed down through the filters of the ministries. Political parties were not active but relied on inputs from ministries. As such, the same conflicting structures among ministries were formed within the ruling party. The reason the Petroleum and Coal Tax was introduced was because of the consensus between MOE and METI. Such an institutional structure hindered public discourse in society, lowering the possibility of the ETR.

Pillar Design Stage

Supported by previously accumulated knowledge, the pillar of the ETR was built during coalition negotiations over the course of two weeks in Germany. Although Schröder's 6 pfennig declaration was institutionalized and worked as a constraint, it made possible the imposition of taxation on various tax objects. By so doing, the new government secured financial resources for reducing social security contributions, which became the primary object of the ETR. In addition, some opinions by the Greens with strong environmental beliefs were incorporated. In Japan, because parties lacked concrete proposals, they lost an opportunity after the governmental change. For the same reason, the influence of coalition partners was quite small. The main role of DPJ's subcommittee as an arena for policy design was to choose a story submitted by ministries and adjust to different interests. This means the pillar was established again through the filters of MOE and METI. The choice of the budget effects reflects politicians' doubts toward price signal and policy preferences of Japanese citizens. Interestingly, both countries used their existing tax systems with more practical and political reasons.

Detail Design Stage

In Germany, ministries finally participated in the ETR discussion from this stage. It was the BMF's role to form a closed informal working group and to lead drafting work. The EU also appeared to be an actor who imposed conditions. After writing the ETR bill, open public hearings were conducted to collect opinions from various sectors. This improved the bill in a way by increasing the understanding by the public. In Japan, the sub-committee continued its work. There was no opportunity to hear public opinions during and after drafting details of the system, though it may have enhanced the possibility of introducing a carbon tax without getting negative attention from the critics. Nevertheless the government also lost an opportunity for improving its bill. From the discussion of revenue usage, we saw the ministries' general behaviour of increasing their budget resources.

CONCLUSION

The most important reason for introducing the ETR/carbon tax in Germany and Japan was governmental change, even though both countries are major car manufacturers, it may be surprising to see those countries increasing transport fuel taxes. However it was only a trigger. It is clear that other reasons related with the contents and levels of policy change depended on policymaking processes. In Germany, there was an arena where various actors with different interests and beliefs could freely participate and compete with their policy ideas. Experts and independent researchers functioned as a basis for policy debates and parties were active in public discourse, refining their policy proposals, thus enabling them to use an opportunity after the governmental change. As the process came to an end, the main focus was on adjusting to the interests of various actors. Nevertheless environmental beliefs were kept at the design stage because of the work of the Greens and the open public hearings. On the other hand, in Japan, ministries took a dominant role in that they hosted a policy arena and set the direction by collecting policy ideas from experts and interest groups. As a result policy ideas which did not invade the jurisdiction of other ministries survived, meaning the option of an ETR was substantially excluded. Politicians mainly chose policy proposals presented by ministries and adjusted to different interests. In other words they were relatively passive. From the above discussion, it can be interpreted that one of the keys to overcoming incrementalism is to incorporate environmental beliefs through the entire process. To do so, institutions, through official rules and procedures, should secure an open arena for considering policy direction and collect opinions widely at the design stage, promoting networking between experts and various actors, and raising a political party which can share common beliefs. In this study, Germany showed better institutions for policy change. Nevertheless, as mentioned before, higher level policy change is not always better or right. The impacts of the taxes, especially Japanese ones, have to be carefully evaluated later.

NOTES

1. In Japan the carbon tax is occasionally called 'environmental tax' or 'global warming tax'.
2. See for example Goldstein and Keohane (1993).
3. Watanabe (2011) uses 'belief' to compare changes in climate change policies in Germany and Japan.
4. In Japan the fiscal year starts in April and ends in March.
5. Both taxes were earmarked. METI and MOE split the increased revenue of the Petroleum and Coal Tax for activities, projects and R&D for energy savings, renewable energies, Kyoto credits, and so on.
6. The Gasoline Tax was JPY53800/kl (incl. JPY25100/kl as a provisional tax rate) and the Diesel Oil Delivery Tax was JPY32100/kl (incl. JPY17100/kl as a provisional tax rate).
7. MOE proposed to increase only the Gasoline Tax because it is a national tax, while the Diesel Oil Delivery Tax is a local tax which is out of MOE's jurisdiction.

BIBLIOGRAPHY

Binswanger, H.C., H. Nutzinger et al. (1983), *Arbeit ohne Umweltzerstörung: Strategien einer neuen Wirtschaftspolitik*, Frankfurt/Main: Fischer Taschenbuch-Verlag.

BMF (Federal Ministry of Finance) (2003), *Promotion of Environmental Protection in German Laws on Taxes and Levies*, retrieved from http://www.bundesfinanzministerium.de/Content/DE/Standardartikel/Themen/Oeffentliche_Finanzen/Wirtschafts_und_Finanzdaten/Foerderung_des-Umweltschutze_im_Deutschen_Abgabenrecht_engl.pdf?__blob=publicationFile&v=2, accessed 30 April 2015.

Bündnis 90/Die Grünen (1998a), *Grün ist der Wechsel. Programm zur Bundestagswahl 1998*, Bonn.

Bündnis 90/Die Grünen (1998b), *Neue Mehrheiten nur mit uns. 1998–2002 Vier Jahre für einen politischen Neuanfang*, Bonn.

DIW (Deutsches Institut für Wirtschaftsforschung) (1994), *Ökosteuer – Königsweg oder Sackgasse*, Berlin, retrieved from http://files.foes.de/de/downloads/studien/WirkungenderOESR.pdf, accessed 30 April 2015.

DPJ (Democratic Party of Japan), *Manifesto 2009*.

DPJ (Democratic Party of Japan), SDP (Social Democratic Party of Japan) and People's New Party (2009), 'Three-party coalition government agreement', retrieved from http://www.dpj.or.jp/news/files/20090909goui.pdf, accessed 6 August 2014.

Goldstein, J. and R.O. Keohane (eds) (1993), *Ideas and Foreign Policy: Beliefs, Institutions, and Political Change*, Ithaca, US and London, UK: Cornell University Press.

Government Tax Commission of Japan (2009), 'List of Materials for 9th Meeting in FY2009', retrieved from http://www.cao.go.jp/zei-cho/history/2009-2012/gijiroku/zeicho/2009/21zen9kai.html, accessed 6 August 2014.

Government Tax Commission of Japan (2010), 'List of Materials for 8th Meeting in FY2010', retrieved from http://www.cao.go.jp/zei-cho/history/2009-2012/giji roku/zeicho/2010/22zen8kai.html, accessed 6 August 2014.

Hall, P.A. (1993), 'Policy paradigms, social learning, and the State: The case of economic policymaking in Britain', *Comparative Politics*, 25 (3), 275–296.

Krebs, C. and D.T. Reiche (1997), Wie die Ökologische Steuerreform beerdigt wurde, *Blätter für deutsche und internationale Politik 7/97* (In: Frankfurter Rundschau, 27 August 1997).

METI (Ministry of Economy, Trade and Industry of Japan) (2010a), 'Basic energy plan', retrieved from http://www.enecho.meti.go.jp/category/others/basic_plan/pdf/100618honbun.pdf, accessed 6 August 2014.

METI (Ministry of Economy, Trade and Industry of Japan) (2010b), 'Interim report of Policy Measures Working Group', retrieved from http://www.meti.go.jp/committee/summary/0004672/report_01_01j.pdf, accessed 6 August 2014.

MOE (Ministry of the Environment of Japan) (2003), 'Agenda and material for the 11th meeting of the Expert Study Commission on Global Warming Tax', retrieved from https://www.env.go.jp/council/16pol-ear/y161-11.html, accessed 14 August 2014.

MOE (Ministry of the Environment of Japan) (2012), 'Details on the carbon tax (Tax for climate change mitigation)', retrieved from https://www.env.go.jp/en/policy/tax/env-tax/20121001a_dct.pdf, accessed 6 August 2014.

MOE (Ministry of the Environment of Japan) (n.d.), 'Greening taxation (environment tax, and so on.)', retrieved from http://www.env.go.jp/policy/tax/kento.html, accessed 14 August 2014.

MOF (Ministry of Finance of Japan) (2012), 'Revision of the Act on Special Measures Concerning Taxation (the petroleum and coal tax [Special Measures on the Tax for Climate Change Mitigation])', retrieved from http://www.mof.go.jp/tax_policy/tax_reform/outline/fy2012/explanation/pdf/p688_699.pdf, accessed 29 July 2014.

Nakatsuka, I. (2010), 'Carbon parity' [Blog of Ikko Nakatsuka], retrieved from http://ikko.typepad.jp/blog/2010/12/%E3%82%AB%E3%83%BC%E3%83%9C%E3%83%B3%E3%83%91%E3%83%AA%E3%83%86%E3%82%A3.html, accessed 14 August 2014.

Reiche, D. and C. Krebs (1999), *Der Einstieg in die ökologische Steuerreform. Aufstieg, Restriktionen und Durchsetzung eines umweltpolitischen Themas*, Frankfurt am Main: Peter Lang.

Schlegelmilch, K. (2005), *Insights in Political Processes on the Ecological Tax Reform from a Ministerial Perspective*, GBG Discussion Paper No. 2005/06, retrieved from http://files.foes.de/de/downloads/diskussionspapiere/GBGDisPap2005_06PoliticalProcesses.pdf, accessed 9 June 2015.

SPD (Sozialdemokratische Partei Deutschlands) (1989), *Fortschritt 90*.

SPD (Sozialdemokratische Partei Deutschlands) and Bündis90/Die Grünen (1998), *Aufbruch und erneuerung – Deutschlands weg ins 21. Jahrhundert*.

Teufel, D. (1988), *Ökosteuern als marktwirtschaftliches instrument – vorschläge für eine ökologische steuerreform*, UPI-Report No. 9, Heidelberg, retrieved from http://www.upi-institut.de/upi9.htm, accessed 30 April 2015.

Watanabe, R. (2011), *Climate Policy Changes in Germany and Japan: A Path to Paradigmatic Policy Change*, Abingdon, Oxon, New York: Routledge.

5. The EU emission trading scheme: first evidence on Phase 3

Claudia Kettner*

INTRODUCTION

Since 2005, the EU emission trading scheme (EU ETS) has been the EU's key instrument for reducing greenhouse gas emissions from industry and from energy supply. Phase 1, the pilot phase, which ran from 2005 to 2007, and Phase 2, which covered the Kyoto commitment period 2008 to 2012, dampened expectations regarding the scheme's performance: due to surplus allocation prices plumped, generating only a weak signal for investment in low carbon technologies. While surplus allocation in Phase 1 was the result of incomplete information, in Phase 2 it was caused by an exogenous effect, that is, the decline in emissions following the financial and economic crisis.

Based on the lessons learnt from the first trading phase, several changes of the design of the EU ETS were adopted in 2008 that should help generate a stringent cap translating into carbon prices inducing low-carbon investment. First evidence on Phase 3 shows, however, persistently low carbon prices in the range of 5–6€ as of October 2014.

In this chapter, the underlying developments will be investigated. After describing the changes in the design of the EU ETS in Phase 3 compared with the previous trading periods, empirical evidence on allocation, emissions and carbon prices in the EU ETS in the period 2005–2013 is presented. Empirical results confirm a structural surplus of allowances that is analyzed in the next section. The final section concludes.

THE DEVELOPMENT OF THE EU ETS FRAMEWORK

Phase 1 (2005–2007) and Phase 2 (2008–2012)

In the first two trading phases, the EU ETS included CO_2 emissions from four emissions-intensive activities: energy activities (that is, large combustion installations, refineries, coke ovens), the production and processing of ferrous metals, activities of the mineral industry (that is, cement and lime production, glass production and ceramic production), and pulp and paper production (Directive 2003/87/EC). The covered activities accounted for 51 per cent of EU CO_2 emissions and 42 per cent of EU greenhouse gas emissions respectively.

Allowances were allocated to sectors and installations by Member States in the National Allocation Plans (NAPs). The NAPs had to follow criteria defined in Annex III of Directive 2003/87/EC. These included that the national emission caps should be consistent with the Member States' emission reduction targets for the Kyoto period (Council Decision 2002/358/EC), that allocation should take the (technical) emission reduction potential into account, and that the NAPs should be consistent with other EU legislative and policy instruments.

The NAPs had to be approved by the European Commission. In the review process the Commission decided whether the NAPs met the criteria defined in the emissions trading directive. For Phase 2, in the review process Member States were required to reduce allocations proposed in the NAPs by 10.4 per cent on average, with the New Member States facing the highest reduction requirements (see Kettner et al., 2010).[1]

Grandfathering of allowances was the main allocation principle in the first two trading phases, in other words, allowances were distributed to installations based on their historical emissions, sometimes including benchmarking elements; only up to 5 (10) per cent of allowances could be auctioned by Member States in Phase 1 (Phase 2).[2]

Allowances issued for Phase 1 could not be transferred to Phase 2, in other words, no 'banking' of allowances was permitted. Allowances issued for Phase 2 could, however, be banked to Phase 3.

The use of international credits for compliance under the EU ETS is provided for in order to increase the economic efficiency of the scheme, in other words, to lower abatement costs. The 'Linking Directive' (Directive 2004/101/EC) regulates the use of project-based credits by installations covered by the EU ETS. Credits from the Clean Development Mechanism (CDM)[3] and from Joint Implementation (JI)[4] are used by firms for compliance since the start of Phase 2. The maximum number of international credits that installations could use for compliance had to be specified in the Member States' NAPs (see above) and ranged between 7 and 21 per cent of free allocation (see for example, Elsworth et al., 2012). The total number of CDM and JI credits eligible for use in Phase 2 amounted to 1.5 billion t CO_2e (14 per cent of EU-wide allocation).

Phase 3

In 2009, the EU Climate and Energy Package was adopted, which set the framework for European climate policy until 2020. The Package also included a new emissions trading directive (Directive 2009/29/EC) bringing about fundamental changes in the design of the EU ETS. These changes apply to Phase 3 of the EU ETS that covers the period from 2013 to 2020 and the subsequent trading periods.

Starting with Phase 3, the EU ETS has been extended to CO_2 emissions from the production of non-ferrous metals (primary and secondary aluminium, other non-ferrous metals), CO_2 emissions from the production of certain chemicals[5] and CO_2 emissions related to carbon capture and storage. Furthermore, the EU ETS now also covers perfluorocarbons from aluminium production and nitrous oxide emissions from the production of certain chemicals.

In contrast to the previous trading phases, for Phase 3 an EU-wide cap and allocation process were established. A greenhouse gas (GHG) emission reduction target of 21 per cent in 2020 compared with 2005 was defined for the EU ETS sector.[6] This target will be approached linearly, that is, each year the cap of the EU ETS will be reduced by 38 Mt.[7]

In the allocation of allowances, sectoral differences regarding the potential exposure to carbon leakage are taken into account. Three categories of sectors and respective allocation procedures are differentiated according to their potential risk of carbon leakage:

- *Power sector*: The power sector faces full auctioning from 2013 on.[8]
- *'Normal' sectors*: 'Normal' sectors, that is, sectors that are not at risk of carbon leakage, receive 80 per cent free allocation in 2013. The share of free allocation is linearly reduced to 30 per cent in 2020.
- *'Exposed' sectors*: Sectors that are potentially at risk of carbon leakage will receive up to 100 per cent free allocation until 2020.[9]

A sector is considered to be at risk of carbon leakage in case of a substantial price increase due to emission trading, that is, if the direct and indirect costs of emission trading amount to at least 5 per cent of sectoral gross value added assuming a carbon price of 30€, and the sector's intensity of trade with third countries, that is, the share of exports and imports in the market, exceeds 10 per cent. Furthermore, sectors with a trade intensity *or* a cost intensity of at least 30 per cent are considered to be at risk of carbon leakage.

Starting from Phase 3, also two liquidity management provisions are implemented in the EU ETS. In Directive 2009/29/EC 'measures in the event of excessive price fluctuations' were provided for, in other words, in case of excessively high market prices, additional allowances could be auctioned. In July 2013, the European Parliament furthermore adopted the proposal of backloading allowances, that is, shifting auctions of allowances from the beginning to the end of Phase 3, in order to strengthen the role of EU ETS carbon prices as an investment signal. In the period 2014 to 2016, a total of 900 million allowances will be withheld and auctioned in the last two years of the third trading phase (Commission Regulation (EU) 176/2014).

Aviation is supposed to be included in the EU ETS since 2012 (Directive 2008/101/EC). Directive 2008/101/EC stipulated the inclusion of all flights departing from and arriving in the EU in the scheme; the inclusion of flights to and from countries not covered by the EU ETS has, however, been suspended for the period until 2016 (Decision 377/2013/EU, Regulation (EU) 421/2014).[10] For these international flights, a global market based mechanism is to be developed that will become effective in 2020.

While the EU ETS aims at significantly reducing GHG emissions from stationary installations, with respect to aviation it rather strives for a stabilization of emissions. For Phase 3, the cap for the aviation sector has been set at 95 per cent of the sector's average annual emissions in the base period 2004 to 2006 which corresponded to 210 million allowances for all flights (Commission Decision 2011/389/EU) and will be adjusted proportionally to limited scope of intra-EEA flights (European Commission 2014a); in contrast to the other ETS sectors, the cap for aviation will not be decreased over Phase 3. Aircraft operators receive special certificates, so-called European Aviation Allowances (EUAAs) that can only be surrendered for compliance by aviation companies in order to relieve pressures from the other EU ETS sectors; the companies can, however, also use 'normal' European Allowances (EUAs) and – up to a certain limit – international credits for compliance.

Changes in the design of the EU ETS as described above are reflected in the results of the empirical analysis described in the next section of this chapter.

EMPIRICAL EVIDENCE

Database

For the analysis of allocation patterns, installation[11] level data on allocation and emissions from the EU Transaction Log (EUTL, 2014) is used that is assigned to sectors using information from the NAPs. The EUTL currently covers more than 11,000 installations in the EU-28, Norway and

Liechtenstein[12] for the period 2005 to 2013. For the analysis a sample of 8,000 installations, for which data are available in all years, is used to assess changes over time. This sample of installations is limited to the EU-28 except Croatia and Bulgaria.[13]

Free Allocation and Emissions

Table 5.1 illustrates the development of free allocation and verified emissions in the EU sample between 2005 and 2013. In Phase 1, allocation exceeded emissions in all years due to overestimated ETS emissions and a corresponding oversupply of allowances.[14] For Phase 2, allocation was reduced during the review of the Member States' NAPs resulting in a stringent cap in 2008, where emissions exceeded free allocation by 9 per cent. The rest of Phase 2 was, however, characterized by a pronounced surplus of allowances as (EU ETS) emissions fell in line with decreasing production in the course of the economic and financial crisis. For 2013, the first year of Phase 3, a different pattern arose: Only 50 per cent of verified emissions were covered by free allocation which corresponds to a net shortage of allowances of 758 Mt CO_2e. This net shortage resulted from a gross shortage of 886 Mt CO_2e and a gross surplus of 128 Mt CO_2e. It is evident that compared with the previous trading phases also the gross surplus of allowances decreased, in other words, less installations saw a surplus of allowances in 2013.

With respect to the sector level, one can see that the power and heat sector has exhibited a net shortage of allowances since the start of the EU ETS. During the first two trading phases, the other sectors on average showed a net surplus of allowances. In 2013, free allocation on average equalled emissions in these sectors reflecting a gross surplus of allowances in the range of Phase 1 and a significantly higher gross shortage of 113 Mt CO_2e.

Price Development in the EU ETS

The allocation patterns as described above are reflected in the development of EU ETS carbon prices. Since 2005, carbon prices have shown a high variability. Various price drivers have been identified in addition to the stringency of the cap, including economic business cycles, fuel prices, regulatory decisions, market conditions and speculation (see for example, Kettner et al., 2010; Feng et al., 2011; Chevallier, 2011; Hintermann, 2010; Kettner et al., 2014; Koch et al., 2014; Aatola et al., 2013; Zhu et al., 2014).

The role of surplus allocation and (expected) shortages of allowances for the development of EUA prices is illustrated in Figure 5.1. Towards the

Carbon pricing

Table 5.1   Free allocation and verified emissions in the EU ETS, 2005–2013

	Free allocation in Mt	Emissions in MT	Surplus/shortage in Mt		
			Net surplus	Gross shortage	Gross surplus
EU ETS					
Phase 1					
2005	1,868	1,809	59	−148	206
2006	1,841	1,829	12	−182	194
2007	1,918	1,917	1	−205	207
Phase 2					
2008	1,679	1,825	−146	−327	181
2009	1,680	1,610	70	−245	314
2010	1,689	1,642	47	−266	313
2011	1,691	1,611	80	−260	340
2012	1,715	1,584	132	−279	411
Phase 3					
2013	791	1,550	−758	−886	128
POWER and HEAT					
Phase 1					
2005	1,133	1,163	−29	−132	103
2006	1,109	1,173	−64	−161	97
2007	1,146	1,219	−73	−176	103
Phase 2					
2008	907	1,145	−238	−292	54
2009	900	1,036	−136	−222	85
2010	898	1,036	−138	−237	99
2011	900	1,019	−119	−233	114
2012	917	1,021	−104	−256	152
Phase 3					
2013	205	963	−759	−773	14
OTHER SECTORS					
Phase 1					
2005	734	646	88	−15	104
2006	732	656	76	−21	97
2007	772	698	75	−29	104
Phase 2					
2008	772	680	92	−36	127
2009	780	574	206	−23	229
2010	792	606	186	−29	214
2011	791	593	199	−27	226
2012	799	563	236	−23	259
Phase 3					
2013	586	586	0	−113	113

Source: EUTL (2014); own calculations. 'Gross shortage' and 'gross surplus' denote the sum of allowance shortages and surpluses on installation level respectively.

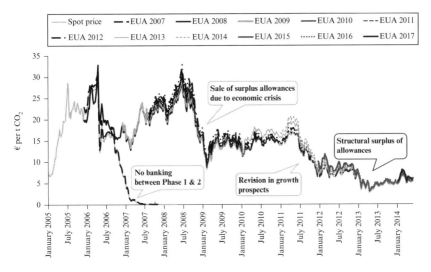

Sources: Adapted from Kettner et al. (2014).

Figure 5.1 *Development of Over-The-Counter (OTC)[15] closing prices in the EU ETS, 2005–2014*

end of Phase 1, spot prices converged towards zero as allowances could not be banked for the second trading phase and thus literally became worthless. In parallel, the price of allowances issued for Phase 2 rose as firms expected a stringent cap due to the European Commission's interventions in the NAPs. In the course of the financial and economic crisis, carbon prices fell reflecting the surplus of allowances in the market caused by this external shock. While low carbon prices alleviate the financial burden for industry during periods of low growth, they also pose an obstacle for the long-term economic efficiency of the EU ETS as they fail to incentivize low carbon investment and may thus contribute to lock-ins in emission-intensive structures (see for example, Kettner et al., 2014).

For Phase 3, no recovery of carbon prices can be observed despite tight allocation in 2013. Instead, the price reflects a structural surplus of allowances that has built up since Phase 2.

STRUCTURAL SURPLUS OF ALLOWANCES IN THE EU ETS

While free allocation in 2013 covered only 50 per cent of verified emissions, the total allowance base accumulated until 2013 considerably exceeded

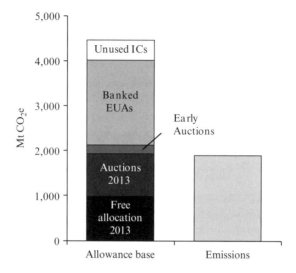

Sources: EUTL (2014), EEA (2014); own illustration.

Figure 5.2   Structural surplus of allowances in Phase 3

verified emissions. The allowance base not only comprised free allocation and auctioned allowances in 2013, but also EUAs banked from Phase 2, and CER and ERU credits from the CDM and JI that have not been used for compliance in Phase 2 (see Figure 5.2). Furthermore, early auctions of Phase 3 allowances contributed to the structural surplus of allowances.

On average, Phase 2 of the EU ETS was characterized by a pronounced surplus of allowances (see above). Cumulative allocation in Phase 2 amounted to 10.2 Gt CO_2e, while only 9.8 Gt CO_2e were emitted in the period 2008 to 2012. This corresponds to an accumulated surplus of allowances of 379 Mt CO_2e (4 per cent of free allocation in Phase 2). This difference between allocation and emissions, however, accounts for only one part of banked EUAs; also allowances that have been substituted by international credits need to be considered. During Phase 2, on average 134 million of CERs and 76 million of ERUs have been used for compliance under the EU ETS each year. Over the five-year period, a total of 1,056 million project-based credits have been surrendered under the EU ETS, substituting EUAs. Furthermore, 442 million allowances auctioned during Phase 2 add to the allowance base. The total number of EUAs transferred to Phase 3 hence can be estimated to have accumulated to 1,878 million.

In Phase 2, a total of 1,500 million CERs and ERUs were eligible for compliance in the EU ETS which corresponded to 14 per cent of free allocation. Until 2012, only 1,056 million project-based credits – 675 million CERs and 381 million ERUs – have been surrendered. The difference of 445 million credits could be banked to Phase 3 representing the second part of the structural allowance surplus.

The third source of the structural surplus is made up by early auctioned allowances from the EU ETS New Entrants Reserve in Phase 3. Early auctioning was intended to raise funds for the EU's NER 300 program[16] for innovative renewable energy technologies and carbon capture and storage pilot projects as well as to meet the hedging demand of the power sector (COM (2012) 652 final). By 2013, 200 million of Phase 3 EUAs have been auctioned to generate funds for the NER 300 program (EEA, 2014).

CONCLUSIONS

The Commission acknowledged in 2013 that the EU ETS 'has not succeeded in being a major driver towards long term low carbon investment' and that the 'low carbon price . . . increases the risk of "carbon lock-in"' (COM (2013) 169 final). Nevertheless, the EU ETS has been confirmed as a cornerstone of EU climate policy beyond 2020; for 2030, an emission reduction of 43 per cent compared with 2005 is stipulated for the EU ETS sector.[17]

Persistent low carbon prices have intensified calls for the introduction of a price stabilization mechanism in the EU ETS. Such a mechanism could either take the form of direct price control (in case of the introduction of a floor price or a price corridor) or liquidity management (see for example, Kettner et al., 2014; Weishaar, 2014).

In January 2014, the European Commission put forward a proposal concerning the introduction of a market stability reserve in Phase 4 starting in 2021. This reserve should handle surplus allocation that accumulated during the previous trading phases and thus help the EU ETS cope with external shocks by an adjustment of the quantity of auctioned allowances. Depending on the number of allowances in circulation, that is, the allowances in the market that are not needed for compliance,[18] allowances will be placed in or released from the market stability reserve. Starting in 2021, 12 per cent of the circulating allowances can be placed in the market stability reserve providing that the amount of circulating allowances is at least 100 million. In contrast, 100 million allowances will be released from the reserve if there are less than 400 million circulating allowances in the market or, over a period of at least six months, the carbon price exceeds the average carbon price of the two previous years by at least 200 per cent (MEMO/14/39).

The envisaged adjustments of the number of allowances in circulation represent a negligible market intervention compared with the structural surplus of allowances in the EU ETS that will likely prevail until the start of Phase 4 (MEMO/14/39). This suggests that more effort will be needed in order to guarantee that the EU ETS will deliver efficient long-term emission reductions. Especially hybrid schemes, that is, introduction of a price floor[19] or a price corridor, would be a way of generating a stable and predictable price signal incentivising low-carbon investment precluding a lock-in in inefficient carbon-intensive structures (see for example, Kettner et al., 2014).

The European Commission is, however, still opposing direct price control mechanisms arguing that these 'would alter the very nature of the current EU ETS being a quantity-based market instrument' and that 'the carbon price may become primarily a product of administrative and political decisions (or expectations about them), rather than a result of the interplay of market supply and demand' (COM (2012) 652 final). This raises doubts whether the EU ETS can initiate the technological changes necessary for climate change mitigation in the next trading phase.

NOTES

*   The author thanks Daniela Kletzan-Slamanig for valuable comments and Katharina Köberl and Susanne Markytan for excellent research assistance.
1. For a discussion of the legal implications of the EC's interventions see Weishaar (2014b).
2. In Phase 1, however, only four EU Member States decided to auction allowances: Denmark, Hungary, Ireland and Lithuania (EEA, 2014). The total volume of auctions amounted to 8.5 million EUAs (2.8 million per annum) which corresponds to 0.13 per cent of EU allocation. In Phase 2, ten EU Member States and Norway initially opted for auctioning (see Neuhoff et al., 2006, and NAPs), while five more countries auctioned left-over certificates from the New Entrants Reserves.
3. The CDM mechanism comprises credits from project-based emission reductions in non-Annex-I countries – so-called Certified Emission Reductions (CERs) – that may be used for compliance in Annex-I countries (Article 12 of the Kyoto Protocol).
4. The JI mechanism as defined in Article 6 of the Kyoto Protocol comprises credits from project-based emission reductions in Annex-I countries – so-called Emission Reduction Units (ERUs) – that may be used for compliance in other Annex-I countries.
5. That is, carbon black, nitric acid, adipic acid, glyoxal and glyoxylic acid, ammonia, bulk organic chemicals, hydrogen and soda ash.
6. EU Non-ETS sectors are obliged to reduce emissions by 10 per cent until 2020 compared with 2005 (Decision 406/2009/EC).
7. This corresponds to 1.74 per cent of average annual allocation in Phase 2.
8. With exceptions for some new Member States, highly efficient co-generation and district heating.
9. The list of sectors exposed to a significant risk of carbon leakage in the period until 2014 has been published in the carbon leakage decision (Commission Decision 2010/2/EU) and the respective amendments (Commission Decisions 2011/745/EU, 2012/498/

EU and 2014/9/EU). For the period 2015 to 2019, the Commission has published a draft decision on sectors exposed to carbon leakage (European Commission, 2014b).

10. In addition, for the period 2013 to 2016 further exemptions for operators with low emissions have been introduced (Regulation (EU) 421/2014).
11. The analysis focuses on installations in the manufacturing sector and for electricity and heat generation; aircraft operators are not considered.
12. The EEA countries Norway and Liechtenstein joined the EU ETS in 2008.
13. Croatia joined the EU ETS when it became a Member State of the EU in 2014. Data on Bulgaria are omitted due to data inconsistencies in the first trading years.
14. For a detailed analysis of the Phase 1, see Kettner et al. (2008).
15. OTC trading refers to transactions between market participants that are not handled at the exchange.
16. The name 'NER 300' refers to the fact that the funds for the program are generated by auctioning 300 million of allowances of the EU ETS New Entrants Reserve in Phase 3 (http://www.ner300.com/).
17. This translates into a linear reduction factor of 2.2 per cent from 2021 on, compared with 1.74 per cent in Phase 3.
18. The number of allowances in circulation is calculated as the total number of allowances issued from 2008 on plus the number of international credits used since 2008 less the cumulated emissions since 2008 and the number of allowances that are currently in the market stability reserve.
19. As implemented for example, in the Californian emission trading scheme or in the Regional Greenhouse Gas Initiative (RGGI) (see Weishaar, 2014a).

REFERENCES

Aatola, P., M. Ollikainen and A. Toppinen (2013), 'Price Determination in the EU ETS Market: Theory and Econometric Analysis with Market Fundamentals', *Energy Economics* **36**, 380–395.
Chevallier, J. (2011), 'A Model of Carbon Price Interactions with Macroeconomic and Energy Dynamics', *Energy Economics* **33** (6), 1295–1312.
COM (2012) 652 final (2012), Report from the Commission to the European Parliament and the Council, The State of the European Carbon Market in 2012, Brussels.
COM (2013) 169 final (2013), Green Paper, A 2030 Framework for Climate and Energy Policies, Brussels.
Commission Decision 2010/2/EU of 24 December 2009 Determining, pursuant to Directive 2003/87/EC of the European Parliament and of the Council, a List of Sectors and Subsectors Which Are Deemed to Be Exposed to a Significant Risk of Carbon Leakage.
Commission Decision 2011/389/EU of 30 June 2011 on the Union-Wide Quantity of Allowances Referred to in Article 3e(3)(a) to (d) of Directive 2003/87/EC of the European Parliament and of the Council Establishing a Scheme for Greenhouse Gas Emission Allowances Trading within the Community.
Commission Decision 2011/745/EU of 11 November 2011 Amending Decisions 2010/2/EU and 2011/278/EU as Regards the Sectors and Subsectors Which Are Deemed to Be Exposed to a Significant Risk of Carbon Leakage.
Commission Decision 2012/498/EU of 17 August 2012 Amending Decisions 2010/2/EU and 2011/278/EU as Regards the Sectors and Subsectors Which Are Deemed to Be Exposed to a Significant Risk of Carbon Leakage.

Commission Decision 2014/9/EU of 18 December 2013 Amending Decisions 2010/2/EU and 2011/278/EU as Regards the Sectors and Subsectors Which Are Deemed to Be Exposed to a Significant Risk of Carbon Leakage.

Commission Regulation (EU) 176/2014 of 25 February 2014 Amending Regulation (EU) 1031/2010 in Particular to Determine the Volumes of Greenhouse Gas Emission Allowances to Be Auctioned in 2013–20.

Council Decision (2002/358/EC) of 25 April 2002 Concerning the Approval, on Behalf of the European Community, of the Kyoto Protocol to the United Nations Framework Convention on Climate Change and the Joint Fulfilment of Commitments Thereunder.

Decision 377/2013/EU of the European Parliament and of the Council of 24 April 2013 Derogating Temporarily from Directive 2003/87/EC Establishing a Scheme for Greenhouse Gas Emission Allowance Trading within the Community.

Decision 406/2009/EC of the European Parliament and of the Council of 23 April 2009 on the Effort of Member States to Reduce Their Greenhouse Gas Emissions to Meet the Community's Greenhouse Gas Emission Reduction Commitments up to 2020.

Directive 2003/87/EC of the European Parliament and of the Council of 13 October 2003 Establishing a Scheme for Greenhouse Gas Emission Allowance Trading within the Community and Amending Council Directive 96/61/EC.

Directive 2004/101/EC of the European Parliament and of the Council of 27 October 2004 Amending Directive 2003/87/EC Establishing a Scheme for Greenhouse Gas Emission Allowance Trading within the Community, in Respect of the Kyoto Protocol's Project Mechanisms.

Directive 2008/101/EC of the European Parliament and of the Council of 19 November 2008 Amending Directive 2003/87/EC so as to Include Aviation Activities in the Scheme for Greenhouse Gas Emission Allowance Trading within the Community.

Directive 2009/29/EC of the European Parliament and of the Council of 23 April 2009 Amending Directive 2003/87/EC so as to Improve and Extend the Greenhouse Gas Emission Allowance Trading Scheme of the Community.

Elsworth, R., B. Worthington and D. Morris (2012), 'Help or Hindrance? Offsetting in the EU ETS', report, London Sandbag.

European Commission (2014a), Frequently Asked Questions on the 2013–2016 Regulation Amending the EU Emissions Trading System for Aviation, Brussels.

European Commission (2014b), Draft Commission Decision Determining, pursuant to Directive 2003/87/EC of the European Parliament and of the Council, a List of Sectors and Subsectors Which Are Deemed to Be Exposed to a Significant Risk of Carbon Leakage, for the Period 2015 to 2019. Brussels.

European Environment Agency (EEA) (2014), 'EU Emissions Trading System (ETS) Data Viewer', http://www.eea.europa.eu/data-and-maps/data/data-viewers/emissions-trading-viewer, accessed 13 October 2014.

EUTL (2014), 'European Union Transaction Log', http://ec.europa.eu/environment/ets/welcome.do, accessed 13 October 2014.

Feng, Z.H., L.L. Zou and Y.M. Wei (2011), 'Carbon Price Volatility: Evidence from EU ETS', *Applied Energy* **88** (3), 590–598.

Hintermann, B. (2010), 'Allowance Price Drivers in the First Phase of the EU ETS', *Journal of Environmental Economics and Management* **59** (1), 43–56.

Kettner, C., D. Kletzan-Slamanig and A. Köppl (2014), 'The EU Emission Trading Scheme: Is There a Need for Price Stabilization?', in Kreiser, L., S. Lee,

K. Ueta, J. Milne and H. Ashiabor (eds), *Environmental Taxation and Green Fiscal Reform*, Cheltenham, UK and Northampton, MA, USA: Edward Elgar Publishing, pp. 113–125.

Kettner, C., A. Köppl and S. Schleicher (2010), 'The EU Emission Trading Scheme: Insights from the First Trading Years with a Focus on Price Volatility', in Dias Soares, C., J.E. Milne, H. Ashiabor, L. Kreiser and K. Deketelaere (eds), *Critical Issues in Environmental Taxation VIII. International and Comparative Perspectives*, Richmond, UK: Oxford University Press, pp. 205–225.

Kettner, C., A. Köppl, S.P. Schleicher and G. Thenius (2008), 'Stringency and Distribution in the EU Emissions Trading Scheme: First Evidence', *Climate Policy* **8** (1), 41–61.

Koch, N., S. Fuss, G. Grosjean and O. Edenhofer (2014), 'Causes of the EU ETS Price Drop: Recession, CDM, Renewable Policies or a Bit of everything? – New Evidence', *Energy Policy* **73**, 676–685.

Kyoto Protocol, Kyoto Protocol to the United Nations Framework Convention on Climate Change.

MEMO/14/39 (2014), Questions and Answers on the Proposed Market Stability Reserve for the EU Emissions Trading System, Brussels.

Neuhoff, K., M. Åhman, R. Betz, J. Cludius, F. Ferrario, K. Holmgren, G. Pal et al. (2006), 'Implications of Announced Phase II National Allocation Plans for the EU ETS', *Climate Policy* **6** (4), 411–422.

Regulation 421/2014 of the European Parliament and of the Council of 16 April 2014 Amending Directive 2003/87/EC Establishing a Scheme for Greenhouse Gas Emission Allowance Trading within the Community, in View of the Implementation by 2020 of an International Agreement Applying a Single Global Market-Based Measure to International Aviation Emissions.

Weishaar, S.E. (2014a), 'Incentivizing Technologic Change in Emissions Trading Systems: The Case of Excess Supply', in Kreiser, L., S. Lee, K. Ueta, J. Milne and H. Ashiabor (eds), *Environmental Taxation and Green Fiscal Reform*, Cheltenham, UK and Northampton, MA, USA: Edward Elgar Publishing, pp. 126–144.

Weishaar, S.E. (2014b), *Emissions Trading Design: A Critical Overview*, Cheltenham, UK and Northampton, MA, USA: Edward Elgar Publishing.

Zhu, B., J. Chevallier, S. Ma and Y. Wei (2014), 'Examining the Structural Changes of European Carbon Futures Price 2005–2012', *Applied Economics Letters*, doi 10.1080/13504851.2014.943875.

6. The Regensburg Model: emission trading between countries based on a global CO_2 budget, national emission pathways and gradual climate justice

Manfred Sargl, Andreas Wolfsteiner and Günter Wittmann*

THE PROPERTIES OF CO_2 EMISSIONS AND THEIR IMPLICATIONS

According to the Intergovernmental Panel on Climate Change (IPCC), global warming can still be limited to 2°C, and, as Professor Otmar Edenhofer (Co-Chair of IPCC Working Group III) noted at a press conference held by his Working Group: 'It wouldn't cost the earth to save the planet'.

Discussions about reaching the 2°C target often dismiss an important property of CO_2: it stays in the atmosphere for a long time. Thus, it will not suffice to determine reduction targets to be reached by one specific point in time. The crucial determining factor is the future cumulative anthropogenic CO_2 emissions.[1] The IPCC has therefore published a cumulative CO_2 budget of 2,900 Gt, starting from the onset of industrialization (with a range of 2,550 to 3,150 Gt depending on non-CO_2 drivers), which will meet the 2°C target with a probability of over 66 per cent. Between then and 2011 about 1,890 Gt had already been emitted.[2]

At the 2010 World Climate Conference in Cancun the 2°C target was set politically, based on scientific evidence. The logical next step would now be to determine a CO_2 budget compatible with this target.

In this chapter, we will present a proposal for the distribution of the remaining budget between the individual countries in a fair and economically sensible way (effort sharing) following a top-down approach, showing how this can be combined with an emission trading scheme between states.

WHY A TOP-DOWN APPROACH?

A binding agreement on a global cap on CO_2 and its distribution among states is currently not part of the political agenda.[3] The question thus arises as to whether it would also be possible to meet the budget by different means. One bottom-up solution without commitment to a global cap could be for the major emitters of CO_2 to realize that there is only a limited budget left, thus inducing them to change their climate policies in such a way as to adapt their emissions to this budget. However, there are several important reasons why such an approach will probably not be successful:

Limits of Pioneering Countries

International competition puts limits on pioneering activities. Electricity generated by brown coal-fired power plants might, for example, be economically more favourable (without internalization of external costs) than the use of renewable energy (also including storage) for too long. The fact that climate protection would pay in terms of economic benefits is not very helpful, as it only applies if enough players collaborate (public good problem).

Zero-sum Situations (Carbon Leakage, Green Paradox)

Without reduction commitments the risk of a zero-sum situation arises: CO_2 emissions saved by one country[4] may lead to lower pressure on the world market price of fossil fuels and therefore they will be emitted by other countries. One form might be that production is shifted to a country with less or no regulation on CO_2 emissions. The announcement of stricter emission targets and climate policies might lead producers to offer more fossil fuels on the world market and thus make the prices fall.[5] Even the stronger engagement[6] of citizens, organizations, local authorities and companies can lead to a zero-sum situation. However, this does not mean that adopting a pioneering role, within certain limits, is not meaningful. Role models can be meaningful in achieving goals. They will, however, probably not be sufficient to ensure that enough fossil fuels stay underground.

It is also conceivable that a binding agreement on a global cap can be negotiated by committing to self-defined reduction goals. Currently hopes are pinned on voluntary contributions of countries that will be declared obligatory in a joint agreement to be approved in 2015 (Durban Platform[7]). Countries have, however, an incentive to keep their reduction offers as low as possible (public good problem). Most likely the commitments made in this way will however not be sufficiently compatible with the remaining budget.

A transitional solution might be to establish an alliance of pioneering states. A helpful aspect would be to introduce a common price for CO_2 with border adjustments. In this way the problems associated with taking a pioneering role could be limited and the acceptance of a global agreement could be enhanced. However border adjustments have to be designed very carefully in order to be compatible with World Trade Organization rules.

In conclusion, there are strong arguments in favour of the further development of the idea of a top-down approach.[8]

A global climate change agreement could include the following steps:

1. Stipulating a global emission budget compatible with the 2°C target (cf. IPCC budget).
2. Agreeing on criteria for the distribution of the remaining budget between countries; one possibility for doing so is the Regensburg Model.
3. Agreeing on emission trading between countries.

At the same time, agreement must be reached on reductions of the other greenhouse gases which, together with the CO_2 budget, are compatible with the 2°C target.

This approach will not solve the public good problem but it will make negotiations more structured and its transparent criteria for the distribution of the remaining budget could enhance political assertiveness, thus making a solution more likely.

PROPOSALS FOR THE DISTRIBUTION OF THE CO_2 BUDGET

There are several proposals on how the global CO_2 budget could be distributed among states following a top-down approach (see Clarke et al. 2014 and Bodansky 2004). The proposals can be classified according to different criteria.[9] We distinguish between economic criteria and climate justice criteria:

1. Economic criteria
   a. Cost effectiveness: using a benchmark such as marginal abatement costs.
   b. Capacity: benchmark for the economic capacity (such as GDP per capita).
      Reciprocal distribution: for example high GDP per capita – lower allowances.
2. Climate justice criteria (When is climate justice achieved?)

a. Immediate climate justice
    Equal distribution per capita of the remaining budget at a set
    date in the future.
b. Responsibility
    Equal distribution per capita of the remaining budget at a set
    date in the past.
c. Gradual climate justice
    Gradual achievement of equal distribution per capita in a set
    period of time in the future by agreement on national emission
    pathways that, taken all together, comply with the remaining
    budget.

Some models including 'gradual climate justice' follow non-monotonic
emission pathways, like the Contracting and Convergence Model (C&C)[10]
or the Static Convergence Model,[11] while the Regensburg Model[12] follows
strictly monotonic emission pathways. We call these models Future
Convergence Models.[13]

In the following section, we will analyse the pros and cons, as well
as the implications of the criterion 'gradual climate justice' in comparison with the other criteria. The criterion 'cost effectiveness' is difficult to apply and should preferably be fulfilled through an emission
trading scheme. The criteria 'capacity' and 'responsibility' were already
identified in the 1992 United Nations Framework Convention on
Climate Change.[14] However, we want to question whether it is reasonable
to apply these criteria, as well as 'immediate climate justice', when distributing the remaining budget in the form of allowances between states.

Pro Future Convergence Models (Criterion 'Gradual Climate Justice')

1. They have a less negative effect on the global economy, since they
    induce structural changes rather than a structural break.
2. They allow industrial states to finance measures for adaptation and
    mitigation better, as well as technology transfers to emerging and
    developing countries.
3. They allow for an easy and transparent determination of national
    emission pathways using one single criterion: equal distribution per
    capita of allowances in the target year. This facilitates negotiations
    and enhances political viability on the national level.

Contra Future Convergence Models

(pro criteria 'capacity', 'immediate climate justice' and 'responsibility')

1. Gradual climate justice contradicts certain notions of justice as it does not take into account the fact that some countries caused a major part of the on-going climate change and gained a certain level of prosperity through this. Achieving real climate justice is further postponed.
2. Emerging and developing countries should not be petitioners for measures for adaptation, mitigation and technological transfers.

Further Implications of these Criteria

Emerging and developing countries will only accept a Future Convergence Model if it is combined with other criteria, for example when setting contributions to the United Nations Framework Convention on Climate Change (UNFCCC) climate funds.

If such criteria as 'historical responsibility', 'immediate climate justice' and 'economic and technological capacity' are accounted for distributing allowances, emerging and developing countries could sell parts of their emission allowances to purchase 'state-of-the-art' technologies, build up know-how and finance climate adjustments. It could be argued however that this would overstretch the instrument of emission trading between states, if it is only supposed to guarantee certain flexibility and cost efficiency and keep trading at a reasonable level. Instead, countries in need of additional allowances because of their path dependency could prefer to contribute to climate funds if they acquire the right to control the use of these funds to a certain degree in exchange.

Emerging and developing countries face the enormous challenge of building up a new welfare model not based on fossil fuels (although emerging and some developing countries have the advantage of being less path dependent),[15] while at the same time being most affected by adaptations to climate changes they have caused the least.[16] It is questionable, though, whether any agreement on climate could account for this injustice. Developed countries are facing major changes too, and are more path dependent. On the other hand, they have the advantage of higher economic performance and better technological know-how.[17]

The analysis demonstrates that Future Convergence Models have important advantages. Thus, the following section will present the Regensburg Model as one alternative and compare it with other Future Convergence Models.

THE REGENSBURG MODEL

Basic Idea of the Regensburg Model

The basic idea of the model is a global emission pathway that meets a budget compatible with the 2°C target. National emission pathways are then determined from this global pathway, while gradually implementing a 'one man – one emission right'. Emission trading between countries allows for flexibility and cost efficiency.

Core Element of the Model: Regensburg Formula

The following formula[18] is the core element for determining the emissions of different countries:

$$\text{Regensburg Formula:} E_t^i = E_{t-1}^i + CR_{t-1} * (E_{t-1}^i - TA^i)$$

Where:
E_t^i = emissions of country i in year t
TA^i = target amount of country i in target year
Annual rates of change (CR_{t-1}) are derived from the global emission pathway:

$$CR_{t-1} = \frac{E_t - E_{t-1}}{E_{t-1} - TA} = \frac{\text{amount by which emissions are reduced in year } t}{\text{amount of emissions which remains to be reduced}}$$

$CR_{t-1} = -1$, if target amount has already been reached in year $t - 1$

Where:
E_t = global emissions in year t
TA = global target amount in target year

How does the Regensburg Formula Work?

In the standard case (decreasing global emissions[19]), CR_{t-1} is negative. The global rate of change (CR_{t-1}) is the percentage by which in year t the amount of CO_2 emissions that remains to be reduced globally $(E_{t-1} - TA)$ decreases according to the global emission pathway. The difference $(E_{t-1}^i - TA^i)$ is the amount which remains to be reduced by country i. If the global rate of change is applied to the amount to be reduced per country, the individual amount of reduction in year t is calculated with: $CR_{t-1} * (E_{t-1}^i - TA^i)$.

Gradual Adjustment Towards Equal Emission Rights (Convergence)

The Regensburg Formula offers the possibility of gradually achieving equal emission rights ('one man – one emission right') using the following calculation of the target amount of a country in target year (TA^i):

$$\frac{TA^i}{TA} = \frac{P^i_{ty}}{P_{ty}} => TA^i = P^i_{ty} * \frac{TA}{P_{ty}}$$

Where:

$\frac{TA^i}{TA}$ = national share of emissions in target year (ty)

$\frac{P^i_{ty}}{P_{ty}}$ = national share of population in target year

The following options with regard to plan population in the target year[20] for example are feasible:

1. Freezing of the population data in the base year.
2. Considering the demographic forecast for the target year.
3. A compromise could be to limit the population in the target year by calculating the population on the basis of a replacement fertility rate.

For countries the emissions of which are below their target amounts (for example developing countries), the difference ($E^i_{t-1} - TA^i$) in the Regensburg Formula is negative. Due to the fact that CR_{t-1} is also negative these countries will receive an upgrading assessment of their emissions viz. emission rights until ($E^i_t - TA^i$).

The target year determines at which point in time climate justice, as defined above, will be reached. The earlier the target year is set, the more emission allowances will in sum be distributed to, for example, least developing countries, because the global emissions per capita used as the distribution criterion will be even higher.

Emission Trading Between Countries

The model allows the implementation of emission trading between states. The national emission pathways are used as a basis for allocating emission allowances to a country. Emission trading is thus also based on gradual climate justice, if this option is selected when determining the target amounts. This is an important difference to other suggested trading systems between states, such as WBGU (2009) for example.

The amount of certificates owned by country *i* in year *t* as well as the respective target amount, as adjusted on the basis of emission trading, result from the following formulae:

$$CE_t^i = CE_{t-1}^i + T_t^i + CR_{t-1} * (CE_{t-1}^i - TA_{t-1}^i)$$

$$TA_t^i = TA_{t-1}^i + T_t^i$$

Where:

CE_t^i = amount of certificates owned by country i in year t

T_t^i = amount of emissions bought or sold by country i in year t

By selling emission allowances to another country, this amount will be added to the target amount and to the annual emissions of the buying country, and deducted from the target amount and from the annual emissions of the selling country. Actual emissions per capita, however, are no longer equal for the target year in this case but are still based on equal rights.

Emission trading has many advantages: it facilitates cost efficient climate protection, countries with lower emissions per capita can receive financial resources[21] helping them to skip the developmental status of a fossil fuel based economy, and countries with high emissions per capita can attenuate high and fast reduction obligations. This flexibility helps with finding consensus on a global climate change agreement. Arrangements can be made with respect to discrepancies between annual emissions according to the emission pathway and actual emissions. Moreover, companies may receive incentives[22] to search worldwide for investment opportunities in energy-efficiency technologies that reduce greenhouse gas emissions.

Comparison of Regensburg Model and other Future Convergence Models

In C&C Models national emission pathways are determined according to the following formula[23] with varying amounts of emissions:

$$E_t^i = \left((1 - C_t) * \frac{E_{t-1}^i}{E_{t-1}} + C_t * \frac{P_t^i}{P_t} \right) * E_t$$

C_t is the weighting of the national population to world population when E_t^i is determined for year t.[24]

We have also developed a formula (Static Convergence Model) that includes a weighted share of the national population. In our formula, the amount of emissions remains constant at the value of the base year (*by*):

$$E_t^i = \left((1 - C_t) * \frac{E_{by}^i}{E_{by}} + C_t * \frac{P_t^i}{P_t} \right) * E_t$$

There are several options for determining C_t:

C&C: exponential specification: $C_t = e^{-a\left(1 - \frac{t-by}{ty-by}\right)}$

C&C: linear specification: $C_t = \dfrac{t - by}{ty - by}$

Quadratic specification: $C_t = a(t - by)^2 + b(t - by) + c; 0 \le C_t \le 1$

By choosing parameter a in the C&C-exponential specification and parameters a, b and c in the quadratic-specification, it can be specified how fast the share of the population determines the emission allowances of countries.

Differences to the Regensburg Model:[25]

- For a small a (< 1.5), the 'exponential specification' results in a relatively high weighting of the share of the national population straight after the base year.
- In the C&C Models and our Static Convergence Model, the emissions and emissions per capita of a country that starts below its target amount could temporarily exceed the target amount (pathways are non-monotonic). In the Regensburg Model on the other hand, the emission pathways of these countries grow steadily until the target year and do not exceed the target amount. This difference leads to more rights for these countries in the C&C Models and in the Static Convergence Model.
- In the Regensburg Model, a country i is given the same budget (BG^i),[26] independent of the concrete trajectory of the global emission path, as long as it adheres to the same global budget and the same global target amount. In the other models, this budget (and thus the extent of climate justice) varies according to the trajectory of the global path. When determining the trajectory of the global path, however, other criteria, such as cost efficiency, should be given priority (cf. Chapter 5).
- The C&C Models and the Static Convergence Model can result in illogical courses of emission pathways (rising – falling – then rising again) for certain global emission pathways.

Direct financing of technological transfers and climate adaptations by the developed countries tend to be more important in the Regensburg Model, since emission trading generates fewer financial means. Countries starting with emissions below their target amount, usually developing countries, would profit more from the other Future Convergence Models.

If the target amount is temporarily exceeded in these models, it could be argued that these pathways partly take into account other criteria such as 'responsibility'. Since it would not be reasonable to build up a CO_2 intensive economy for a rather short time period, these emission allowances could be available for trading. In climate negotiations countries that need to buy these allowances could object to such an allocation of rights and prefer to pay through public transfers in order to achieve influence on the application of financial payments and technology transfers. Basically it is equally possible to integrate restrictions on the revenues by means of emission trading.[27] It could be considered an advantage, however, if a given model requires fewer restrictions on the use of such revenues.

The comparison shows that the Regensburg Model implements a kind of minimum standard of climate justice when aiming at gradually achieving an equal distribution per capita.

APPLICATION OF THE REGENSBURG MODEL

For concrete calculations, the Regensburg Model needs a time frame to achieve gradual climate justice and which is long enough to enable economically sensible transition. We have chosen 2019 as the base year, since the climate agreement of Paris is supposed to enter into force in 2020, and a total time period of 31 years (target year: 2050). The first period of commitment to be set for the national emission pathways should be shorter (for example 2020–2029), in order to review at certain intervals whether adaptation is necessary on the grounds of new findings. Considering the emissions until 2019 and the emissions after 2050, and subtracting them from the total cumulative global budget (2,900 Gt), results in a budget of 650 Gt for 2020 until 2050 under certain assumptions.[28]

In order to deduct national emission pathways, a global emission pathway compatible with the 2°C climate target must be defined. Ideally, the trajectory of this pathway should be set in a way that mitigation costs are minimized. In order to move away from a fossil fuel based economy, new products have to be developed, investments in new infrastructure have to be made, and new lifestyles have to be generally accepted. All of this needs time for preparation. The earlier political decisions are taken, the cheaper mitigation will be.[29]

Cost effective pathways are in principle described by UNEP (2013) and the IPCC-AR5.[30] The IPCC scenario RCP2.6,[31] which is the only scenario of the Working Group I compatible with the 2°C target, would result in the annual reduction rates depicted in Figure 6.1.

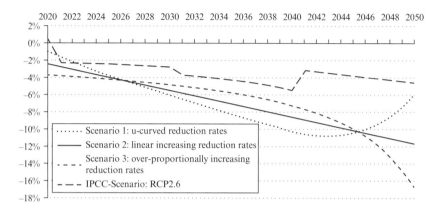

Note: The RCP2.6 scenario does not follow the same boundary conditions as the other scenarios.

Figure 6.1   Annual percentage change of global emission pathways (RR_t)

However, there are reasons why the global emission pathway of scenario RCP2.6 cannot be used to calculate national emission pathways from 2020 to 2050, which are needed to determine the distribution of allowances between states in the Regensburg Model:

1. For the period of 2010 to 2019 the pathway assumes emissions that are no longer realistic. In 2010, the actual emissions were already 1.3 Gt higher than forecast. We assume an average annual increase of 1.5 per cent until 2019. Hence, we evaluate emissions that are 28 Gt higher than in the RCP2.6 scenario for the period of 2012 to 2019.

2. The CO_2 emissions in the RCP2.6 scenario from 2012 to 2100 total 1,188 Gt and thus overshoot the budget of 2,900 Gt by 178 Gt. This scenario still lies within the range of 2,550 to 3,150 Gt determined by IPCC, depending on non-CO_2 drivers. If within a climate agreement the remaining budget is distributed to countries based on the scientific evidence then existing and agreed restrictions of non-CO_2 drivers, an exact budget has to be decided.

3. Figure 6.1 illustrates that the trajectory of the annual reduction rates shows leaps. This can happen if one supposes that at certain points in time new technologies are put into practice. To determine national emission pathways necessary for the distribution of allowances, however, it is more useful to presuppose a steady course of the annual reduction rates.

In view of the negotiations in Paris in 2015 it could be useful if the IPCC were to present updated scenarios with an explicit CO_2 budget to be complied with.

We have developed a tool[32] which allows the determination of global emission pathways adhering to a given CO_2 budget for the period 2020 to 2050. The tool permits the determination of a trajectory of the global emission pathway by choosing, for example a reduction rate for 2050 compared with 1990, a starting reduction rate in 2020 and a certain type of scenario.

A fundamental finding when determining global emission pathways is that a relatively low reduction in 2050 compared with 1990 (emissions 1990: 28.5 Gt)[33] first reduces the budget available for the period 2020 to 2050, since more of it needs to be reserved for the time after 2050. Second, it means that the relatively high target amount needs to be reached before 2050 in order to comply with the overall budget. Therefore a higher reduction in 2050 compared with 1990 allows for more time to adapt to a less fossil fuel intensive economy (trade-off).[34] In our scenarios we therefore use a reduction of 85 per cent.[35] This implies CO_2 emissions of 4.3 Gt in 2050 and an emission per capita of 0.5 t (today: about 6 t), based on an estimated world population of 9.6 billion people.

The most important difference between the global pathways is the trajectory of the annual reduction rates. There are four main variations for these trajectories:

1. A u-shaped reduction rate
    This trajectory is based on the assumption that the reduction of 'the last Gt CO_2' is especially expensive.
2. A linear increase in the annual reduction rate
    This one assumes a linear development of technology and adaptation of infrastructure.
3. An over-proportional increase in the annual reduction rate
    This trajectory is based on the assumption that an early political decision on reduction rates will enable very high reduction rates.
4. A constant annual reduction rate
    This trajectory assumes a continuous development of technology and adaptation of infrastructure.

The trajectories 1 to 3, depicted in Figure 6.1, follow the same basic assumption that, if political decisions are taken soon enough, it is technically possible to achieve high annual reduction rates in the future with relatively low mitigation costs.[36] For example, the necessary investments can be made in the ordinary investment cycles, which will devaluate existing investments to a lesser extent. This is however only possible if political commitments are reliable and trustworthy.[37]

The over-proportionally increasing trajectory has high potential to minimize mitigation costs. However, it also needs a high level of trust and a strong commitment to the political decisions. Constant annual reduction rates would enhance the credibility of policies, because they start with relatively high reduction rates. However, within our boundary conditions, no constant reduction rate exists that complies with the global budget and the target amount at the same time. A constant reduction rate of 4.9 per cent would stick to the budget but would lead to emissions of 8.9 Gt in 2050.

On the basis of a politically determined global emission pathway compatible with the 2°C target, the Regensburg Formula can calculate national emission pathways. Figure 6.2 shows the results based on a global emission pathway following scenario 1 of Figure 6.1 for different country groups. For a concrete example of a national emission pathway, we chose Eritrea, a country starting with very low emissions per capita (0.15 t). For the population figures, we used the recent forecasts of the UN.[38] Obviously, developed as well as emerging countries will have to reduce their emissions massively. Least developed countries will get considerably more allowances. In the target year, emission rights per capita will converge.

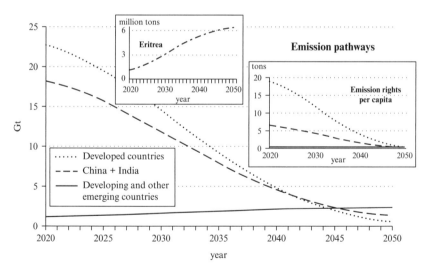

Figure 6.2   Emission pathways calculated with the Regensburg Formula on the basis of the global emission pathway of scenario 1 in Figure 6.1

CONCLUSION

Climate negotiations can be simplified and made more transparent by applying the Regensburg Model in two important areas, namely 'adhering to the remaining CO_2 budget' and 'climate justice', since it only uses one criterion: gradual climate justice in target year.

The Regensburg Model might not represent the subjective notions of justice of all parties concerned. However, if the Rawls theory of justice is applied, which asks from a neutral standpoint which distribution would be picked if one were under a 'veil of ignorance' and did not know in which position one would be once the veil is lifted, then the model does quite well. Furthermore the model combines an objective notion of justice with economic rationality, since it induces structural changes rather than a structural break.

There are many strong reasons to assume that a bottom-up approach will not result in compliance with the remaining budget. We therefore hope that the international community can reach agreement on a top-down approach that distributes the remaining global budget between the states in a fair and economically reasonable manner. An emission trading scheme will assure the necessary flexibility and cost efficiency. The Regensburg Model offers a framework for achieving these goals.

The national emission pathways derived by the Regensburg Model can also be used as a point of reference for the intended nationally determined contributions (INDC) which the countries have to present preparatory to the climate conference in Paris in 2015.

The annual reduction rates (see Figure 6.1) show the magnitude of the challenge we are facing. This challenge can be dealt with in an economically reasonable way if the political decisions are taken in the next years. Further delay will lead to higher costs of emission reduction and increase the probability of ultimately missing the 2°C target.

NOTES

*   We should like to thank Jens Hirsch and Sebastian Wolfsteiner for their contributions to this chapter.
     Contact to all authors: save-climate@email.de.
1.   Anthropogenic CO_2 emissions include all types of CO_2 caused by human intervention: emissions from fossil fuel combustion, emissions from industrial processes (for example production of cement), and other causes of human-induced reduction of CO_2 stored in biomass, such as FOLU (Forestry and Other Land Use).
2.   Source: IPCC WGI AR5 SPM – 2013, p. 27 and IPCC SYR AR5 SPM – 2014b, p. 8.
3.   WBGU (2014), p. 54 and Radermacher (2014), p. 12.
4.   This leading role might produce other benefits, leading to technological innovations

with spillover effects and first-mover advantages. Dependence on importing fossil fuels from politically unstable regions can be lowered as well. However, we need to keep in mind that we are talking about a reduction of emissions in industrial countries by over 90 per cent.

5. Cf. Sinn (2012).
6. Cf. WBGU (2014).
7. A new working group ('Ad Hoc Working Group on the Durban Platform for Enhanced Action (ADP))', which will elaborate corresponding rules of commitment, was established at the world climate conference in Durban 2011. The roadmap established in Durban arranges for the enacting of this new regulation at the 21st COP 2015 in Paris as a follow-up of the Kyoto protocol in 2020.
8. For a varying opinion, see for example Geden (2011).
9. Cf. Höhne et al. (2014).
10. Cf. Meyer (1998), Spencer (1998) and Meyer (2014).
11. Another model developed by the authors of this chapter.
12. Described first in Sargl et al. (2011) and in Wolfsteiner and Wittmann (2011).
13. We would like to point out Baer et al. (2014), who deduct national emission pathways as well. However, they follow the criteria 'capacity' and 'responsibility'.
14. UN (1992), Article 3 (1).
15. WBGU (2009), p. 3.
16. Cf. Cameron et al. (2013).
17. Cf. WBGU (2014), p. 39.
18. For mathematical proof, see appendix in Sargl et al. (2014).
19. For consideration of potential (further) increase of global emissions after base year, see corresponding chapter in Sargl et al. (2014). The alternative Future Convergence Models can also be used without further changes if emissions grow worldwide in a first period of time.
20. Climate justice based on actual population development remains an objective even after the target year.
21. Scope depends on concrete distribution of emission rights (for example selected target year).
22. For more information, see corresponding chapter in Sargl et al. (2014).
23. Cf. Meyer (1998) and Spencer (1998). We have changed their notations to make comparison of the models easier.
24. The Regensburg Formula cited above can also be shown as a weighting formula: $E_t^i = (1 - C_t) * E_{by}^i + C_t * TA^i$ where: $C_t = (E_{by} - E_t)/(E_{by} - TA)$. For mathematical proof and the interpretation of the formula, cf. Sargl et al. (2014).
25. A detailed (graphical) representation can be downloaded at www.save-the-climate.info.
26. $BG^i = TA^i * (ty - by) + (BG - TA * (ty - by)) * (E_{by}^i - TA^i)/(E_{by} - TA)$. BG is the global budget which must be adhered to. For mathematical proof and the interpretation of the formula, cf. Sargl et al. (2014).
27. Cf. WBGU (2009), p. 35.
28. Calculation: 1,890 Gt CO_2 were already emitted by 2011 (source: IPCC WGIII AR5 SPM – 2014a, p. 27). 37.2 Gt CO_2 were emitted in 2010 (source: WGIII AR5 Figure SPM.1.). Taking into account an annual growth rate of 1.5% per cent, we get total emissions of 324 Gt for the period 2012–2019 and 43 Gt in base year 2019. For the years after 2050 we assume a net remaining budget of only 36 Gt. We assume negative emissions of 24 Gt from 2080 onwards until 2100. The IPCC report of Working Group III contains scenarios with much higher negative emissions. This requires on an active removal of CO_2 from the atmosphere such as by a combination of bioenergy with carbon dioxide capture and storage (BECCS). We do not currently consider such over-optimistic scenarios regarding negative emissions as feasible because of the uncertainties connected with them (cf. WBGU 2014, S. 36).
29. Cf. UNEP (2013), p. 13.
30. Cf. van Vuuren et al. (2011), p. 3 and UNEP (2013), p. 13.

31. Sources for the annual CO_2 emissions 2011–2100 according to the RCP2.6 scenario: downloaded from the website: www.iiasa.ac.at/web-apps/tnt/RcpDb/. The website asks for the following sources for the RCP2.6 scenario to be used: van Vuuren et al. (2007).
32. For more information, see corresponding chapters in Sargl et al. (2014). Download Tool: www.save-the-climate.info.
33. Source: IPCC SYR AR5 SPM – 2014b, Figure SPM.2.
34. Cf. UNEP (2013), p. 15.
35. A small reduction is possible if higher negative emissions are supposed in the second half of the century (cf. note 28).
36. Cf. Jakob et al. (2011).
37. Cf. Brunner et al. (2012).
38. Source: http://esa.un.org/unpd/wpp/unpp/panel_population.htm.

REFERENCES

Baer, P., Athanasiou, T., Kartha, S. and Kemp-Benedict, E. (2014), website 'Greenhouse Development Rights', www.gdrights.org, accessed 17 November 2014.

Bodansky, D. (2004), 'International Climate. Efforts Beyond 2012: A Survey of Approaches', Center for Climate and Energy Solutions (successor to the Pew Center on Global Climate Change), www.c2es.org/docUploads/2012%20new.pdf, accessed 17 November 2014.

Brunner, S., Flachsland C. and Marschinski R. (2012), 'Credible commitment in carbon policy', *Climate Policy*, **12** (2), 255–271.

Cameron, E., Shine, T. and Bevins, W. (2013), 'Climate Justice: Equity and justice informing a new climate agreement', Working Paper, World Resources Institute, www.wri.org, accessed 17 November 2014.

Clarke, L., Jiang, K., Akimoto, K., Babiker, M., Blanford, G., Fisher-Vanden, K., Hourcade, J.C., Krey, V., Kriegler, E., Löschel, A., McCollum, D.L., Paltsev, S., Rose, S., Shukla, P.R., Tavoni, M., van der Zwaan, B. and van Vuuren, D.P. (2014), 'Assessing transformation pathways', Chapter 6 in IPCC (eds), *Climate Change 2014, Mitigation of Climate Change, Contribution of Working Group III to the Fifth Assessment Report.*

Geden, O. (2011), 'Bottom-Up statt Top-Down: Die international Klimapolitik vor dem Paradigmenwechsel', *Energiewirtschaftliche Tagesfragen*, (12), 60–62.

Höhne, N., den Elzen, M. and Escalante, D. (2014), 'Regional GHG reduction targets based on effort sharing: a comparison of studies', *Climate Policy*, **14** (1), 122–147.

IPCC (IPCC WGI AR5 SPM – 2013), *Summary for Policymakers*, in: Climate Change 2013: The Physical Science Basis. Contribution of Working Group I to the Fifth Assessment Report.

IPCC (IPCC WGIII AR5 SPM – 2014a), *Summary for Policymakers*, in: Climate Change 2014: Mitigation of Climate Change. Contribution of Working Group III to the Fifth Assessment Report of the Intergovernmental Panel on Climate Change.

IPCC (IPCC SYR AR5 SPM – 2014b), *Climate Change 2014*, Synthesis Report, Approved Summary for Policymakers, version: 1 November 2014.

Jakob, M., Luderer, G., Steckel, J., Tavoni, M. and Monjon, S. (2011), 'Time to act now? Assessing the cost of delaying climate measures and benefits of early action', *Climate Change*, **114** (1), 79–99.

Meyer, A. (1998), 'The Kyoto Protocol and the Emergence of "Contraction and Convergence" as a Framework for an International Political Solution to Greenhouse Gas Emissions Abatement', in Hohmeyer, O. and Rennings, K. (eds), *Man-made Climate Change, Economic Aspects and Policy Options*, Germany, Physica Verlag Heidelberg, 291 ff.

Meyer, A. (2014), website 'Contraction & Convergence (C&C)', www.gci.org.uk, accessed 17 November 2014.

Radermacher, F.J. (2014), 'Kann die 2-Grad-Obergrene noch eingehalten werden? Ansätze für einen neuen Klimavertrag', full version, www.faw-neu-ulm.de/Potsdam-Paper-2Grad-Ziel, accessed 17 November 2014.

Sargl, M., Wolfsteiner, A. and Wittmann, G. (2011), 'Neue Weltklimaordnung: Emissionshandel zwischen Staaten mit schrittweiser Klimagerechtigkeit', *Wirtschaftsdienst*, (11), 704–711.

Sargl, M., Wolfsteiner, A. and Wittmann, G. (2014), 'Background Paper Regensburg Model', www.save-the-climate.info.

Sinn, H-W. (2012), *The Green Paradox, A Supply-Side Approach to Global Warming*, Cambridge, MA: The MIT Press.

Spencer, T. (1998), 'Climate Change and the G8. A Guide for Parliamentarians', www.gci.org.uk/Documents/globe_.pdf, accessed 17 November 2014.

UN (1992), *United Nations Framework Convention on Climate Change*.

UNEP (2013), *The Emissions Gap Report 2013*, a UNEP Synthesis Report.

van Vuuren, D., den Elzen, M., Lucas, P., Eickhout, B., Strengers, B., van Ruijven, B., Wonink, S. and van Houdt, R. (2007), 'Stabilizing greenhouse gas concentrations at low levels: An assessment of reduction strategies and costs', *Climatic Change*, **81** (2), 119–159.

van Vuuren, D.P., Stehfest, E., den Elzen, M.G.J., Kram, T., van Vliet, J., Deetman, S., Isaac, M., Klein Goldewijk, K., Hof, A., Mendoza Beltran A., Oostenrijk, R. and van Ruijven, B. (2011), 'RCP2.6: exploring the possibility to keep global mean temperature increase below 2°C', *Climatic Change*, **109** (1–2), 95–116.

Wissenschaftlicher Beirat der Bundesregierung Globale Umweltveränderungen (WBGU 2009), *Kassensturz für den Klimavertrag – Der Budgetansatz*, Sondergutachten 2009.

Wissenschaftlicher Beirat der Bundesregierung Globale Umweltveränderungen (WBGU 2014), *Klimaschutz als Weltbürgerbewegung*, Sondergutachten 2014.

Wolfsteiner, A. and Wittmann, G. (2011), *Nur Egoismus kann das Klima retten*, Gütersloh, Germany: Gütersloher Verlagshaus.

7. Carbon tariffs and developing countries: the case for special and differential treatment

Selina Cheng and Bill Butcher

INTRODUCTION

Economic instruments, including environmental taxes, have long been considered an effective and cost-efficient means of achieving lower carbon emissions. However, environmental taxes raise two prominent concerns: first, that they will lower international competitiveness for a taxing country's exports and second that they will lead to 'carbon leakage', whereby producers will relocate to non-taxing countries. These concerns can be addressed, at least in part, by the imposition of border adjustment measures (BAMs), which create a more level playing field by imposing on imports from countries without a comparable environmental impost a charge (known as a 'carbon tariff') equivalent to the environmental tax imposed on domestic products; and by exempting exports from the tax.

The prospect of carbon tariffs will raise concerns among countries without comparable carbon pricing mechanisms, whose exports will be the potential objects of such tariffs. Indeed, one of the objectives of carbon tariffs is to incentivize the introduction of carbon pricing regulation in non-taxing countries. Particularly concerned will be producers and governments from developing countries, whose economies could be especially challenged by any imposition of carbon tariffs on their products.

The issues around carbon tariffs and developing countries have been brought into sharper focus by the recent United States–China agreement to limit carbon emissions.[1] If this initiative has its desired effect of stimulating greater international action on climate change, two of the consequences will have a direct impact on carbon tariffs and developing countries. First, among the tools available to meet their obligations under the commitment, both the USA and China will need to consider the imposition of new forms of environmental impost. This in turn will lead to reinvigorated calls for carbon tariffs to protect domestic producers. Second, China's commitment will be seen as an exemplar for developing countries, leading to higher expectations of them in the environmental protection sphere.

This chapter examines the legality under World Trade Organization (WTO) jurisprudence of carbon tariffs and their current and potential application to imports from developing countries. The chapter proposes that developing countries can and should be subjected to a lighter regime of carbon tariffs and, to the extent that this is not currently provided for in WTO rules, that explicit provision should be made for it. In recognition of the heightened expectations of developing countries, the authors do not propose that all developing countries should be exempted from all carbon tariffs but rather, that there be a graduated imposition of such tariffs according to each developing country's current stage of economic development.

CARBON TARIFFS

'Carbon tariff' refers to a carbon-based border adjustment imposed on imported goods which have not been subject to any comparable domestic carbon emission reduction impost in their source country. The form of a carbon tariff will differ according to the form of emissions reduction scheme operated by the importing country: when the importing country's emissions reduction scheme operates through a carbon tax, the carbon tariff takes the form of a tax payment and when the importing country's emissions reduction scheme operates through an emissions trading system (ETS), the carbon tariff takes the form of a requirement on the importer to surrender emissions allowances.

These in turn will be subject to different WTO rules: a carbon tariff in the form of a tax will primarily be subject to challenge under the General Agreement on Tariffs and Trade (GATT) Articles I (Most Favoured Nation Treatment) and III (National Treatment) while a carbon tariff in the form of an allowance may be challenged under Article XI (General Elimination of Quantitative Restrictions). If a carbon tariff violates any of these provisions, the implementing country can turn to GATT Article XX to argue its WTO consistency.

PREVIOUS CARBON TARIFF PROPOSALS

In the USA, several bills called for carbon tariffs through a requirement that energy-intensive imports surrender permits. The (Low Carbon Economy Act) Bingaman-Specter Bill 2007[2] included a mild form of border adjustment by requiring importers to surrender emissions permits when the emissions in the unregulated (or under-regulated) producing country sector rose above a baseline level. The Lieberman–Warner Bill 2008[3] required importers to purchase and surrender 'international reserve allowances' to cover goods imported from countries that had not under-taken adequate steps to mitigate greenhouse gas emissions. The (American Clean Energy and Security Act) Waxman–Markey Bill 2009[4] similarly required importers of certain products to surrender emission allowances.

In the European Union (EU), the prefatory note to the 2008 proposal to amend Directive 2003/87/EC, to take into account concerns about carbon leakage stemming from the operation of the EU Emissions Trading System (EU ETS), discusses the possibility of carbon tariff measures requiring importers to acquire and surrender allowances on terms 'no less favour-able to institutions within the EU'.[5] In preparing the third phase of the EU ETS, Directive 2009/29/EC contains various provisions to address 'sectors at risk' of carbon leakage, including adjusting the amount of free allowances and inclusion of importers in the EU ETS as possible options to address leakage from those sectors deemed to be at significant risk of carbon leakage.[6]

The US and EU proposals have several similarities: first, the proposed carbon tariffs are all based on the inclusion of importers in their domestic ETS and take the form of allowances. Second, both the USA and the EU state their proposals on carbon tariffs are to reduce carbon leakage and maintain the competitiveness of their domestic industries in international trade. Third, both affirm that international negotiations to persuade other Members to adopt comparable emission reduction actions would be their first choice to address carbon leakage and competitiveness concerns and that carbon tariffs would only be adopted as a last resort should those negotiations fail.

CARBON TARIFFS AND THE WTO

Do Carbon Tariffs Conform with WTO Rules?

The Preamble of the Marrakesh Agreement Establishing the WTO (the WTO Agreement) recognizes five objectives: (1) improve living stand-ards, ensure full employment, higher real income and effective demand; (2) expand the production and trade of goods and services; (3) adhere to sustainable development, rational use of the world's resources, protect-ing the environment; (4) ensure the trade and economic development of developing country members; and (5) establish an integrated multilateral trading system. Broadly, these five objectives are coordinated with each other and can be attributed to the core principle of the WTO – trade liberalization. However, trade measures taken for the purpose of environment protection, such as carbon tariffs, may generate conflict between the objective of protecting the environment and that of promoting free trade. In *United States – Import Prohibition of Certain Shrimp Products*, the panel observed that although environmental protection is one of the objectives of the WTO agreements, its primary goal remains the promotion of economic development through trade liberalization.[7] The authors of this chapter take the view that the principle of trade liberalization should be balanced with the specific Preamble objectives and that, in the case of conflict, neither should necessarily 'trump' the other. While it is appropriate that the WTO take a broad view of carbon tariffs, it is also true that given the primacy afforded in the WTO Preamble to the international improvement of living standards and to ensuring the trade and development of developing country members, a strong case can be made for the non-imposition of carbon tariffs on imports from developing countries.

Emission Allowances and GATT Article XI – General Elimination of Quantitative Restrictions

Article XI:1 states 'No prohibitions or restrictions other than duties, taxes or other charges, whether made effective through quotas, import or export licences or other measures, shall be instituted or maintained by any contracting party on the importation of any product of the territory of any other contracting party or on the exportation or sale for export of any product destined for the territory of any other contracting party'. The WTO panel in *Japan – Trade in Semi-Conductors* explained that this provision applied to 'all measures instituted or maintained by a contracting party prohibiting or restricting the importation, exportation or sale for export of products other than measures that take the form of duties, taxes or other charges'.[8] The panel in *India – Quantitative Restrictions on Imports of Agricultural, Textile and Industrial Products* found that India's import restriction measures including an import licensing system, imports canalization through government agencies and actual user requirement for import licences were inconsistent with the broad scope of a general ban on import restrictions embodied in Article XI:1 and thus not compliant. The panel in *Turkey – Restrictions on Imports of Textile and Clothing Products* held that Turkey's quantitative import restrictions imposed pursuant to the *Turkey – EC customs union* were inconsistent with Article XI:1. Similarly, carbon tariffs in the form of emission allowances are likely to be considered as having a quantitative restrictive effect on imports and be held to violate Article XI:1.[9]

Carbon Taxes and GATT Article I:1 – Most Favoured Nation Treatment

Article I:1 provides for non-discriminatory treatment between like foreign products. It covers border measures such as customs duties, import/export charges, methods of levying duties and charges and exportations rules, as well as national taxes and regulations under Articles III:2 and III:4.[10] Analysing whether carbon tariffs meet the requirement of this provision involves two aspects: first, whether, otherwise 'like' products can be differentiated based on different carbon emissions generated through different production and processing methods (PPMs), and second, whether there is discrimination between the same products produced in different countries. In the most recent relevant WTO dispute, the panel in *Canada – Certain Measures Affecting the Automotive Industry* held that a non-product-related PPM will be consistent with Article I provided it is origin neutral. Commentators have observed that origin-neutral PPM-based measures are more likely to be found consistent with certain provisions of the GATT than country-based PPM-based measures.[11] Carbon tariffs are origin neutral PPM-based measures and as such unlikely to be found inconsistent with Article I:1.

Carbon Taxes and GATT Article III – National Treatment

Article III contains three provisions most relevant to carbon tariffs: the first sentence of Article III:2 with respect to internal tax or charges on 'like' products, the second sentence of Article III:2 with respect to tax or charges on 'directly competitive or substitutable products' and the first sentence of Article III:4 with respect to taxes and regulations not covered by Article III:2.

The first sentence of Article III:2 states: 'The products of the territory of any contracting party imported into the territory of any other contracting party shall not be subject, directly or indirectly, to internal taxes or other internal charges of any kind in excess of those applied, directly or indirectly, to like domestic products.' As interpreted by the panel in *Argentina – Measures Affecting the Export of Bovine Hides and the Import of Finished Leather*, for an infringement of this provision, there must be an affirmative conclusion as to three matters: (1) that the measure is the type of tax covered, (2) that the taxed imported and domestic products are 'like', and (3) that the imported product is taxed in 'excess' of like domestic products.[12] In *Japan – Taxes on Alcoholic Beverages*, the Appellate Body explained that the term 'like' under this provision should be interpreted 'narrowly' and the factors for determining likeness of products include the product's end use in a given market, consumers' tastes and habits in the importing country; and the product's properties, nature, quality and tariff classification.[13] Regarding the meaning of 'excess', the Appellate Body in *Japan – Taxes on Alcoholic Beverages* confirmed that even the smallest amount of 'excess' was too much, and that it was irrelevant to consider whether protectionism was an intended objective of the excessive tax. From these cases, this chapter argues that 'like product' is interpreted more strictly in Article III:2 than Article I:1 and imported products that are manufactured under different non-product-related PPMs are likely to be deemed as 'like products' under this provision.

The second sentence of GATT Article III:2 states: 'Moreover, no contracting party shall otherwise apply internal taxes or other internal charges to imported or domestic products in a manner contrary to the principles set forth in paragraph 1'. This means internal taxes or other internal charges should not be applied to imported like products 'so as to afford protection to domestic production'.[14]

As the objective of carbon tariffs is to reduce carbon leakage and to maintain competitiveness of domestic industries in international trade (as expressed by both the USA and the EU in their carbon tariff proposals), carbon tariffs may be regarded as being for the purpose of affording protection to domestic production and hence inconsistent with Article III:2.

The first sentence of Article III:4 states 'The products of the territory of any contracting party imported into the territory of any other contracting party shall be accorded treatment no less favourable than that accorded to like products of national origin in respect of all laws, regulations and requirements affecting their internal sale, offering for sale, purchase, transportation, distribution or use.' According to the Appellate Body in the *European Communities – Measures Affecting Asbestos and Asbestos-Combining Products*, the concept of 'like products' in Article III:4 is broader than 'like products' under the first sentence of Article III:2 and should also include 'directly competitive or substitutable' products.[15] The phrase 'no less favourable' has been interpreted in several cases. The Appellate Body *in Korea – Measures Affecting Imports of Fresh, Chilled, and Frozen Beef*, explained that whether a measure causes 'less favourable' treatment depends on whether it 'modifies the conditions of the competition in the relevant market to the detriment of imported products'.[16] The Appellate Body in *Dominican Republic – Measures Affecting the Importation and International Sale of Cigarettes* further explained that a detrimental effect on a foreign product alone does not necessarily cause 'less favourable' treatment if the measure at issue does not discriminate on the basis of the origin of the product and the detrimental effect is caused by 'factors or circumstances unrelated to the foreign origin of the product'.[17] As with Article III:2, imported products and domestic products using different PPMs are thus likely to be considered as 'like products' under Article III: 4. However, when calculating carbon tariffs, it would be impractical for the implementing jurisdiction to determine the individual emissions of each producer so the calculation is more likely to be based on a blanket industry average of emissions (as was intended in the USA proposals).[18] This could constitute a breach of Article III:2 as it would entail treating foreign firms less favourably than domestic producers as it would mean that the carbon impost would be charged differently because of the foreign origin of the product. To overcome this, an alternative approach to achieve consistency with Article III:2 is to base the tariff on an assumption that the imported products were produced using the lowest polluting technology available, regardless of the PPMs actually employed,[19] but in most cases this would mean the tariff would reflect less emissions than those actually generated.

Justification under GATT Article XX – General Exceptions

If a carbon tariff is found inconsistent with Articles I, III or XI, it might still be considered as GATT-compliant through the exceptions provided in Article XX which, most relevantly, provides as follows:

> Subject to the requirement that such measures are not applied in a manner which would constitute a means of arbitrary or unjustifiable discrimination between countries where the same conditions prevail, or a disguised restriction on international trade, nothing in this Agreement shall be construed to prevent the adoption or enforcement by any contracting party of measures:
> (*b*) necessary to protect human, animal or plant life or health; . . .
> (*g*) relating to the conservation of exhaustible natural resources if such measures are made effective in conjunction with restrictions on domestic production or consumption . . . . .

A carbon tariff is likely to satisfy the requirements of Article XX(b). Given the environmental purpose of a carbon tariff, it is most likely that it would be held to protect human, animal or plant life or health. It would also be held 'necessary' to those ends.[20] Similarly, as a carbon tariff relates to the conservation of exhaustible natural resources (clean air)[21] and is implemented in conjunction with a domestic carbon tax or ETS, it is likely to be found consistent with Article XX(g).

Regarding the Article XX chapeau, however, a carbon tariff calculated individually for domestic firms but according to an industry average for foreign firms may well be regarded as 'arbitrary or unjustifiable discrimination' and thus fail on this point. A tariff would be more likely to succeed if calculated based on the assumption described above in the discussion of Article III:2 – that the products were produced using the best available technology.

SPECIAL TREATMENT FOR DEVELOPING COUNTRIES

What are Developing Countries and Least Developed Countries

There is no WTO definition of 'developing country'. Each WTO member can simply declare itself to be 'developing', which, as such status brings with it certain trade-related advantages, is then subject to challenge by other members. The factor most commonly considered when determining the developmental status of a country is gross national income (GNI) per capita.[22]

The WTO adopts the meaning of least developed country (LDC) by reference to the list compiled by the United Nations Office of the High Representative for the Least Developed Countries, Landlocked Developing Countries and Small Island Developing States.[23] The countries listed are those with the lowest levels of socio-economic development, determined according to three criteria:

- Per capita income (gross national income per capita)
- Human assets (indicators of nutrition, health, school enrolment and literacy)
- Economic vulnerability (indicators of natural and trade-related shocks, physical and economic exposure to shocks, and smallness and remoteness).[24]

As at 21 November 2014, there are 48 countries listed – 34 in Africa, 9 in Asia, four in Oceania and one in the Americas[25] – of which 34 are WTO members.[26]

While the WTO affords LDCs additional preferential treatment, they are nonetheless considered a subset of developing countries.[27] Consistent with this approach, references in this chapter to 'developing countries' includes LDCs, except where otherwise stated.

Common but Differentiated Responsibility

The notion of common but differentiated responsibility has long been at the forefront of global cooperation on responses to climate change.

The *Rio Declaration* states: 'In view of the different contributions to global environmental degradation, States have common but differentiated responsibilities. The developed countries acknowledge the responsibility that they bear in the international pursuit of sustainable development in view of the pressures their societies place on the global environment and of the technologies and financial resources they command.'

Similarly, the *Framework Convention on Climate Change* states that parties' responses to climate change should be 'on the basis of equality and in accordance with their common but differentiated responsibilities and respective capabilities'.

The principle of common but differentiated responsibility has two core elements. The first is that all states bear a responsibility for the protection of the environment. The second is that in considering the extent of each state's responsibility, account should be taken of the different circumstances, particularly each state's contribution to the problem and its capability to contribute to the global response.

The bases for differentiated responsibility include recognition that developing countries:

- pollute less per head than developed countries
- have less financial capacity to 'green' their economies
- have less access to 'green' technology
- have not contributed as much historically to environmental damage as have developed countries
- are in some instances 'importing' the emissions of developed countries through their production of goods for the latter.

In the specific context of international trade and its regulation, can be added:

- developing countries have less developed infrastructure, which impedes their capacity to export
- developed countries have more sophisticated ways to frame laws that would be trade-restrictive yet WTO-friendly[28]
- developing countries and LDCs often have excessive reliance on export of raw materials and should be encouraged to develop value-adding processes
- excluding developing countries from carbon tariffs responds to claims of 'economic imperialism'.[29]

The Enabling Clause

The Enabling Clause was adopted in 1979 and subsequently incorporated into the GATT 1994.[30] It provides that 'contracting parties may accord differential and more favourable treatment to developing countries, without according such treatment to other contracting parties' and applies this exception to, inter alia, preferential tariff treatment in accordance with the Generalized System of Preferences (GSP).[31] 'GSP' had earlier been defined as 'a system of generalized, nonreciprocal and non-discriminatory preferences beneficial to the developing countries'.[32] Thus, it is the Enabling Clause that allows developed countries to offer unilateral, non-reciprocal preferences to imports from developing countries.

A WTO Member wishing to offer preferential trade treatment beyond that permitted under the Enabling Clause may seek a waiver of any of its GATT commitments (including Articles I, III and XI) under Article IX:3 of the WTO Agreement. This authorizes WTO Members as a whole to waive obligations imposed on a Member by any of the WTO's multilateral trade agreements, including the GATT. Unusually for the WTO, which normally requires consensus decisions, a decision to grant a waiver only requires the support of three fourths of the Members. Examples of successful USA applications for waivers include the Caribbean Basin Economic Recovery Act (CBERA),[33] the Andean Trade Preference Act (ATPA),[34] and the African Growth and Opportunity Act (AGOA).[35]

Other Special and Differential Treatment Provisions

In addition to the specifically trade-related preferential treatment permitted under the Enabling Clause and the waiver procedure, there are a number of other preferential treatment provisions in WTO agreements. According to the WTO Committee on Trade and Development,[36] special and differential treatment provisions in the WTO can be divided into six categories:

Provisions aimed at increasing the trade opportunities of developing countries
These provisions require Members to take action to increase trade opportunities available to developing countries. Examples include Article IV:1 of the General Agreement on Trade in Services (GATS), which requires Members to negotiate specific commitments to increase the participation of developing country Members in world trade; and the Preamble of the Agreement on Agriculture, which requires developed country Members to take into account the particular needs and conditions of developing

country Members by providing improved opportunities and terms of access for agricultural products.

Provisions for safeguarding the interests of developing countries[37]
These provisions require developed country Members to safeguard the interests of developing countries when adopting trade measures. For example, Article 10.1 of the Agreement on the Application of Sanitary and Phytosanitary Measures (SPS Agreement) requires Members to take account of the special needs of developing country Members, and in particular of the LDC Members. Article 12.3 of the Agreement on Technical Barriers to Trade (TBT Agreement) requires Members to take account of the special development, financial and trade needs of developing country Members, with a view to ensuring that their technical regulations, standards and conformity assessment procedures do not create unnecessary obstacles to exports from those Members.

Flexibility of commitments, of action, and use of policy instruments[38]
These allow developing country Members exemptions (or reduced levels of commitment) from disciplines and commitments otherwise applying to the membership in general. For example, Article 6.2 of the Agreement on Agriculture allows government subsidies to encourage agricultural and rural development as an integral part of the development programs of developing country Members and it also allows domestic support to encourage diversification away from growing illicit narcotic crops. Article 12.4 of the TBT Agreement states that developing country Members should not be required to comply international standards which are not appropriate to their development, financial and trade needs.

Transitional time periods[39]
These allow developing countries longer time limits on meeting certain new obligations. For example, the Agreement on Trade-Related Aspects of Intellectual Property Rights (TRIPS) allows developing country Members and LDC Members five year and 11 year transition periods respectively, compared with the one year transition period granted to developed country Members. Similarly, the Agreement on Trade-Related Investment Measures (TRIMS) allows developed country Members a two year transitional period but gives five years to developing country Members, and seven years to LDC Members.

Technical assistance[40]
Developing country Members must provide technical assistance to developing country Members. For example, Article 9.2 of the SPS Agreement

requires importing developed country Members to provide technical assistance to exporting developing country Members to meet their sanitary or phytosanitary requirements.

Provisions relating to least-developed countries[41]
These provisions entitle LDC Members to further protections and exemptions than developing country Members in the five types of provisions discussed above. An example is the longer transition period allowed under TRIPS.

Problems with Special and Differential Treatment Provisions

From the foregoing, it can be seen that the WTO recognizes the importance of environmental protection (albeit subject to the WTO's paramount concern for open trade) and, with that confers a broad legitimacy on carbon tariffs, and that it also recognizes the appropriateness of affording preferential treatment, in certain circumstances, for developing countries. It is likely that under current WTO rules, particularly the Enabling Clause, developed country Members which chose to impose carbon tariffs on imports would be permitted to grant exemptions from those tariffs to developing country Members.

Moreover, a Member imposing a carbon tariff is not obliged to give all developing country Members the same level of exemption and could, for example, give differentiated special treatment to developing countries according to their development level. The result will be that some developing countries will gain exemption from some carbon tariffs, while others will not. This, too, is consistent with WTO jurisprudence. A WTO Appellate Body decision in 2004 determined that developed countries could give benefits to some developing countries but were not required to provide the same benefits to all developing countries.[42]

While this flexibility in WTO jurisprudence is to be welcomed, it can be argued that in light of the special development needs of developing countries set out earlier in this chapter, consideration should be given to reaching further and *requiring* developed countries to grant waivers from carbon tariffs in certain cases.

This should not be applied to all exports from all developing countries, however, as to do so could compromise the environmental goals of the country imposing the carbon tariffs and may provide an unwarranted trade advantage to the exporting country whose products have not been subjected to any meaningful emissions-based impost. A balance is needed between two potentially competitive global concerns: the protection of the natural environment and the economic improvement of developing countries.

Where that balance falls will require consideration of three factors in particular: the level of development of the exporting country and the impact a carbon tariff could have on that development (and in this the Gross National Income of the exporting country would be a major factor); the impact of imports from that country on the market in the importing country (and in this the volume and price of such imports would play a major part); and the impact of those imports on the environmental goals of the importing country.

Questions will arise about the consideration of non-economic and non-environmental factors. Commonly, where special treatment is afforded by developed countries under GSP arrangements it is made subject to special, non-economic, conditions. For example, ATPA provides that the United States will not afford preferential treatment to a country if it: is communist; has allowed the expropriation or nationalization of the property of a citizen of the United States or a corporation owned by the United States; provides preferential treatment to the products of another developed country that could negatively affect trade with the United States; does not adequately protect intellectual property rights; and fails to afford internationally recognized workers' rights.[43] Ideally, such factors should be irrelevant to the granting of carbon tariff exemptions but attempts to exclude them from consideration would meet with resistance from at least some importing countries. Allowing those factors to be considered would not be fatal to the spirit of an agreement on compulsory exemptions however, provided safeguards were in place to prevent such factors being used purely for trade protection ends.

CONCLUSION

With the recent US–China agreement on carbon emissions, and heightened expectations for the 2015 United Nations Climate Change Conference in Paris, there is renewed focus on the use of economic instruments to achieve positive environmental outcomes. To protect domestic producers, those countries which implement such instruments can be expected to consider the imposition of carbon tariffs on imports. This is appropriate and, depending on the form of the carbon tariff, conforms to WTO rules. It does, however, raise concerns about the impact of carbon tariffs on the development of developing countries, which are already disadvantaged for a range of reasons including under-performing infrastructure and slow transition to the most up-to-date 'green' technology. While some developed countries will afford exemptions from carbon tariffs and other special treatment in line with existing GSP regimes (a form of discriminatory treatment but one which is also generally permitted under WTO rules) there will be instances where this will not be done. This chapter advocates that, with a view to safeguarding the progress of the more vulnerable developing country economies, the WTO should adopt regulations over carbon tariffs, including a requirement that countries applying them must afford exemptions and other forms of special treatment to developing countries.

NOTES

1. Mark Lander (2014), 'US and China Reach Climate Accord After Months of Talks', *the NYTimes.com*, 11 November 2014, retrieved from: http://www.nytimes.com/2014/11/12/world/asia/china-us-xi-obama-apec.html?_r=0 (accessed 5 March 2015).
2. Low Carbon Economy Act of 2007, retrieved from: http://www.gpo.gov/fdsys/pkg/BILLS-110s1766is/pdf/BILLS-110s1766is.pdf (accessed 5 March 2015).
3. Lieberman–Warner Climate Security Act of 2008, retrieved from: http://www.gpo.gov/fdsys/pkg/BILLS-110s3036pcs/pdf/BILLS-110s3036pcs.pdf (accessed 5 March 2015).
4. American Clean Energy and Security Act of 2009, retrieved from: http://www.gpo.gov/fdsys/pkg/BILLS-111hr2454eh/pdf/BILLS-111hr2454eh.pdf (accessed 5 March 2015).
5. Proposal for a Directive of the European Parliament and of the Council amending Directive 2003/87/EC so as to improve and extend the greenhouse gas emission allowance trading system of the Community, retrieved from: http://eur-lex.europa.eu/legal-content/EN/TXT/PDF/?uri=CELEX:52008PC0016&from=EN, p8 (accessed 5 March 2015).
6. Directive 2009/29/EC of The European Parliament and of The Council of 23 April 2009, retrieved from: http://faolex.fao.org/docs/pdf/eur88008.pdf (accessed 5 March 2015).
7. Panel Report, United States-Import Prohibition of Certain Shrimp Products, 15 May 1998, WT/DS58/R, para 7.42.
8. Panel Report, *Japan – Trade In Semi-Conductors*, adopted on 4 May 1988, L/6309 – 35S/116, 104.
9. J. Pauwelyn (2007), 'US Federal Climate Policy and Competitiveness Concerns – The Limits and Options of International Trade Law', Working Paper, Nicolas Institute for Environmental Policy Solutions, Duke University, p. 12.
10. For a general review, see M. Matsushita et al. (2006), *The World Trade Organization: law, practice, and policy*, Oxford: Oxford University Press.
11. R. Howse and Regan, D. (2000). 'The Product/Process Distinction – An Illusory Basis for Disciplining Unilateralism', *European Journal of International Law* 11(2), 249–289; S. Charnovitz (2002), 'The Law of Environmental "PPMs" in the WTO: Debunking the Myth of Illegality', *The Yale Journal of International Law* 27(1), 59–110.
12. Panel Report, *Argentina-Measures Affecting the Export of Bovine Hides and the Import of Finished Leather*, WT/DS155/R (December 19 2000), para. 11.131.
13. Appellate Body Report, *Japan – Taxes on Alcoholic Beverages*, WT/DS8/AB/R,WT/DS10/AB/R, WT/DS11/AB/R, pp. 20–21.
14. GATT Article III:1 states: 'The contracting parties recognize that internal taxes and other internal charges, and laws, regulations and requirements affecting the internal sale, offering for sale, purchase, transportation, distribution or use of products, and internal quantitative regulations requiring the mixture, processing or use of products in specified amounts or proportions, should not be applied to imported or domestic products so as to afford protection to domestic production'.
15. Appellate Body Report, *European Communities – Measures Affecting Asbestos and Asbestos-Combining Products*, WT/DS135/AB/R (12 March 2001), para. 99.

16. Appellate Body Report, *Korea – Measures Affecting Imports of Fresh, Chilled, and Frozen Beef*, WT/DS161/AB/R,WT/DS169/AB/R (11 December 2000), para. 144.
17. Appellate Body Report, *Dominican Republic – Measures Affecting the Importation and International Sale of Cigarettes*, WT/DS302/AB/R (25 April 2005), para. 96.
18. For example, Sec. 768 (p. 1123) of the American Clean Energy and Security Act of 2009 requires 'submissions of appropriate amounts of such allowances for covered goods with respect to the eligible industrial sector that enter the customs territory of the United States' in contrast to domestic 'reporting entities' are accessed on their individual circumstances as shown in Sec. 713 (p. 71).
19. Roland Ismer and Neuhoff, K. (2004), 'Border Tax Adjustments: A Feasible Way to Address Nonparticipation in Emission Trading' *DAE Working Paper Series* (CMI Working Paper 36, University of Cambridge) 15. See also, Mary Kate Crimp (2008), 'Environmental Taxes: Can Border Tax Adjustments Be Used to Counter Any Market Disadvantage?' *New Zealand Journal of Environmental Law*, 12, 39–63. http://search.informit.com.au/documentSummary;dn=747250399896222;res=IELHSS. ISSN: 1174-1538.
20. The test of necessity set out in *Brazil – Measures Affecting Imports of Retreaded Tyres* WT/DS332/AB/R (3 December 2007) at para 136 is 'In order to determine whether a measure is "necessary" within the meaning of Article XX(b) of the GATT 1994, a panel must assess all the relevant factors, particularly the extent of the contribution to the achievement of a measure's objective and its trade restrictiveness, in the light of the importance of the interests or values at stake. If this analysis yields a preliminary conclusion that the measure is necessary, this result must be confirmed by comparing the measure with its possible alternatives, which may be less trade restrictive while providing an equivalent contribution to the achievement of the objective pursued.' A carbon tariff can be expected to satisfy this test.
21. Appellate Body Report, *United States – Standards for Reformulated and Conventional Gasoline (US – Gasoline)*, WT/DS2/AB/R (20 May 1996).
22. The World Bank defines all low- and middle-income countries as 'developing', while recognizing that these are not all experiencing similar levels of development. The World Bank defines all low- and middle-income countries as 'developing', while recognizing that these are not all experiencing similar levels of development. https://datahelpdesk.worldbank.org/knowledgebase/articles/378834-how-does-the-world-bank-classify-countries. 'For the current 2015 fiscal year, low-income economies are defined as those with a GNI per capita, calculated using the World Bank Atlas method, of $1,045 or less in 2013; middle-income economies are those with a GNI per capita of more than $1,045 but less than $12,746; high-income economies are those with a GNI per capita of $12,746 or more. Lower-middle-income and upper-middle-income economies are separated at a GNI per capita of $4,125' http://data.worldbank.org/about/country-and-lending-groups.
23. http://unohrlls.org/.
24. UN Commission on Trade and Development ('UNCTAD'), 2014: http://unctad.org/en/Pages/ALDC/Least%20Developed%20Countries/UN-recognition-of-LDCs.aspx.
25. Refer to http://unctad.org/en/pages/aldc/Least%20Developed%20Countries/UN-list-of-Least-Developed-Countries.aspx.
26. Refer to http://www.wto.org/english/thewto_e/whatis_e/tif_e/org7_e.htm.
27. Appellate Body Report, *European Communities – Conditions for the Granting of Tariff Preferences to Developing Countries*, WT/DS246/AB/R (7 April 2004).
28. P. Kishore (2012), 'Revisiting the WTO Shrimps Case in the Light of Current Climate Protectionism: A Developing Country Perspective', *Journal of Energy and Environmental Law*, Winter, pp. 78 and 84.
29. 'The whole debate … boils down to countries wanting to assert their jurisdiction over priorities and policies of other countries. To that end, the attempt is being made by some to "legitimize" trade restrictions that are otherwise inconsistent with WTO obligations for the purpose of protecting the environmental resources, that lie outside

the member's jurisdiction': Trade and Environment: Issues in the WTO and Proposals, Submission by Egypt, 10/11 September 1996, at 3.

30. Agreement Establishing the World Trade Organization, Annex 1A, General Agreement on Tariffs and Trade 1994, para. 1(b)(iv). For detailed review of the Enabling Clause, see Appellate Body Report, *European Communities – Conditions for the Granting of Tariff Preferences to Developing Countries*, para. 90.3, WT/DS246/AB/R (7 April 2004).

31. GATT, *Differential and More Favourable Treatment, Reciprocity and Fuller Participation of Developing Countries*; Decision of 28 November 1979, L/4903 (3 December 1979).

32. GATT, Generalized System of Preferences; Decision of 25 June 1971, L/3545 (28 June 1971).

33. Caribbean Basin Economic Recovery Act (CBERA), P.L. 98–67, as amended, 19 U.S.C. §§2701-2706.

34. Andean Trade Preference Act (ATPA), P.L. 102–182, as amended, 19 U.S.C. §§3201-3206.

35. African Growth and Opportunity Act (AGOA), P.L. 106–00, Title I, as amended, 19 U.S.C. §§2466a-2466b, 3701–3722.

36. WTO, Committee on Trade and Development, *Implementation of Special and Differential Treatment Provisions in WTO Agreements and Decisions*, WT/COMTD/W/77(2000), p. 3.

37. Ibid., p. 5.

38. Ibid.

39. Ibid., p. 6.

40. Ibid.

41. Ibid.

42. Appellate Body Report, *European Communities – Conditions for the Granting of Tariff Preferences to Developing Countries*, WT/DS246/AB/R (7 April 2004).

43. Section 3202(c) Andean Trade Preference Act 1991, Section 201 of title II of Pub. L. 102–182.

PART II

Energy and excise taxes

8. Reforming the EU VAT system to support the transition to a low-carbon and resource efficient economy

Bettina Bahn-Walkowiak and Henning Wilts

INTRODUCTION

This chapter discusses the question of ecologically differentiated value added taxes (VAT) as a tool to overcome tax-related cognitive barriers by connecting to an existing tax system. This is elaborated along several aspects: (a) The role indirect of consumption taxes for the economy, (b) the legal issues of the VAT system, (c) the EU harmonization efforts in this context, (d) the distributional implications of value added taxes.

Following this, the chapter develops a proposal for a VAT reform (e). To this end, it looks at potential and existing differentiations between sectors, products and services, and product and service groups and turns to those consumption areas that are widely identified as particularly resource *and* carbon intensive and sets out how a harmonization of the overall system and an ecological differentiation in single consumption areas could be brought together. Potential impacts and effects are briefly discussed (f) and some conclusions are drawn (g). The subject addressed in the chapter is relevant from a policy perspective but mainly descriptive: It does not use innovative qualitative and quantitative tools.

THE VALUE ADDED TAX (VAT) SYSTEM IN THE EUROPEAN UNION

Despite efforts to expand the portfolio of environmentally oriented market-based instruments (EEA 2005), recently renewed by the 'getting the prices right and reorienting the burden of taxation' objective of the EU Roadmap (EC 2011a, p.10), the use of economic incentives such as taxes is reluctant. The share of environmental taxes in the total tax revenue of the EU (approximately 6 per cent in 2011) seems too low for substantial progress towards a low-carbon and resource efficient economy. According to the EU Roadmap, all Member States have to 'review their fiscal policies and instruments with a view to supporting resource efficiency more effectively, and in this context reflect on incentives to support consumer choices and producer action in favour of resource efficiency' by 2013. Although the public rarely pays attention to economic instruments as strongly as to the value added tax (VAT) and the VAT system affects the households' consumption decisions due to its price impacts (Albrecht 2006), it is rarely discussed as an environmental instrument as such (Sterner and Coria 2011; Kosonen and Nicodème 2009) or as element of an environmental tax reform (Ekins and Speck 2011). VAT is levied in all European countries and, apart from the US, in all OECD countries. 'The spread of VAT has been the most important development in taxation over the last half century. Limited to less than ten countries in the late 60s, it has now been implemented by more than 150 countries' (OECD 2012, p. 44).

The Role of Indirect Consumption Taxes for the Economy

Indirect consumption taxes[1] are one of the main sources of income in developed countries. In OECD countries, the share of the indirect consumption taxes in the overall government revenues is approximately 34 per cent. On average, about two thirds come from the VAT; one third comes from other consumption taxes such as excise duties on mineral oil, tobacco or alcoholic beverages (OECD 2012).

The VAT is a transfer tax triggered by transactions between economic actors. All upstream services are entitled to the deduction of the input tax, provided they have been charged in commercial transactions before. The cumulative tax burden is usually passed on to the consumers all along the value chain where it is an excise tax charged on end users.

The EU VAT Directive 2006/112/EC allows flexibility in formulating the national VAT system but stipulates that a tax of at least 15 per cent have to be collected. Standard rates vary from 15 per cent (Luxembourg) to 27 per cent (Hungary). Two reduced rates of at least 5 per cent are allowed but currently restricted to 21 categories of product and services, mainly on the basis of social motives (for example, foodstuffs, water, pharmaceuticals, medical equipment, books, and so on). Reduced rates vary from 5 per cent (for example, UK) to 15 per cent (Czech Republic) and additional super reduced rates (for example, France, Ireland, Italy, Luxembourg, Spain) are in the range of 2–4 per cent. Further zero rates/exemptions for public

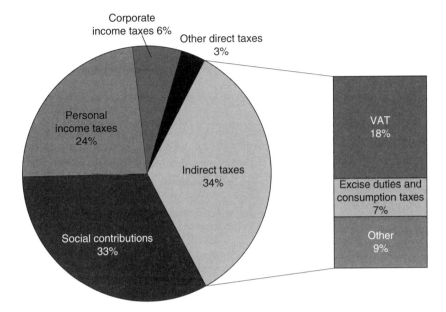

Source: Own compilation on the basis of Eurostat data.

Figure 8.1   *Direct and indirect taxes, EU 2011, as percentage of total tax revenue*

services are common (in other words, they are taxable for VAT but the rate is zero) (EC 2014).

There is no European-wide consensual rationale for standard rates, exemptions and zero rates. Hence, VAT rates are widely inconsistent due to different cultures and traditions (EC 2014; Eurostat 2013; OECD 2012).

The Legal Context of the EU VAT System and the Harmonization Efforts

The first European VAT directives were adopted in 1967. Under Article 93 EC a modification of the VAT Directive requires unanimity voting of the European Council, for example, for the introduction of additional products and services subject to a reduced rate.

There are currently 21 categories of products and services for which the EU directive allows reduced VAT rates (IFS 2011), essentially corresponding to those also known as merit goods.[2] Tax neutrality is considered to be an important principle in the EU, stating that regardless of the length of the value chain like-products should have the same tax burden (Lohse

1999). The term 'like-products', however, does not refer to the manufacturing processes or the material input of the goods and calls for interpretation. The extended Ecodesign Directive acknowledges 'very different degrees of environmental impact despite similar functional performances' (EC 2009a, para. 3) pointing to the inhomogeneity of products. In the absence of effective resource efficiency labels, this provision could serve as a suitable starting point for the introduction of ecologically oriented VAT rates.[3]

A European Commission proposal for a Council Directive amending the VAT Directive of 2006 as regards reduced VAT rates first brought up the question of 'a reduced rate to energy saving materials and to other environmentally beneficial products or services' and 'of eliminating reduced rates for environmentally prejudicial products such as pesticides' (EC 2008, p. 2f.; EC 2007). In the follow up, the EU commissioned several studies on the VAT system and its economic effects (for example, CEP 2009; IVM 2008).

Some studies conclude that an ecological VAT differentiation would only result in minor or no consumption shifts (CE 2007, 2008; CEP 2009) in the realm of energy or energy efficient products and services and emphasized state revenues losses and market distortions. Other studies expect positive interactions of the impacts on environment and innovation (for example, IVM 2008; De Camillis and Goralczyk 2013).

A Green Paper then called for 'maximizing revenue collection' and initiated a consultation process with stakeholders and Member States (MS) (EC 2010; EC 2011b, 2011c). Estimations comparing the actual and theoretical VAT revenues conclude that revenues could almost be twice as high (Eurostat 2013) when a harmonized single rate was introduced and evasion could be avoided. Simultaneously, there have been significant movements in most MS. Only five out of 28 countries have left their tax rates completely unchanged in the last decade (Eurostat 2014). Eighteen countries have particularly modified the reduced rates and eight countries have even introduced additional reduced rates. Despite strong interest in harmonizing the tax rates by abolishing reduced rates and exemptions and avoiding evasion in order to raise the tax revenues, a near-term convergence of the different frameworks and an implementation of a single rate seem rather unlikely.

THE DISTRIBUTIONAL IMPLICATIONS OF VAT CHANGES

Conflicts particularly arise in the context of reduced VAT rates (Albrecht 2006; ZEW 2004; Peffekoven 2009; UBA 2010). The distributional effects of the VATs are – especially in the public debate – highly sensitive. It is argued that the VAT is not based on the financial capacity of the taxpayers, different than the income tax. Households with a low income would therefore bear a proportionately heavier burden through the VAT than households with a high income (ZEW 2004). While the regression effect is largely undisputed, estimations on the extent differ greatly (Kosonen 2012). In a study on the distributional effects of a potential German VAT reform, a regressive but rather moderate effect was revealed: The relative burden of the net income by the VAT for the bottom tenth of the households is about 10 per cent, whereas the relative burden for the upper tenth of the households is about 6 per cent (Ochmann et al. 2012).

While one position holds on to the exemptions for food and rents motivated by distribution policy, another position argues for a full elimination of VAT reductions and notes that an abolition of reduced rates would have only a slight regressive effect (ZEW 2004). In addition, life cycle effects can become relevant in terms of distributional effects, for example in the case of household appliances and mobility (Ochmann et al. 2012; De Camillis and Goralczyk 2013). A tax reduction or exemption is often rather a disguised industry subsidy than a social policy tool (Experian 2009). Sometimes, resource- and carbon-intensive sectors and product groups such as the agricultural and food system benefit from a two-level subsidization, in other words, the sector receives on-budget subsidies at the beginning of the value chain as direct financial support and a preferential treatment through VAT reductions as off-budget subsidies at the end of the value chain (IEEP 2012). These points contribute to the fact that VAT rates are a hotly contested terrain, both as a direct incentive as well as an indirect subsidy.

POTENTIAL SCOPE OF DIFFERENTIATIONS IN THE VAT SYSTEM AND REFORM PROPOSALS

Current VAT differentiations and exemptions follow social, educational, cultural or health reasons. There is sectoral differentiation, differentiation between products and services, and product and service groups. Although differentiations of tax rates can lead to market distortions and macroeconomic disadvantages (EC 2011c), the state distinguishes between eligible and less eligible purposes, such as tax benefits for foundations and other non-profit organizations.

The simple idea behind ecologically differentiated VAT rates is to give subsidies or tax exemptions ('bonus') for environmentally friendly products and/or additional fees/higher taxes ('penalty') for the purchase of less green alternatives (BIO IS 2012). The comparative advantage of tax preferences is in providing support for positive externalities generating additional social benefits (Greene and Braathen 2014). The following will outline the potential scope of differentiations and give some examples (Bleischwitz 2012; Bahn-Walkowiak et al. 2010).

Differentiations between Sectors

In 2009, the European Parliament voted for a sectoral differentiation: the introduction of reduced VAT rates for locally supplied labour-intensive services (EC 1999; EC 2009b) affecting various sectors, inter alia, the hotel and catering industry, parts of skilled craft and trades, such as renovation and repair of private dwellings and services of barbers, shoe-makers and bicycle craft. The services have to be labour-intensive, largely provided to end users, be mainly local, not create distortions of competition, and there must be a close link between the reduction of prices resulting from the VAT rate reduction and a foreseeable increase in demand and employment. The clause specifically refers to industries that are partly competing with private labour-intensive services and illegal employment (EC 2009b).

Standard VAT rates for resource and carbon-intensive food

The example of the food sector demonstrates that sectoral tax benefits hinder the access to resource efficiency potentials. The sector is not only one of the sectors with the strongest environmental impacts (EEA 2013; UNEP 2010), it also entails an enormous amount of wastage. At the same time, the raw materials are comparatively cheap and partially subsidized by the governments (for example, milk and dairy products). Since food is considered as merit goods by legislation they are, regardless of the production methods and the associated consequences for the environment and health, favoured by tax cuts.

Westhoek et al. (2011) indicate that European meat consumption is twice as high and the consumption of dairy products is three times higher than the world average. An analysis of meat and dairy products revealed that the sector – while constituting 6 per cent of the economic value of the total final consumption – contributes 24 per cent of the environmental impacts in EU-27 (JRC 2008). As a full abolition of the reduced rates on food would very likely run into major opposition of businesses and consumer organizations, a normal VAT rate on the most resource and carbon-intensive food could thus gain acceptance. These include mainly meat, dairy and frozen products (EEA 2012). Calculations of IVM (2008) showed that an increase in VAT for conventional meat and dairy

*Table 8.1   Ex ante estimation of demand shifts and GHG reduction
potentials in million tonnes by specific VAT rate changes in
selected product groups*

Product category	Demand increases/ decreases	Estimated GHG emissions reduction in EU*
Energy efficient central heating boilers Application of reduced rates	2004–2014: + 43%–75%	18 million tonnes; approx. 5%
Energy efficient refrigerators, fridge freezers, washing machines (A+/A++) Application of reduced rates	up to + 15%	3 million tonnes; approx. 5%
Thermal insulation materials Application of reduced rates	+ 3.0–12.2%	23–36 million tonnes
Electricity Application of the individual standard rates in those 10 EU countries which use the reduced rates	− 3–4%	20 million tonnes (in 2005)
Electricity Application of reduced rates for electricity from renewable energy	+ 2.5%	2.8 million tonnes
Meat and dairy products Application of standard rates with a possible exemption for organic products	Meat: − 2–7% Dairy products: − 2–5% Organic meat/ dairy products: + 6–16%	12–21 million tonnes

Note: * in Mt CO_2-eq. /a.

Source: IVM 2008.

products to the standard rate in all MS would result in a consumption decrease of 2–7 per cent for meat and 2–5 per cent for dairy products. Taking into account possible shifts in organic products and conventional foods, this would result in a CO_2 reduction of 12–21 million tonnes of CO_2 per year (IVM 2008; see Table 8.1). Most MS currently use one or more of the reduced tax rates. Only Bulgaria, Denmark, Estonia, Lithuania, Romania and Slovakia raise standard rates of at least 20 per cent on food. Alternatively, it could be a useful measure to support the organically produced meat and dairy products with a VAT reduction.

Differentiations among Functionally Identical Products

Differentiations can also be made within a group of functionally identical products. Then criteria verifying resource-efficient or carbon-intensive products are needed. Ideally, life cycle analyses regarding resource and carbon intensity and environmental impacts would be available for all products (as suggested by De Camillis and Goralczyk 2013). The Ecodesign Directive for energy-using equipment does not cover all products and only takes a limited number of indicators for energy efficient devices into account (EC 2005). Nevertheless, the use of such complex eligibility and differentiation criteria would require specialized staff that is likely to be more expensive and less effective (Greene and Braathen 2014). Alternatively, a variety of eco-labels exist and could be employed for VAT differentiations. They would be favourably dynamic (for example, Top Runner lists)[4] because products considered to be resource-efficient at their market introduction will probably be average performers after a few years. This also calls for regular monitoring.

Reduced VAT rates on energy- and resource-efficient household appliances
In 2010, the residential sector accounted for almost 30 per cent of total final electricity consumption, thus playing an important role for efficiency programmes and policies. Only the industry sector had a larger share (36 per cent); the services sector 29 per cent and transport 2 per cent (JRC 2012). Up to 20 per cent of the electricity consumption of private households is caused by cooling and freezing of food alone (Barthel et al. 2005).

Although the average energy consumption of household per year drops already by 1–5 per cent (IVM 2008), the proportion of A++ appliances of refrigerators and freezers sold in 2007 were only 8 per cent and 11 per cent respectively. Due to the fact that aspirations rise and life cycles and innovation cycles are dramatically shortening, electrical appliances are among the top sectors in terms of sales and earning potential. Although the penetration rate is almost 100 per cent for refrigerators, 4.3 million units are still sold each year in Germany (Barthel et al. 2005). The 'Retailers' Environmental Action Plan' (ERRT 2012) calls for advancing innovation for resource-saving and energy efficient appliances.

Household appliances are subject to a standard rate all over Europe and the sector is characterized by a strong competition; a nearly 100 per cent transfer of the tax reduction to the consumers can be expected. Little data exists concerning the price elasticity of demand, especially for large household appliances. However, there have been positive experiences in some EU countries with direct government subsidies for energy-efficient products. In the Netherlands, a programme has led to an increase in sales of about 15 per cent and a market share of 15–40 per cent. In Italy, there is a rebate on income tax, in Spain a discount sale for old products (IVM 2008). It is proposed to allow for reduced VAT rates on labelled energy and material efficient and low carbon products and services in the household appliances sector.

Differentiations between Product/Service Groups

The current VAT system already differs between product and service groups. In the EU, especially the domestic transport is treated very differently. Rates range from 0 per cent (UK) up to 27 per cent (Hungary) (EC 2014).

The intra-community and international air transport is not VAT charged by any European country, whereas a number of countries, including Belgium, Greece, Netherlands and Spain apply a reduced VAT rate for long-distance passenger transports by rail; Germany and Austria even use a standard rate. As regards domestic public transport, 14 European MS collect reduced or zero tax rates. Eight countries use a standard rate of more than 15 per cent. Rail transport is strongly competing with road transport, also concerning freight. This fact is supported by a large share of EU subsidies directed toward road investments (Bahn-Walkowiak et al. 2012).

Harmonization of the system regarding sustainable transport modes
In the current design of the VAT system in Germany, for example, regional public transport is favoured by 7 per cent, long-distance rail transport is subject to the standard rate of 19 per cent, while flight transport is fully exempted. Despite air ticket charges that have been introduced in Germany, France, England and the Netherlands (Greenpeace 2008; FÖS 2008) VAT exemptions for international flights are still classified as harmful to the environment (UBA 2010; Rave 2008) – a disguised transport subsidy promoting an unsustainable means of transport. The European Parliament (EP) consequently notices market distortions and an uneven playing field in the transport 'since all modes of transport are competing for the same crossborder transport services' (EP 2011, p. 5). In order to promote sustainable transport in times of growing inter-community transport, the relevant mechanisms should systematically be re-focused on urban and regional public transport for passengers and an intermodal infrastructure shifting of freight from road to rail. VAT adaptation could be one element and harmonization of tax rates should be fostered.

POTENTIAL IMPACTS AND EFFECTS

An instrument can be described as efficient, when a given environmental objective cannot be achieved at lower costs; only less ambitious environmental targets may be reached at given costs. In this sense, an instrument can be considered suitable if it can bring about a change in the desired direction (CEP 2009). Regarding the effectiveness of VAT increases and reductions, there is little doubt that they have an impact on the demand due to subsequent price changes (CE 2007). An important factor for the market effect is the intensity of competition of the goods involved: In highly competitive markets a 100 per cent pass-through of reductions to consumers is more likely than in monopolistic markets. The rate of price adjustment is also dependent on the capital intensity of production. When an expansion of production capacities is associated with high costs, a price reduction is passed on to consumers much more slowly due to longer depreciation periods (CE 2008). It is also possible that VAT increases result in price increases due to overcompensation or reductions that are not fully passed through.[5] Those effects are more pronounced with increases than decreases (asymmetric cross-price elasticity).

Ecologically differentiated VAT rates, as proposed in the previous sections, could contribute to the overcoming of barriers for resource efficient or less carbon intensive consumption decisions. The abolition of VAT reductions for products associated with strong negative externalities would lead to a reduction of the external costs to be borne by society and tax-cuts for environmentally friendly innovations and products would lead to positive externalities. Table 8.1 gives an overview on estimated demand changes and related GHG emissions reduction potentials based on previous VAT changes.[6]

A quantitative analysis of the economic effects of a resource efficiency strategy for Germany simulated modified VAT rates for long-distance passenger transport services by rail (introduction of reduced rates) and air (abolition of exemption/introduction of standard rates). The case study revealed that the price signals would induce demand shifts and thus reduce energy consumption and CO_2 emissions. As regards material consumption, the results showed interactions between a decline of air travel contributing to reductions in oil consumption and increases in the consumption of coal and gas for the electricity generation due to an increasing rail travel (Distelkamp et al. 2010).

The signalling effect of decreasing or increasing sales triggered by a tax reduction or an abolition of exemptions of a product or service is sometimes critically assessed in comparison with direct incentives (Kosonen and Nicodème 2009) but should give incentives to producers to expand resource efficiency potentials of their products and services. A dynamic design of the tax categories allowing for an exchange between higher and lower tax classes could give an additional impetus for companies to provide information on the resource intensity of their products when they are rewarded with a lower VAT rate in case of compliance. It can also lead to a sectoral benchmark serving as an opportunity to break established path dependencies and to strengthen the focus on successful first-movers. A coupling of differentiated VAT rates to a benchmarking system could be an interesting perspective.

VAT exemptions or advantages for resource-efficient products are thus used to reduce price barriers for final consumers. A VAT reduction for a commodity such as a refrigerator or a national rail ticket could result in significant price reductions and further contribute to social benefits. A certain tax rate could become an environmental selection criterion for end users. It may be argued that labels can do the job more effectively which is true. In view of the existing label overload and the high level of public attention to VAT changes in general, it can however be assumed that changes of VAT rates for specific products and services can contribute to the reduction of information asymmetries.

Finally, an increase in demand for 'green' products may lead to innovative learning curve effects. If a breakthrough from a niche market to mass production can be achieved through the reduction of the VAT rate economies of scale lead to further dynamic price and innovation effects. Compared with the administrative costs for the banning of single polluting products (for example, the light bulbs ban due to the EU ecodesign directive) tax incentives can be a smart solution that could meet more consent and allow for better adaption of the economy.

CONCLUDING REMARKS

From an economic perspective, taxes are usually second-best policies due to their inherent impreciseness (Söderholm 2011). From an environmental perspective, taxes are a step towards reflecting the full external and social costs of resource use. In general, price increases by implementation of taxes should create incentives to reduce the use of the product or service (depending on the range of the rate) or substitute it by an alternative product or service. Like all subsidies also tax preferences should ideally be established for a defined time period, and their costs and benefits should be assessed at appropriate intervals (Greene and Braathen 2014).

At present, differentiations are made within the VAT system predominantly for social but not for environmental reasons and without considering the social distribution of ecological positive and negative externalities. Aside from that, a very substantial feature of a tax is the ability to influence behaviour if one wants to modify patterns of consumption. A proposal of the European Parliament 'calls for a Green VAT strategy to be devised, centred on reduced rates for energy-efficient and environmentally friendly products and services, counterbalancing unfair competition which results from externalities not reflected in the price of a good or service' (EP 2011, p. 6). The consumption tax rates provide a good basis to make resource consumption and environmental effects visible. The possibilities for differentiation of consumption taxes should therefore be expanded to include ecological options by expanding the Annex III of the VAT Directive (EC 2006) and the harmonization efforts should focus on adjusting and correcting distorting and environmentally harmful reduced rates. This will nevertheless require clear and transparent eligibility criteria in order to minimize additional administrative efforts.

NOTES

1. Indirect taxes include the value added tax and excise taxes (energy tax, tobacco tax, electricity tax, taxes on alcoholic beverages or alcopops, and so on). Direct taxes refer to personal income and property; they include corporate taxes.
2. Food, water, pharmaceuticals, medical equipment, children's car seats, passenger transport, books, newspapers, periodicals, cultural services and amusement and sport events, TV, writers/composers, social housing, renovation and repairing of private dwellings, cleaning in private households, agricultural inputs, hotel accommodation, restaurant and catering services, sporting facilities, social services, services of undertakers and cremation, medical and dental care, domestic waste collection and street cleaning, minor repairing (bicycles, shoes, clothing), domestic care services, hairdressing.
3. European law exclusively backs the implementation of reduced VAT rates in national legal frameworks within the given framework of the Articles 98 and 106 and Annexes III and IV (EC 2006).
4. The Eco Top Ten rating system created for Germany shows up-to-date market surveys for ecological products in various product fields, such as living, mobility, textiles, food, home appliances and consumer electronics, information and communication technologies and investments (www.ecotopten.de). Other countries use such approaches too.
5. An increase of the VAT by 10 per cent for magazines in Italy, for example, led to an increase of prices by 14 per cent. The reduction of the VAT on books in Sweden by 19 per cent led to a lowering of prices by 12 per cent (CE 2007).
6. The table summarizes results from comprehensive modelling exercises of the Institute for Environmental Studies in the year 2008 which are cited here for illustrating the potential order of magnitudes.

REFERENCES

Albrecht J. (2006), 'The use of consumption taxes to re-launch green tax reforms', *International Review of Law and Economics* **26** (1), 88–103. DOI:10.1016/j. irle.2006.05.007.
Bahn-Walkowiak B., Usubiaga A. and Schepelmann P. (2012), 'EU structural and cohesion policy and sustainable development', in Kreiser L. et al. (eds), *Carbon Pricing, Growth And The Environment – Critical Issues in Environmental Taxation*, Vol. XI, Cheltenham, UK and Northampton, MA, USA: Edward Elgar Publishing, 17–32.
Bahn-Walkowiak B., Wilts H., Bleischwitz R. and Sanden J. (2010), *Differenzierte Mehrwertsteuersätze zur Förderung eines ressourceneffizienteren Konsums*, Ressourceneffizienz Paper 3.6, Project Material Efficiency and Resource Conservation (MaRess), Wuppertal Institute for Climate, Environment, Energy.
Barthel C., Irrek W., Thomas S. and Hohmeyer O. (2005), 'Energieeffiziente Kühl- und Gefriergeräte. Beschreibung eines möglichen Förderprogramms eines Energieeffizienz-Fonds', Wuppertal Institute/University Flensburg, http://wup perinst.org/uploads/tx_wupperinst/EnEff-Fonds_Anhang2_Programm8.pdf, accessed at 15 January 2015.
BIO IS (2012), *Policies to Encourage Sustainable Consumption*, Paris: Bio Intelligence Service.
Bleischwitz R. (2012), 'Towards a resource policy – unleashing productivity dynamics and balancing international distortions', *Miner Econ* **24** (2–3), 135–144, DOI: 10.1007/s13563-011-0114-5.
CE (2007), *Study on Reduced VAT Applied to Goods and Services in the Member States of the European Union*, Copenhagen: Copenhagen Economics.
CE (2008), *Reduced VAT for Environmentally Friendly Products*, Copenhagen: Copenhagen Economics/DG TAXUD.
CEP (2009), *Ermäßigte Mehrwertsteuersätze als Instrument der Umweltpolitik in der EU*, Freiburg, Centrum für Europäische Politik. http://www.foes.de/pdf/CEP-Studie%20Mehrwertsteuer.pdf, accessed 15 January 2015.
De Camillis C. and Goralczyk M. (2013), 'Towards stronger measures for sustainable consumption and production policies: Proposal of a new fiscal framework based on a life cycle approach', *International Journal of Life Cycle Assessment* 18, 263–272, DOI 10.1007/s11367-012-0460-5.
Distelkamp M., Meyer B. and Meyer M. (2010), *Quantitative und qualitative Analyse der ökonomischen Effekte einer forcierten Ressourceneffizienzstrategie*, Ressourceneffizienz Paper 5.6, Project Material Efficiency and Resource Conservation (MaRess), Wuppertal Institute for Climate, Environment, Energy.
EC (1999), *Council Directive 1999/85/EC of 22 October 1999 amending Directive 77/388/EEC as regards the possibility of applying on an experiment basis a reduced VAT rate on labour-intensive services*, OJ L 277/34.
EC (2005), *Council Directive 2005/32/EC of 6 July 2005 establishing a framework for the setting of ecodesign requirements for energy-using products and amending Council Directive 92/42/EEC and Directives 96/57/EC and 2000/55/EC of the European Parliament and of the Council*, OJ L 191/29.
EC (2006), *Council Directive 2006/112/EC of 28 November 2006 on the common system of value added tax*, OJ L 347/1.

EC (2007), *Communication from the Commission to the European Parliament and the Council on VAT rates other than standard VAT rates*, 5 July 2007, COM(2007) 380.

EC (2008), *Proposal for a Council Directive amending Directive 2006/112/EC as regards reduced rates of value added tax*, 7 July 2008, COM(2008) 428.

EC (2009a), *Council Directive 2009/125/EC of 21 October 2009 establishing a framework for the setting of ecodesign requirements for energy-related products (recast)*, OJ L 285/10.

EC (2009b), *Council Directive 2009/47/EC of 5 May 2009 amending Directive 2006/112/EC as regards reduced rates of value added tax*, OJ L 116/18.

EC (2010), *Green Paper on the future of VAT – Towards a simpler, more robust and efficient VAT system*, 1 October 2010, COM(2010) 695.

EC (2011a), *Roadmap to a Resource Efficient Europe*, COM(2011) 571, Brussels, European Commission.

EC (2011b), *Summary Report of the Outcome of the Public Consultation on the Green Paper on the Future of VAT – Towards a Simpler, More Robust and Efficient VAT System* (1 December 2010 to 31 May 2011), Brussels, European Commission.

EC (2011c), *Communication from the Commission to the European Parliament, the Council and the European Economic and Social Committee on the future of VAT – Towards a simpler, more robust and efficient VAT system tailored to the single market*, 6 December 2011, COM(2011) 851.

EC (2014), *VAT Rates Applied in the Member States of the European Union*, Brussels, European Commission.

EEA (2005), *Market-based instruments for environmental policy in Europe – EEA Technical Report No. 8/2005*, Copenhagen, European Environment Agency.

EEA (2012), *Consumption and the environment – 2012 update; the European environment – state and outlook 2010*, Copenhagen, European Environment Agency.

EEA (2013), *Environmental pressures from European consumption and production – EEA Technical Report No 2/2013*, Copenhagen, European Environment Agency.

Ekins P. and Speck S. (eds) (2011), *Environmental Tax Reform (ETR) – A Policy for Green Growth*, Oxford: Oxford University Press.

EP (2011), *Report on the future of VAT*, Plenary sitting, A7-0318/2011, Brussels, European Parliament, Committee on Economic and Monetary Affairs.

ERRT (2012), *REAP – Retailers' Environmental Action Programme* – revised 14 June 2012, Brussels, European Retail Round Table, http://ec.europa.eu/environment/industry/retail/pdf/reap_tor.pdf, accessed 15 January 2015.

Eurostat/European Commission (2013), *Taxation trends in the European Union, Data for the EU Member States, Iceland and Norway*, 2013 edition, Luxembourg: EC.

Eurostat/European Commission (2014), *Taxation trends in the European Union, Data for the EU Member States, Iceland and Norway*, 2014 edition, Luxembourg: EC.

Experian (2009), *The Opportunities and Costs of Cutting VAT – The Effects of Selected Reductions in the rate of VAT on the Labour Element of Housing Repair Maintenance and Improvement*, London, Cut the VAT campaign, www.fmb.org.uk/EasySiteWeb/GatewayLink.aspx?alId=161361, accessed 15 January 2015.

FÖS (2008), *Umweltschädliche Subventionen und Steuervergünstigungen des Bundes*, Hamburg, Greenpeace.

Greene J. and Braathen N.A. (2014), *Tax Preferences for Environmental Goals –
Use, Limitations and Preferred Practices*, OECD Environment Working Papers,
No. 71, OECD Publishing, http://dx.doi.org/10.1787/5jxwrr4hkd6l-en, accessed
8 January 2015.
Greenpeace (2008), *Umweltschädliche Subventionen und Steuervergünstigungen des
Bundes*, Hamburg.
IEEP (2012), *Study supporting the phasing out of environmentally harmful subsi-
dies* – Final Report for the European Commission, DG Environment, Brussels,
Institute for European Environmental Policy (IEEP), Institute for Environmental
Studies – Vrije Universiteit (IVM), Ecologic Institute, VITO.
IFS (2011), *A retrospective evaluation of elements of the EU VAT system* – Final
Report for the European Commission, TAXUD, London, Institute for Fiscal
Studies.
IVM (2008), *The use of differential VAT rates to promote changes in consump-
tion and innovation* – Final Report, Commissioned by European Commission,
DG Environment, Amsterdam, Vrije Universiteit, Institute for Environmental
Studies.
JRC (2008), *Environmental Improvement Potentials of Meat and Dairy Products*,
Seville, Joint Research Centre Institute for Prospective Technological Studies.
JRC (2012), *Energy Efficiency Status Report 2012*, Ispra, Joint Research Centre.
Kosonen K. (2012), 'Regressivity of environmental taxation: Myth or reality?' in
Milne J.E. and Skou-Andersen M. (eds), *Handbook of Research on Environmental
Taxation*, Cheltenham, UK, and Northampton, MA, USA: Edward Elgar
Publishing, 161–174.
Kosonen K. and Nicodème G. (2009), *The Role of Fiscal Instruments in
Environmental Policy*, Taxation Papers, Working Paper No. 19, Luxembourg.
Lohse C.W. (1999), *Die Zuordnung im Mehrwertsteuerrecht*. Bd. 13 von Schriften
zum Umsatzsteuerrecht, Berlin, Otto Schmidt.
Ochmann R., Bach S. and Beznoska M. (2012), *The Retrospective Evaluation
of Elements of the VAT System – The Case of Germany*, Research project on
behalf of the European Commission, TAXUD, Berlin, Deutsches Institut für
Wirtschaftsforschung.
OECD (2012), *Consumption Tax Trends 2012: VAT/GST and Excise Rates, Trends
and Administration Issues*, Paris: OECD, DOI: 10.1787/ctt-2012-en.
Peffekoven R. (2009), 'Mehrwertsteuererhöhung: Keine nachhaltige
Konsolidierung', *Wirtschaftsdienst*, 7, 426–427.
Rave T. (2008), 'Subsidy impact assessment and subsidy monitoring: opportunities
to advance the reform of environmentally harmful subsidies in Germany', in
Chalifour N. et al. (eds), *Critical Issues in Environmental Taxation: International
and Comparative Perspectives*, Volume V, Oxford: Oxford University Press,
621–648.
Söderholm, P. (2011), 'Taxing virgin natural resources: Lessons from aggre-
gates taxation in Europe', *Resources, Conservation and Recycling*, 55, 911–922,
DOI:10.1016/j.resconrec.2011.05.011.
Sterner T. and Coria J. (2011), *Policy Instruments for Environmental and Natural
Resource Management*, 2nd edn, New York, London: RFF Press.
UBA (2010), *Umweltschädliche Subventionen in Deutschland*, Dessau, Federal
Environment Agency.
UNEP (2010), *Assessing the Environmental Impacts of Consumption and
Production – Priority Products and Materials*, A Report of the Working Group on

the Environmental Impacts of Products and Materials to the International Panel for Sustainable Resource Management, Nairobi, United Nations Environment Programme (UNEP).

Westhoek H.J. et al. (2011), 'The protein puzzle: The consumption and production of meat, dairy and fish in the European Union', *European Journal of Food Research and Review*, **1** (3), 123–144.

ZEW (2004), *Allokative und distributive Effekte einer Abschaffung des ermäßigten Umsatzsteuersatzes*; Commissioned by Federal Ministry of Finances, Mannheim, Centre for European Economic Research.

9. Long-term climate mitigation and energy use in Austria: the impacts of carbon and energy prices

Kurt Kratena, Ina Meyer and Mark Wolfgang Sommer

INTRODUCTION

The chapter presents energy use scenarios for the Austrian economy up to 2030. These scenarios represent a national approach to forecast energy demand which is embedded in the integrated European strategy to a climate and energy policy that aims to combat climate change, increase the EU's energy security and strengthen its competitiveness. The scenarios serve as input data for calculating greenhouse gas (GHG) emissions, and as reporting requirements under the Monitoring Mechanism 2013 of the United Nations Framework Convention on Climate Change (UNFCCC). Finally, the energy scenarios serve as a source of information with respect to the European 20-20-20 targets which are also headline targets in the Europe 2020 strategy for smart, sustainable and inclusive growth (European Commission, 2010), namely:

a) Reducing GHG emissions by 20 per cent (to 1990 levels)
b) Generating 20 per cent of energy use from renewable energy resources
c) Improving energy efficiency by 20 per cent.

Within the EU climate and energy package (targets a and b), the Effort Sharing Decision establishes binding annual GHG emissions targets for Member States for the period 2013–2020 from sectors not included in the EU Emissions Trading System (EU ETS) such as transport (except aviation), buildings, agriculture and waste. Emission targets within the Effort Sharing Decision have been allocated at the national level of Member States according to their national per capita GDP levels. For Austria, GHG emissions should be reduced by 16 per cent as compared with the 2005 emission level. By 2020, the national targets will collectively deliver a reduction of around 10 per cent in total EU emissions covered under the Effort Sharing Decision. Together with a 21 per cent cut in European GHG emissions covered by the EU ETS, the main instrument for cutting industrial GHG emissions, this will accomplish the overall emission reduction goal of a 20 per cent cut in GHG emissions from 1990 levels by 2020. Based on the actual data, the Environment Agency Austria (Anderl et al., 2012) calculated the target for Austria's GHG emissions in 2020 to be 47.7 $MtCO_2e$ for the non-ETS sectors. In October 2014 the European Council agreed on the 2030 climate and energy policy framework for the European Union and endorsed a binding EU target of reducing at least 40 per cent of domestic GHG emissions by 2030 compared with 1990 levels. The target reflects the EU's goal of reducing GHG emissions by 80–95 per cent below 1990 levels by 2050 as part of the mitigation efforts needed from industrialized countries.

The Austrian target regarding the share of renewable energy sources in gross final energy consumption in 2020 is 34 per cent (European Commission, 2009). In order to support the renewable energy objective, each Member State is requested to submit a national renewable energy action plan (NREAP) detailing how they will reach their individual targets (Karner et al., 2010). Since Austria's share of renewable energy sources was at 31 per cent in 2011 (Statistik Austria, 2012a) the target must be viewed as somewhat lacking in ambition.

The aim of the Energy Efficiency Directive (2012/27/EG; target c) is to cut energy consumption by 20 per cent by the year 2020. This corresponds to 368 Mtoe less energy use in 2020 to be achieved by the EU as a whole with regard to the baseline development. Energy efficiency is one of the cornerstones of the Europe 2020 flagship initiative for a resource-efficient Europe (European Commission, 2010). Energy efficiency is considered the most cost-effective way to increase the security of supply and, at the same time, to reduce the GHG emissions responsible for climate change. The desired decrease in energy consumption should also help to achieve the target for the share of energy from renewable sources. Finally, producing more using less energy input should improve the competitiveness of industries and thus allow energy efficient technologies to sustain their lead in the global markets. Member States have committed to achieving the 2020 targets for energy efficiency in terms of primary energy savings or absolute energy use in 2020. According to its Energy Strategy, Austria has committed to an indicative energy use reduction target of 7.16 Mtoe of primary energy consumption or 300 PJ by 2020 with regard to its baseline development (or 200 PJ with respect to final energy consumption). This corresponds to freezing its primary energy consumption at the 2005 level (BMLFUW/BMWFJ, 2010).

The chapter is structured as follows: the first section deals with scenario assumptions, the next section delineates the methodology, and the following section sketches the data input. Next, scenario results are presented, followed by concluding remarks.

SCENARIO DESCRIPTION

Given this policy background, the chapter presents the WAM+ energy scenario, which relates to the WAM (with additional measures) scenario. The WAM scenario describes the effects of climate and energy policy measures in Austria on energy demand until 2030. The main climate policy modelled in the WAM scenario deals with energy efficiency according to the objectives of the energy efficiency directive (2012/27/EU) and the discussions related to an Austrian energy efficiency act, targeting a reduction in energy use of 8.14 PJ or a 1.5 per cent p.a. increase in energy efficiency. A further major policy implemented in the WAM scenario is an increase in the mineral oil tax of 6 cents per litre of diesel and gasoline in 2015 and 2019. In addition, the WAM+ scenario evaluates the effects of a more stringent climate mitigation policy after 2020, thus placing the focus on the long-term climate and energy policy perspective for Austria. The climate mitigation measures analyzed are:

- higher CO_2 certificate prices in ETS sectors during the 2020–2030 period
- introduction of a CO_2 tax on the non-ETS sectors in the same order of magnitude as the ETS scheme, with the exception of transport
- an additional increase in the mineral oil tax during the 2020–2030 period.

The WAM+ scenario thus assesses the impact on energy use and energy efficiency resulting from significantly higher carbon and fossil fuel prices, which are assumed to become significant after 2020. Table 9.1 shows the assumptions in an overview of all scenarios. In WAM+, the CO_2 certificate real price increases steeply to 70 €$_{2010}$/t CO_2 in the 2020–2030 period, beginning with 20 €$_{2010}$/t CO_2 in 2020. The imposition of the CO_2 tax on the non-ETS sectors (comprising the non-ETS parts of industrial and energy-producing sectors and the household and service sectors, but omitting the transport sector), follows the same CO_2 pricing pattern as the ETS scheme, rising to 70 €$_{2010}$/t CO_2 in 2030. Furthermore, a significant rise in the mineral oil tax is assumed for diesel and gasoline fuels, while the spread between diesel and gasoline largely levels out. In nominal terms, the fuel price increase lies at 56 per cent/48 per cent for diesel/gasoline during the

Table 9.1   Overview of scenarios

Scenario	WEM	WAM	WAM+
	Economic Growth		
Ø GDP – Growth p.a. 2012–2030	1,5%	~1.5 %	1.49%
	Carbon and Energy Prices		
Price of CO_2-Certificates ETS Sectors	20 €/t CO_2 in 2020 30 €/t CO_2 in 2030	= WEM	20 €/t CO_2 in 2020 70 €/t CO_2 in 2030
CO_2 Tax non-ETS Sectors	n.a.	n.a.	20 €/t CO_2 in 2020 70 €/t CO_2 in 2030
Mineral Oil Tax incl. VAT, nominal	n.a.	Diesel/Gasoline +6 ct in Jan 2015 +6 ct in Jan 2019	2020–2030 Diesel +27% Gasoline +25%
	Methodological Settings		
Energy efficiency coefficients of the ETS sectors	estimated econometrically	increased	= WAM
WAM+ Specific Implementations			Disaggregation of 4 energy intensive sectors
	Demographic Development		
Ø Population – Growth p.a. 2012–2030	0.35%	= WEM	= WEM
Ø Households – Growth p.a. 2012–2030	0.52%	= WEM	= WEM

Source: Own representation.

2015–2030 period, whereas fuel prices in real terms remain constant. The benchmark data for the increase in the mineral oil tax (including value added tax) amounts to 11 cents (2020) and 17 cents (2030) for diesel, and 6 cents (2020) and 9 cents (2030) for gasoline. This is equivalent to a nominal price of about 41.5 €/t CO_2 and 64.2 €/t CO_2 for diesel and 25.9 €/t CO_2 to 38.8 €/t CO_2 for gasoline.[1]

In order to reflect the impacts of assumed CO_2 and energy price increases on the final energy demand of the production sector, the energy-intensive production sectors 'iron and steel/non-ferrous metals', 'chemical and petrochemical', 'non-metallic minerals', 'pulp, paper and print' were disaggregated into energy-intensive and non-energy-intensive production sub-sectors beginning in 2012 (WAM+). The price elasticity of energy demand depends on the share of energy as a production factor; a higher share results in a larger demand reaction to energy price increases. Disaggregating these sectors leads to a more adequate representation of energy demand reaction of the respective energy-intensive production sectors. Fossil fuel price increases act as a trigger for interfuel substitution and are responsible for repercussions on the energy efficiency of the production processes. The total energy demand of the 4 energy-intensive production sectors absorbs about 200 PJ of energy in 2010, amounting to about 60 per cent of energy use in all production sectors.

The baseline scenario is represented by the WEM (with existing measures) scenario reflecting existing measures and policies on climate mitigation and energy use enacted before 8 March 2012 (Kratena et al., 2013; UBA, 2013).

METHODOLOGY

The methodological approach to modelling energy scenarios takes a top-down macroeconomic perspective based on the dynamic econometric Input–Output model DEIO in order to generate national economic and energy data, in other words, GDP and the final energy demand of households and industries. This top-down economic model is interlinked with bottom-up models that derive sectoral energy demands for transport and buildings (space and water heating, cooling) and electricity demand and electricity and district heat generation from a micro-data perspective (Müller and Kranzl, 2013; Hausberger and Schwingshackl, 2013; Baumann and Lang, 2013). The data of the bottom-up models are used as exogenous variables with regard to the DEIO model while macroeconomic data derived from the top-down economic perspective such as the GDP is employed as input data in the bottom-up models. The different energy-economy models use a consistent set of economic, technological, demographic and climate data that built a common thread and a solid link between the top-down and bottom-up spheres.

The model approach used for the projection of the energy scenarios can best be described as a dynamic (macro-)econometric input–output (DEIO) model, as elaborated in Kratena and Streicher (2009). The first step in developing this model for Austria is described in Kratena and Wüger (2010) and has been used for the energy scenarios 2030, and published by WIFO in 2011 (Kratena and Meyer, 2011). Further developments to this model type led to a first operational version being evolved for the EU 27, named FIDELIO (Full Interregional Dynamic Econometric Long-term Input–Output model) and described in Kratena et al. (2012).

In contrast to the FIDELIO the emphasis here is given to all relevant aspects of energy demand and emission generation. Therefore several unique features were implemented such as the link to physical energy demand of industries, price and trend depending interfuel substitution functions as well as the demand for durable goods and energy demand of private households.

Production

The model structure and core data is based on Supply and Use Tables (SUT) 1995–2005 of Austria (59 industries and commodities in the NACE Rev 1 classification). The production activities are determined by the SUT-structure itself and by the structure and magnitude of total final demand. By using SUT – instead of a mere input–output structure – it was possible to integrate a wider range of data and furthermore the implementation of an iterative solution algorithm instead of a Leontief inverse.

$$(1) \quad SEQ_{jt} = SEQ_{jt-1} + \rho_j + \gamma_j * ln(PE_{jt})$$

$$(2) \quad E_j = SEQ_j * Q_j$$

$$(3) \quad Energ\_Demand_j = real\_E_j * Z_j$$

The determination of the energy demand of the domestic production is summarized in functions (1) to (3). SEQ – the nominal share of energy goods in the industry's production – is calculated for each economic sector (j) and depends on the sector's average energy price (PE) as well as estimated parameters (taken from FIDELIO cf. Kratena and Wüger, 2012) that represent the sectors price elasticity (γ) and technological improvement over time (ρ).

In the next step (2) the nominal energy demand (E) is calculated and then finally (3), a set of coefficients 'Z' is applied which links the real value of energy goods demand in economic terms (in other words, deflated nominal values) to physical energy unit demand. These 'Z' coefficients are based on Austria's historic energy balance and economic activities and represent the energy inputs in energy per unit of real input.

Final Demand

The modelling of final demand is split into private consumption and the rest of final demand categories. The other final demand categories are treated as exogenous and have therefore been extrapolated on the basis of historic developments and the short term forecasts of WIFO.

Private consumption is modelled according to the buffer stock model of consumption, differentiating between durable and non-durable goods where the demand of non-durable goods have been extrapolated based on historic trends.

For durable stocks (electricity consuming equipment, heating appliances and vehicles) a mix of calibrated functions – considering interest rates, prices, population, income and wealth, and extrapolations, based on these variables (especially population) – have been applied.

Some stocks use energy inputs to provide the services demanded (for example, gasoline for passenger car use). Energy efficiency has an impact on the cost of using this service. This differentiation allows a 'service price' to be calculated which drives the demand for the service consumption and thereby for energy and goods. Consequently service prices decrease if energy efficiency increases, thereby causing the 'rebound effect' on energy demand.

$$(4) \quad log\left(\tfrac{Service}{Capital\ Stock}\right) = \alpha_0 + \gamma * log(P_s) + \theta_1 Param_1 + \theta_2 Param_2$$

$$(5) \quad where\ P_S = \tfrac{PE_C}{\eta}$$

For different durable stocks we model service demand separately and not as part of non-durable consumption. The general formula of the demand estimation can be found in (4) where the service per unit of stock (in other words, the utilization of the stock on an annual basis) is linked to the service price and one or two stock specific parameters. The service price is calculated by the division of a capital stock specific aggregated energy price (PE_C) and efficiency.

The sum of energy demand from domestic production and private household results in Austria's final energy demand. Due to the interfuel substitution functions and fuel specific buffer stock functions it is possible to derive energy demand in terms of fuel type (electricity, oil products, renewable sources, natural gas, gasoline, diesel and coal products).

DATA

Future trends in energy demand are determined by a number of interplaying factors. GDP as a measure of economic growth is considered one of the main drivers of energy demand and GHG emissions. Economic growth in turn is influenced inter alia by demographic developments, technological change, and energy prices. These data are exogenous to the present model of Austria's economic growth and energy demand and to interlinked bottom-up models.

Energy Prices

The crude oil price is considered a proxy for international energy price developments and is one of the main determinants of energy demand. Demand for energy is derived from a specific demand for energy services, for example, kilometres travelled by passenger cars or in industry where energy demand is determined by the functional relationships with production. In real world conditions the crude oil price is influenced by a multitude of factors, in other words, supply and demand, factors relating to the structure of the crude oil market (OPEC), speculative behaviour of financial market participants as well as geopolitical events such as for example the civil unrest in north Africa and the Middle East (Breitenfellner et al., 2009; IEA, 2012). The recent past has shown significant fluctuations in the crude oil price, for example as a corollary of the economic and financial crisis 2008–2009. The present study employs crude oil price trajectories based on the International Energy Agency World Energy Outlook 2011 (IEA, 2011). These price trajectories do not represent any forecasts in the sense of a trend extrapolation or econometric estimations. They are a reflection of prices needed to encourage sufficient investment in supply to meet projected demand of oil over the observation period. That is, they approximately represent the marginal costs of oil production at the expected demand. The real crude oil price is assumed to rise steadily throughout all three scenarios. It rises from US$90 in 2012 to US$118 in 2020 and US$135 in 2030. Thus oil prices show an average annual growth of 7.2 per cent from 2010 to 2014 and of 1.7 per cent from 2014 to 2030.

Natural gas prices follow the assumptions on gas price development of the European import price (IEA, 2011). Thereafter, real gas prices rise to 11 US$/MBtu in 2020 and 12.5 US$/MBtu in 2030, showing an average annual growth of 6 per cent between 2010 and 2014 and of 1.8 per cent p.a. between 2014 and 2030 (2.6 per cent p.a. 2010–2030). Natural gas prices are thus following the growth pattern of the crude oil price trajectory.

Coal prices have fallen relative to both oil and gas prices in the decade prior to 2010. This is partly due to different market conditions and to growing environmental constraints on coal use in OECD countries but also due to stable production costs. However coal prices have recently rebounded because demand from emerging economies such as China is soaring (IEA, 2011). Coal prices are assumed to rise gradually throughout the projection period. The coal price assumptions are like the oil and natural gas price trajectories taken from the IEA (2011) and grow much more slowly than oil and natural gas, at an average annual growth rate of 1.1 per cent in 2010–2014 and 0.7 per cent in 2014–2030.

End-user price trajectories for Austrian households and industries are calculated on the basis of the growth rates of fossil fuels prices and are represented in detail in Kratena et al. (2013).

Demographic and Climate Trends

Future energy demand is also determined by demographic factors such as population growth or the number and structure of households. In particular, demand for heating and cooling depends inter alia on the structure and growth of households. The population in Austria is assumed to grow on average by 0.35 per cent per year from 8.45 million inhabitants in 2012 to 9 million in 2030 (Statistik Austria, 2012b). The historic trend from 1995 to 2012 exhibits a slightly higher average annual growth rate of 0.37 per cent (Statistik Austria, 2012b). The number of households is projected to increase at a rate of 0.52 per cent p.a. from 3.67 million to 4.03 million households and hence it shows a higher growth rate than that of the population (Statistik Austria, 2012c). This indicates a continuous trend towards a growing number of single-households. Empirical data on household growth lies at 0.83 per cent from 1995 to 2012 (Statistik Austria, 2012b).

Heating degree days are employed in the model analysis as an exogenous variable that influences heating or cooling demand and thereby energy use. Heating degree days are assumed to continuously decrease throughout the projection period. This trend basically reflects the growing impacts of climate change. The trend has been calculated as an average between the Holt–Winters trend extrapolation and the moving average extrapolation of heating degree days in the past (Kratena et al., 2013).

Energy Efficiency

Energy efficiency indices of the energy consuming capital stocks of households constitute another exogenous input data and are the output of detailed bottom-up studies. The different energy efficiency indices of durable goods such as the passenger car fleet, the heating system and building stock or the electrical household appliances determine the specific energy service price and thereby the energy service demand of households. The relevant literature indicates that if energy efficiency increases, the per unit price of energy services decreases (c.p.) thereby causing a rebound in energy demand. The increased energy consumption partially offsets the impacts of efficiency gains (Greening et al., 2000; van den Bergh, 2011;

Sorrell, 2009). The present model approach does take the rebound effect into account.

Energy efficiency of industries is calculated using historical trends adopted from econometric estimations of factor demand in European industries (Kratena and Wüger, 2012). In addition, experts from the Environment Agency Austria gave their estimates on the potential for further growth in energy efficiency in the manufacturing industries. These estimates laid the groundwork for quantitative suggestions on future efficiency improvements in the WAM scenario. Three clusters of manufacturing sectors were grouped according to the industry sectors mostly covered by the EU ETS (1), partly covered by the EU ETS (2) and not covered by the EU ETS (3). Assumptions on efficiency improvements in the three industry clusters suggest a growth in efficiency in manufacturing of about 7,374 TJ (cluster 1), 2,578 TJ (cluster 2) and 4,174 TJ (cluster 3) until 2020 compared with WEM. These efficiency gains are derived on the basis of the requirements of the Energy Efficiency Directive that involves a rate of 1.5 per cent average annual efficiency improvements for the Austrian economy. Given early action, this figure reduces to about 1.125 per cent p.a. efficiency gains.

Due to the efficiency improvements and thus a lower demand for relevant energy products in the industry, real output production from energy sectors decreases. These sectors are 'mining', 'coke and refined petroleum' as well as 'electricity', 'gas', 'steam and hot water supply' where production deviates from the WEM level by −1.5 per cent, −0.7 per cent and −1.6 per cent in 2020.

SCENARIO RESULTS

In the WAM+ scenario, total final energy demand amounts to 1,083 PJ in 2020 and 1,152 PJ in 2030 (Table 9.2). The additional carbon and energy pricing (policy measures) in the second decade of the observation period thus show a potential for energy savings in terms of total final energy demand of 44 PJ in 2020 and 100 PJ in 2030 (compared with WEM). In WAM+, average annual growth of total final energy demand lies at 0.4 per cent between 2012 and 2030 only compared with 0.7 per cent in WAM and 0.8 per cent in WEM. Furthermore, in terms of total growth, WAM+ shows a much lower rate, in other words, total final energy demand rises by 0.95 per cent in the first decade (2012–2020) and 6.4 per cent in the second decade (2020–2030), and increasing by 7.41 per cent in total. Growth rates of total final energy demand in WAM lie significantly above these rates.

Economic performance measured as GDP or value added is considered

Table 9.2   Total final energy demand, 2020, 2030

	WEM	in PJ WAM	WAM+
2020	1,127	1,111	1,083
2030	1,251	1,210	1,152
Ø % Δ p.a. 2012–2030	0.83	0.66	0.40
% Δ 2012–2020	4.50	3.27	0.95
% Δ 2020–2030	11.06	8.92	6.40
% Δ 2012–2030	16.06	12.48	7.41

Source: Own calculation.

to strongly correlate with energy demand and GHG emissions. However, despite substantially reduced energy use, the average annual growth in GDP lies at 1.49 per cent p.a. in the WAM+ scenario, which is similar to the GDP growth in WAM and WEM scenarios (Table 9.1).

Strong additional price incentives in WAM+ are not only responsible for reduced energy demand, but also for an increase in the energy efficiency of the energy-consuming capital stock and production processes. The economy's energy efficiency (in other words, energy use/real GDP) is thus a factor for decoupling economic growth from energy use. Growth in energy efficiency per output production is significantly higher in WAM+ than in WAM, mainly due to carbon and energy price incentives. In the model-based simulation of WAM+, energy efficiency improvements have c.p. positive impacts on GDP. But these positive impacts are compensated by higher carbon and energy prices that have a negative impact on GDP caused by a decline in income due to higher expenses for energy goods and services. In the sum, the effects of the assumed higher carbon and energy prices on Austria's GDP growth are insignificant (Table 9.1).

Of the four energy-intensive production sectors, the 'iron and steel/non-ferrous metals' and the 'chemical and petrochemical' sectors show average annual growth in both output and energy demand, although energy demand rises at a lower rate (relative decoupling). In contrast, energy demand in the energy-intensive sectors 'non-metallic minerals' and 'pulp, paper and print' remains constant, while output is on the rise. Absolute decoupling (negative annual average energy demand and positive output) prevails in the 'mining and carrying', 'food, tobacco and beverages', 'wood and wood products', 'textiles and leather', 'construction' and 'commercial and public services' sectors. In the sum of all production sectors, energy use and output growth are positive, but average annual energy demand rises at a much lower rate (relative decoupling).

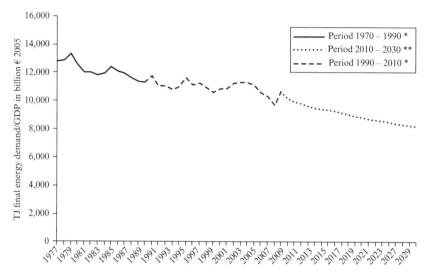

Source: Own calculations, Statistik Austria (2012a).

Figure 9.1   Energy intensity of Austria's economy, 1977–2030

The development of Austria's energy intensity per unit of GDP is depicted
as a time series from 1977 until 2030 in Figure 9.1. Energy intensity shows
a continuous decline over the entire observation period. However, growth
rates in average annual energy efficiency[2] vary across time. While energy
efficiency grew at 0.9 per cent p.a. between 1970 and 1990, the 1990 to
2010 period showed a much smaller improvement in energy efficiency of
only 0.3 per cent p.a. In contrast, WAM+ scenario simulations show that
significant carbon and energy pricing can trigger a higher growth in energy
efficiency of 1.3 per cent p.a. between 2010 and 2030. The scenario-based
calculation comes close to the objective of the 1.5 per cent p.a. increase
in energy efficiency stipulated by the EU directive on energy efficiency;
however, these are not comparable, because the energy efficiency directive
does not, for instance, address the transport sector.

CONCLUSIONS

The model analysis demonstrates no stabilization of final energy demand
in Austria given scenario assumptions and model settings. Given an
average annual GDP growth of 1.5 per cent and an increase in energy efficiency of 1.3 per cent on average, final energy demand declines in relative

terms only. From this analysis one can derive the policy conclusion that carbon and energy prices need to be increased above the levels of this study in order to achieve a higher technological and behavioural progress in energy efficiency.

The WAM+ scenario nevertheless shows a stabilization of the final energy demand at below 1.100 PJ in 2020; reaching the target of the Austrian energy strategy in contrast to the WAM scenario which lies slightly above 1.100 PJ. Higher fuel taxes and additional CO_2 taxes on the non-ETS sectors appear to be adequate instruments to stabilize energy demand.

ACKNOWLEDGEMENTS

This research was supported by the Austrian Climate and Energy Fund. We thank Ilse Schindler and Thomas Krutzler as well as other colleagues from the project consortium for helpful insight and expertise that greatly assisted the research. Technical research assistance from Katharina Köberl is kindly acknowledged.

NOTES

1. Model assumptions on energy and carbon price policies were jointly determined with stakeholders from governmental bodies and research institutions representing Austrian energy expertise.
2. Energy efficiency is reciprocal to energy intensity.

REFERENCES

Anderl, M., Bednar, W., Fischer, D., Gössl, M., Heller, Ch., Jobstmann, H., Ibesich, N., Köther, T., Kuschel, V., Lampert, Ch., Neubauer, Ch., Pazdernik, K., Perl D., Poupa, St., Purzner, M., Riegler, E., Schenk, C., Schieder, W., Schneider, J., Seuss, K., Sporer, M., Schodl, B., Stoiber, H., Storch, A., Weiss, P., Wiesenberger, H., Winter, R., Zechmeister, A. and Zethner, G. (2012), 'Klimaschutzbericht 2012', Reports Bd. REP-0391, Umweltbundesamt, Wien.
Baumann, M. and Lang, B. (2013), 'Entwicklung energiewirtschaftlicher Inputdaten und Szenarien für das Klimaschutzgesetz und zur Erfüllung der österreichischen Berichtspflichten des EU Monitoring Mechanismus 2013', Austrian Energy Agency, AEA, Wien.
Breitenfellner, A., Crespo Cuaresma, J. and Keppel, C. (2009), 'Determinants of Crude Oil Prices: Supply, Demand, Cartel or Speculation?', *Monetary Policy and The Economy* **Q4/09**, *Quarterly Review of Economic Policy*, Österreichische Nationalbank, Wien.
Bundesministerium für Land- und Forstwirtschaft, Umwelt und Wasserwirtschaft

(BMLFUW) und Bundesministerium für Wirtschaft, Familie und Jugend (BMWFJ) (2010), *Energiestrategie Österreich, Maßnahmenvorschläge*, Wien.

European Commission (EC) (2009), *Directive 2009/28/EC of the European Parliament and of the Council of 23 April 2009 on the promotion of the use of energy from renewable sources and amending and subsequently repealing Directives 2001/77/EC and 2003/30/EC*, Brussels.

European Commission (2010), *EUROPE 2020, A strategy for smart, sustainable and inclusive growth*, COM(2010) 2020 final, Brussels.

Greening, L.A., Greene, D.L. and Difiglio, C. (2000), 'Energy efficiency and consumption – the rebound effect – a survey', *Energy Policy*, **28**, 389–401.

Hausberger, S. and Schwingshackl, M. (2013), 'Monitoring Mechanism 2013 – Verkehr', Institut für Verbrennungskraftmaschinen und Thermodynamik, IVT, TU-Graz, Graz.

IEA (2011), 'World Energy Outlook 2011', International Energy Agency, Paris.

IEA (2012), 'Medium-Term Oil Market Report 2012, Market Trends and Projections to 2017', International Energy Agency, Paris.

Karner, A., Koller, S.-Ch., Kettner, C., Kletzan-Slamanig, D., Köppl, A., Leopold, A., Lang, R., Nakicenovic, N., Reinsberger, K., Resch, G., Schleicher, St., Schnitzer, H. and Steininger, K. (2010), 'Nationaler Aktionsplan 2010 für erneuerbare Energien für Österreich', accessed 30 June 2010; http://www.igwindkraft.at/redsystem/mmedia/2011.02.02/1296653537.pdf.

Kratena, K. and Meyer, I. (2011), 'Energy Scenarios 2030, A Basis for the Projection of Austrian Greenhouse Gas Emissions', Vienna.

Kratena, K. and Streicher, G. (2009), 'Macroeconomic input–output modeling: Structures', Working Papers in Input–Output Economics (ed. By the International Input–Output Association), WPIOX 09-009 (available at: http://www.iioa.org/workingper cent20papers/WPs/WPIOX09-009.pdf).

Kratena, K. and Wüger, M. (2010), 'An intertemporal optimization model of households in an E3 (Economy/Energy/Environment) framework', WIFO Working Papers, 382/2010.

Kratena, K., Meyer, I. and Sommer, M.W. (2013), 'Energy scenarios 2030, model projections of energy demand as a basis to quantify Austria's greenhouse gas emissions', *WIFO Monographs*.

Kratena, K., Streicher, G., Neuwahl, F., Mongelli, I., Rueda-Cantuche, J.M., Genty, A., Arto, I. and Andreoni, V. (2012), 'FIDELIO: A new econometric input–output model for the European Union' (available at: http://www.iioa.org/Conference/20th-downableper cent20paper.htm).

Müller, A. and Kranzl, L. (2013), 'Energieszenarien bis 2030: Wärmebedarf der Kleinverbraucher', Energy Economics Group, EEG, TU-Wien, Wien.

Sorrell, S. (2009), 'Empirical estimates of the direct rebound effect: A review', *Energy Policy*, **37**, 1356–1371.

Statistik Austria (2012a), Energiebilanzen, Wien.

Statistik Austria (2012b), Bevölkerungsprognose, Wien.

Statistik Austria (2012c), Haushaltsprognose, Wien.

UBA (2013), 'Energiewirtschaftliche Inputdaten und Szenarien, Grundlage für den Monitoring Mechanism 2013 und das Klimaschutzgesetz, Syntheseberich 2013', Umweltbundesamt, Wien.

van den Bergh, J.C.J.M. (2011), 'Energy conservation more effective with rebound policy', *Environmental Resource Economics*, **48**(1), 43–58.

10. Urban road pricing: the experience of Milan

Edoardo Croci and Aldo Ravazzi Douvan

THE RATIO OF URBAN ROAD CHARGING

Negative externalities generated by mobility have been studied by economists since the nineteenth century (Newbery, 1988, 1990). Main categories of externalities concern environmental impacts, accidents and congestion.

Environmental impacts refer to local air quality degradation due to traffic emissions (causing health consequences, life expectancy reduction, real estate values reduction and damages to cultural heritage), noise (causing health consequences, stress, real estate values reduction), contribution to global climate change through CO_2 emissions.

Accidents involve material damages to vehicles, injuries and deaths to people.

Congestion is responsible for time loss, economic productivity decrease, extra fuel consumption and frustration.

Externalities can vary with respect to three main aspects: place where they are generated, time, type of vehicle (CE Delft, 2011).

Mobility in dense, highly populated and attractive areas, like city centres or main commuting roads, generates higher levels of congestion and other externalities than in scarcely populated and isolated areas.

Mobility in peak hours generates higher levels of congestion and other externalities than in daytime off-peak and night hours.

Private motorized traffic generates higher per capita emissions than public transportation and non-motorized modes. Trucks give a higher contribution to congestion than cars and motorbikes.

Road users impose externalities (of variable value) to other road users and bear externalities (of variable value) from other road users. But road users also impose unilateral externalities to residents. Recent studies assess the relevance of health consequences on people resident in proximity of congested areas and roads (Invernizzi, 2011).

Estimates of externalities generated by mobility in urban areas vary depending on the specific factors described. An average estimation for European cities amounts to 55.4 €/year per person (CE Delft, 2008).

The adverse impact of traffic resulting in air pollution, noise, greenhouse gas emissions, delays and traffic accidents causes in European cities an economic damage estimated at 100 billion euros each year, corresponding to about 1 per cent of the EU's GDP (European Commission, 2007; Erdmenger-Frey, 2010).

Externalities can be treated in various ways. Economic instruments have proven particularly effective for this purpose. In the case of urban mobility, park pricing has been widely introduced; road pricing schemes only in a limited number of cases, but more and more cities are considering whether to adopt it. The European Commission (2011, 2013) is pushing in this direction.

Actual road pricing schemes charging private vehicles have been introduced by municipal authorities mainly in an attempt to price the externalities caused by traffic.

These externalities, created by the fact that road users tend to disregard the impact they cause on others, lead to a gap between private costs, as faced by the decision-maker, and social costs, as incurred by society at large; they prevent the market from reaching an efficient outcome. The introduction of a pricing scheme reduces these distortions leading to higher efficiency: journeys would occur only when benefits from driving outweigh the sum of costs, including all priced externalities (Newbery, 1988, 1990).

Charges are not set at the efficient level that equals the marginal social damage, providing a full internalization of externalities, following Pigouvian criteria (Pigou, 1920), mainly because of political and social reluctance in raising it up to the appropriate level. Moreover the amount of charges is the same for all social groups while a Pigouvian approach would require differentiated charges depending on the damage caused.

Unfortunately in a world of imperfect information such degree of differentiation is unachievable, and introducing a flat tax or a differentiated but not personalized tax, would never lead to the efficient market solution, leading to second-best solutions.

In this sense road charges are not a panacea: as the economic theory of 'second best' suggests, they may cause distortions, as well as unwanted redistributive effects.

A relevant topic is the destination of revenues from charges. Another is the need for dynamic variations in order to maintain the charge impacts: the effects can attenuate over time, either because drivers 'get used to charges' ('acquaintance effect'), or because the freed-up road space is filled up by new groups of drivers, returning to the same congestion levels as before the charges ('rebound effect').

THE EXPERIENCE OF MILAN[1]

Scheme Description

Milan is the capital of Lombardy, one of the wealthiest European regions. Population reaches 1.3 million, the Metropolitan area 3 million, the wider industrial urbanized area, extending beyond Lombardy, 10 million.

Traffic emissions are mainly responsible for poor air quality in Milan and Lombardy, reinforced by geo-climatic conditions adverse to particulate dispersion.

In January 2008, Milan introduced a cordon pricing scheme called 'Ecopass', with a 'pollution charge' to be paid by most polluting vehicles to access the city centre.

Ecopass was a daily charge, operating 7.30am to 7.30pm Monday to Friday, proportional to vehicles' PM10 tail emissions. The system started as a one year trial and was extended year by year.

In January 2012, Ecopass was replaced by a congestion charge scheme, called 'Area C', characterized by a flat charge.

The cordon toll area, common to both Ecopass and Area C, is 8 km^2 covering 4.5 per cent of Milan historic urban district and 6 per cent of urban population (90,000 people). The area attracts daily about 500,000 people.

The 43 toll entrance gates are monitored by an electronic system of cameras, reading the license plates of vehicles accessing the area.

The key assumption to design the Ecopass system was that the responsibility for emission externalities varies among vehicle categories. Charges are described in Table 10.1.

Class 1 and 2 vehicles were exempt from the charge, class 3 vehicles charge was €2, class 4 charge was €5 and class 5 (in large majority commercial vehicles) charge was €10.

Overall potentially charged vehicles amounted to 50 per cent of total circulating vehicles (apart from exempt ones), but a temporary exemption was also set for diesel Euro 4 cars without particulate filter (covering about 10 per cent of circulating vehicles), then extended over time. So actual chargeable vehicles in the base year, before implementing the charge, were 41.8 per cent. Charged vehicles in the first month of implementation amounted to 25.3 per cent of vehicles entering the area and progressively dropped to about 10 per cent in 2011.

The original idea was that the rules could be made stricter dynamically, for example, charging class 2. This never happened because of opposition by political parties.

The system allowed for a few exemptions, mainly public transportation vehicles, taxis, vehicles transporting disabled, and motorcycles.

Table 10.1   Milan Ecopass system: class vehicle category and charges

Class	Category of vehicle	Daily charge (€)	PM 10 Emission factors
Class 1	Low emission vehicles (LPG, methane, hybrid, electric)	free	
Class 2	Petrol Euro 3+	free	≤ 10 mg/km
	Diesel Euro 3+ with particulate filter installed before sale		
	Diesel Euro 5 with particulate filter installed after sale		
Class 3	Petrol Euro 2 and Euro 1	€ 2	≤ 10 mg/km
Class 4	Petrol Euro 0	€ 5	> 10 mg/km
	Diesel cars Euro 1, 2, 3 (and 4 without particulate filter)		≤ 100 mg/km 5
	Diesel commercial vehicles Euro 4 without particulate filter		
	Diesel commercial vehicles Euro 3		
Class 5	Diesel cars Euro 0	€ 10	> 100 mg/km 10
	Diesel commercial vehicles Euro 0, 1, 2		

Residents in the area had the option to buy yearly discounted permits. Other multiple discounted tickets could be bought, but proved scarcely popular.

In the first year the system proved very efficient in reducing congestion and emissions, thanks to both traffic reduction and substitution of older polluting vehicles with new cleaner ones. Then the effect on congestion and emissions progressively decreased because of car substitution.

As the local government was not willing to update the system, a citizens committee led by the first proponents of the charge, called *MilanosiMuove*,[2] promoted a referendum, under the Municipality rules for public participation, with five questions one of which regarded the future development of Ecopass. The question asked for the evolution to a congestion charge: 'Would you like to extend the charged zone to the whole city and to all vehicle categories to fund policies for sustainable mobility?'.

The voter turnout was 49 per cent, a significant participation rate compared with similar experiences, and the majority (80 per cent) was clearly in favour of the proposed extension.

The vote happened in coincidence with new municipal elections in June 2011.

As a result, the pollution charge 'Ecopass' was replaced by the congestion charge 'Area C' in the same central area. The new system entered into force in January 2012 for a trial period and turned permanent from April 2013.

Under the Area C scheme, vehicles entering the area between 7.30am and 7.30pm have to pay a €5 daily charge.

Gasoline vehicles (category Euro 0) and Diesel vehicles (categories Euro 0–1–2) are prohibited access to the area.

Exemptions have been extended to utility vehicles. Commercial vehicles are entitled to a discounted ticket of €3. More recently, another discounted ticket of €3 has been allowed to cars parking in private parkings.

Residents are allowed 40 free entrances per year after which any additional entrance will cost €2.

The charge payment must be done by midnight of the next day of access. A fine of about €80 is applied to violators. Since 2014 a reduced fine is applied, if paid within two weeks.

Impacts

Main results of the Ecopass and Area C schemes regard congestion reduction, public transport speed increase and air quality improvement.

Main traffic results are summarized in Table 10.2.[3]

Traffic reduction dropped from −20.8 per cent in the first year to −10.8 per cent in 2011, because of car substitution of older charged vehicles with new uncharged vehicles. In 2010 the temporary exemption for Euro IV diesel vehicles was abolished, so traffic decreased. In 2012–2013 Area C substituted Ecopass and traffic decreased by about 38 per cent with respect to base year 2007.

Traffic composition in the tolled area improved as most polluting vehicles (the tolled classes 3–4–5) decreased by 70 per cent by 2011 with respect to base year 2007 and the number of 'ecological' vehicles (class 1) increased six fold.

It is estimated that Ecopass reduced the area's total PM10 emissions by 15 per cent compared with the prior period without Ecopass. PM10 emissions were reduced by a further 18 per cent after the first year of the Area C system in 2012 compared with 2011 levels.

A large effect on vehicles composition entering the Ecopass area happened since the first year. A 60.5 per cent reduction of passenger chargeable vehicles occurred in the first year, as well as an impressive 47.5 per cent reduction of commercial vehicles. The Ecopass long term effect is showed in Table 10.3.

With the passage to Area C, while more vehicles are chargeable, exemptions have increased. Only 40.7 per cent of vehicles entering Area C are fully charged.

Table 10.2 *Road charges as reported by AMAT*

	No charge	Ecopass				Area C	
Year	2007(4)	2008	2009	2010	2011	2012	2013
Average number of vehicles entering	90,582 (of which 77,540 passenger)	71,729 (of which 62,120 passenger)	75,097 (of which 65,332 passenger)	73,103 (of which 64,072 passenger)	80,799 (of which 72,378 passenger)	55,670 (1)	56,478 (1)
Charged	*38,081*	*16,322*	*12,255*	*12,224*	*11,431*	*n.a.*	*n.a.*
Not charged	*52,501*	*55,407*	*62,842*	*60,879*	*69,368*	*n.a.*	*n.a.*
Average number of accesses (2)	159,328	136,136	n.a.	n.a.	131,898	90,849	92,175
Traffic inside Area Variation compared to 2007 (3)		−20.8% −19.8% for passenger cars	−17.0% −15.7% for passenger cars	−19.3% −17.4% for passenger cars	−10.8% −6.7% for passenger cars	−38.8% (1) −31.1% compared to 2011	−37.6% (1) −30.1% compared to 2011

Notes:
(1) Our estimate applying the same variation as number of accesses.
(2) Notice that the total number of entrances differs from the number of individual vehicles entering (they may enter more than once in the area).
(3) Excluding exempt vehicles.
(4) Average of 10 days period 26–30 October and 12–16 November 2007.
(5) Provisional data.

Source: AMAT (2009, 2010, 2010b, 2012b).

Table 10.3   Composition of total traffic entering Ecopass Area in 2011

	Reference pre-Ecopass	2011	Variation #	Variation %
Class 1	1,194	7,348	6,154	515.4%
Class 2	51,307	62,020	10,713	20.9%
Class 3	11,939	2,353	−9,586	−80.3%
Class 4	23,167	8,709	−14,458	−62.4%
Class 5	2,973	367	−2,606	−87.7%
Total vehicles	90,580	80,797	−9,783	−10.8%
Total vehicles paying classes	38,079	11,429	−26,650	−70.0%

Source: AMAT (2012).

Costs and Revenues

Investment costs for Ecopass mainly regarded installation of cameras and system software: they amounted to 7 million €. The cost was limited thanks to sunk costs and in particular to the pre-existence of a technologically advanced traffic management centre. Operational costs of both Ecopass and Area C schemes amount to 14 million € per year, directly funded by the scheme's revenues.

Annual revenues decreased progressively from 12.1 million € in 2008 to 5.9 in 2011 in the Ecopass period.

Concerning Area C and considering the period January–June 2012, revenues are equal to 11.2 million €. In subsequent years, Area C revenues amounted to about 30 million €.

An even higher amount of revenues refer to traffic sanctions of system violators.

Revenues are mainly destined to increase in public transport service.

Elasticity to Charge

Price elasticity can be measured in any point of the demand function with the following equation:

$$\varepsilon = \frac{\%\Delta Q}{\%\Delta p} \tag{10.1}$$

where Q is the quantity demanded and p is the price, computable in each point of the demand curve by taking the inverse of the slope of the demand function and multiplying it by p/Q.

An alternative measure to point elasticity is arc-elasticity, which measures elasticity between two points on a curve, and is calculated as follows:

$$\varepsilon = \frac{\Delta Q}{\Delta p} * \frac{(p_1 + p_2)/2}{(Q_1 + Q_2)/2} \tag{10.2}$$

Referring to Q as traffic and p as congestion charge, Q_1 is traffic at time 1, after the introduction of the charge, Q_0 is traffic at time 0 before the charge introduction (baseline), p_1 is the charge amount and p_0 is 0. If the charge has varied over time, elasticity can be measured in correspondence of the difference price variations, where p_1 is the new charge amount and p_0 the old charge amount.

In the case of cost increase and traffic reduction, the arc-elasticity value results slightly higher than the point elasticity value. In case of cost reduction and increased traffic, the arc-elasticity value results slightly lower.

Demand elasticity is always negative because of the inverse relation between quantity and price in the demand curve. We will consider its value in absolute terms.

To assess the contribution of a congestion charge to traffic reduction is quite complex. In order to take a decision about travelling, a rational traveller should consider the full cost of a trip, or at least all components of the variable costs involved in a trip. So elasticity of traffic (demand) to the whole cost of a trip should be measured, where a congestion charge is just one of the components contributing to the cost.

In theory, travellers should be indifferent to which cost component of a trip varies. In this case we should expect that the elasticity value of traffic to the price of a single component, like gasoline, is the same as elasticity to any other component, like a congestion charge. In reality a congestion charge seems to weigh more than the increase in gasoline price or other costs in the perception of drivers. We expect elasticity values of traffic to congestion charges to be more similar to elasticity values of traffic to tolls.

In the road toll systems analyzed in economic literature, the typical elasticity value range is between −0.20 and −0.50 (see Wuestefeld-Regan, 1981; White, 1984; Goodwin, 1992, 2004; Jones and Hervik, 1992; Harvey, 1994; Hirschman et al., 1995; Mauchan-Bonsall, 1995; Gifford and Talkington, 1996; Burris, 2001, 2003; Matas and Raymond, 2003). In some studies, elasticity was analyzed in the short and medium-long terms, showing evidence of a general trend towards a 20–50 per cent increase (Odeck and Bråthen, 2008; Fonti, 2012).

In our specific analysis on elasticity of traffic to the Milan urban road charge scheme, some considerations are due.

It is necessary to define the variable indicating the quantity of traffic Q. Available data for congestion charges can regard number of trips, number of entries or crossings in the cordon area, travelled kilometres and a congestion index. To use one measure or another is not always equivalent, they could involve different trends.

The contemporary presence of other policies and measures for traffic reduction can make it difficult to distinguish the effects attributable only to congestion charging.

Even the definition of a baseline quantity of traffic Q_0 is difficult as a 'standard day' does not exist. Traffic flows vary by month and day conditions (meteorology, road works, big events, and so on).

Moreover it is almost impossible to isolate the effect of a congestion charge on traffic from other factors (economic activity, behaviour, infrastructure).

Many factors also influence the real price of a trip (like inflation, gasoline price, other car use costs, public transport price, fiscal regulation on charge deductibility).

Most factors are not relevant in the short term, while their influence grows in the long term. So it is possible to measure short- and long-term elasticities with a different degree of accuracy.

The elasticity formulas introduced provide a rough measure, as they attribute the whole impact of traffic variation to the charge introduction or variation.

A more accurate measure of elasticity needs to consider all factors influencing the traffic variation in the period between time 0 and time 1, to describe a model where traffic (Q) is a dependent variable and considered factors – among which the congestion charge – are independent variables, and to measure the influence of each variable on traffic variation. This requires the availability of time series of traffic and considered independent variables.

Even if some of these factors have been included in previous econometric analysis, a comprehensive framework is still lacking.

In this chapter only a comparison of rough measurements of elasticities will be provided, with the risk of overestimating their values.

In the case of Milan, the difference in charge levels (depending on vehicle emission factors) determines a renunciation to the use of the private vehicle according to the corresponding charge level.

The Ecopass charge categories have been selected following a criterion of potential to deter private vehicle use. The evaluation was based on a survey of Stated Preferences (SP) that took place in fall 2006.

Around 2,200 interviews were conducted with drivers at the 58 main entrance points of the city between 7am and 9pm on a weekday to assess

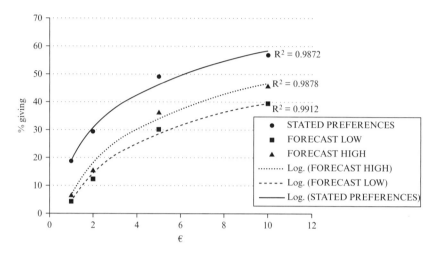

Source: Croci (2008).

*Figure 10.1   Stated preferences in the renounce to use of cars as a function
of level of charge in Milan*

the reaction of people to a proposed implementation of a road charge. For
each proposed charge amount, the proposed alternatives were: (a) confirm
the use of car and pay the charge, (b) park&ride outside the charged area,
(c) public transport, (d) car pooling, (e) motorcycle or bicycle, (f) renounce
the trip.

Three curves were derived, showing the will to continue to access the city
by car in function of an extra cost, corresponding to:

- Obtained data (from interviews);
- A maximum forecast (High);
- A minimum forecast (Low).

Elasticity of traffic to cost of charge can be derived from the curves in
Figure 10.1.[4]

An average elasticity of −0.40 is estimated by AMAT. AMAT used the
subsample of drivers directed within the 'Bastioni ring' to measure elasticity only for drivers entering what later on became the Ecopass area. The
average elasticity drops to about −0.24.

Stated preferences were compared with revealed preferences obtained by
real behaviours of car drivers after the first nine months of Ecopass, shown
in Figure 10.2.

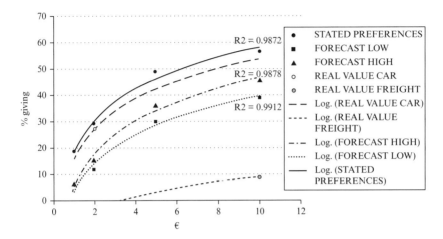

Source: Croci (2008).

Figure 10.2 *Observed behaviours in the renounce to use of cars as a function of level of charge in Milan*

A charge of €2 causes a renunciation by 27 per cent of drivers to enter the Ecopass area. A charge of €5 a renunciation of 43 per cent. For commercial vehicles, the renunciation rate is not relevant when the charge amounts to €2; at €5 the renunciation is around 3 per cent, reaching almost 9 per cent when the charge is €10.

The deterrent effect resulted higher than expected. Renunciation to private car use rates were close to those obtained with the Stated Preferences survey, but it is also possible to observe renunciation among commercial heavy duty vehicles.

In this chapter we provide a new measure of arc-elasticity of Ecopass for passenger cars referred to year 2011 (the last one for Ecopass) using more recent AMAT data reported in Table 10.1. We estimate a long term value of −0.66 for class 3 and −0.46 for class 4. It is not possible to provide a measure for class 5 as too few passenger cars fall into class 5.[5]

Values for commercial vehicles show lower values (between −0.15 and −0.17).

COMPARISON WITH OTHER EUROPEAN URBAN ROAD PRICING SCHEMES

The two main road pricing systems at city level, currently operating in Europe beyond Milan, are in London and Stockholm. The three systems have some common as well as differentiated features, as shown in Table 10.4.

The main aim for all systems is reducing congestion. A secondary aim is to reduce air pollution (this aim was prevalent in the first phase in Milan).

In all systems a flat rate is imposed. In the first phase in Milan, the charge was differentiated on the basis of PM10 emission factors.

Charges are on daily basis in London and Milan and on number of accesses in Stockholm and operate only in the daytime.

In London circulation in the area is charged, in Milan access to the area is charged, in Stockholm crossing of the area is charged.

Similar technologies are in place, using cameras automatically recognizing car plates.

All systems evolved through time in aspects like area, charge level, exemptions, and so on. In the case of Milan there was a major change in the structure of the scheme itself, shifting from a pollution charge to a congestion charge.

Political and public debates were relevant factors in setting up and decide permanency of the systems. In the cases of Stockholm and Milan, a referendum was a key factor to that purpose.

The ratio operating costs/revenues fell from 42 per cent to 37 per cent for London, from 40 per cent to 25 per cent for Stockholm (Erdmenger and Frey, 2010) and from 40 per cent to 22 per cent for Milan.

In all cases a robust increase of public transportation was announced and implemented, and a substantial part of revenues are invested for sustainable mobility.

In all cases the following trend effects, though in different measures, are demonstrated: traffic reduction and modal shift, mainly through an increase of passengers of public transport. A huge pollution emissions' reduction happened in Milan and a significant one in Stockholm, while the effect was negligible in London. In Stockholm and Milan accident reduction and speed increase in public transportation were experienced (in London a connection with accidents does not seem to exist, while bus speed decreased). In all cases, traffic reduction happened also in the area surrounding the charged one. No negative effects were registered on retail and real estate values in the area.

All cases show a high deterrent effect of the charge, as measured on

Table 10.4   Urban road pricing comparison: London, Stockholm and Milan

		London	Stockholm	Milan
Main features of the schemes	Starting year	February 2003[a]	January 2006 (7 months trial) Permanent from August 2007[d]	Pollution charge from January 2008 Congestion charge from January 2012 (formally a trial until April 2013)[f]
	Area	21 km² (1.3% of the city surface) Western extension from February 2007 to January 2011 Metropolitan area 14 m inhab.[a]	30 km² (16% of the city surface) Stockholm County 1.9 m inhab.[d]	8 km² (4.5% of the city surface) Metropolitan area 3 m inhab.[f]
	Charge level	£5 £8 from July 2005 £10 from January 2011 £11.50 (about €14.50) from June 2014[a]	SEK20 (about € 2.16) during peak periods (7:30–8:30, 16:00–17:30), SEK15 30 minutes before and after the peak periods and SEK10 during the rest of the period 6:30–18:30. The total charge per day is capped at SEK60.[d]	Pollution charge: proportional to vehicles' emission class, of € 0, 2, 5 or 10 per day. Congestion charge: flat charge of €5 per day.[f]
	Application of charge	Cordon pricing Daily fee Pay for entrance, exit, intra-area trips[a]	Cordon pricing Single passage fee (with daily limit) Pay for entrance and exit of the area[d]	Cordon pricing Daily fee Pay for entrance in the area[f]
	Time of application	Weekdays, 7:00–18:00[a]	Weekdays, 6:30–18:30[d]	Weekdays, 7:30–19:30[f]

Table 10.4 (continued)

		London	Stockholm	Milan
Results	Reduction of whole traffic with respect to reference year	−14% (2003)[b, c] −16% (2006)[b, c] −21% (2008)[b, c]	−21% (2006)[e] −19% (2007)[e] −18% (2008)[e] −18% (2009)[e] −19% (2010)[e] −20% (2011)[e]	Ecopass: −20.8% (2008)[g] −17.0% (2009)[g] −19.3% (2010) euro IV diesel charged[g] −10.8% (2011)[g] Area C: −38.8% (2012)[g] −37.6% (2013)[g]
	Congestion reduction	−30% (2003)[b] −22% (2005)[b] −8% (2006)[b] 0% (2007)[b]		
	Reduction of potentially chargeable traffic	−33% (2003)[c] −36% (2006)[c] £8 charge drove to a 53% reduction of fully chargeable traffic in 2007[c]		After the first year (2008) Ecopass reduced chargeable passenger traffic on average by 60.5% and in the last year (2011) by 79.8% and 63.2%, respectively for a €2 and €5 charge

		London	Stockholm	Milan
Costs and revenues	Set up investment	160 m £ (203.5 m€)[a]	1,900 mSEK (207.2 m€)[d]	7 m€ (excluding sunk costs)[f]
	Annual operating cost	90 m£ (114.4 m€)[a]	220 mSEK (23.9 m€)[d]	14 m€[f]
	Gross revenues per year (excluding fines)	from 138 m£ to 227 m£ in 2012 (from 175.5 m€ to 288.6 m€ in 2012)[a]	763 mSEK (83.2 m€)[d]	from 12 m€ in 2008 to 5.9 m€ in 2011 (Ecopass); 30 m€ in 2012 (Area C)[f]
	Ratio operating costs/ revenues	37% (in 2008; falling from initially 42%)[a]	25% (in 2010 falling from initially 40%)[d]	22% (falling from initially 40%)[f]

Table 10.4   (continued)

		London	Stockholm	Milan
Elasticity	Elasticity values	0.47[b]	0.70 in 2006 to 0.85 in 2009 onwards[e]	0.46–0.66 (for different classes of emissions of vehicles). (own estimation)

Notes:
a   http://tfl.gov.uk/modes/driving/congestion-charge.
b. Transport for London (2008).
c. Transport for London (2008b).
d. http://www.stockholmsforsoket.se/.
e. Börjesson M. et al. (2012).
f. http://www.comune.milano.it/portale/wps/portal/!ut/p/c1/04_
    SB8K8xLLM9MSSzPy8xBz9CP0os_hAc8OgAE8TIwMDJ2MzAyMPIzdfHw8_
    Y28jQ_1wkA6zeD9_o1A3E09DQwszV0MDIzMPEyefME8DdxdjiLwBDuBooO_
    nkZ-bql-QnZ3m6KioCADL1TNQ/dl2/d1/L2dJQSEvUUt3QS9ZQnB3LzZfQU01U1
    BJNDIwT1RTMzAySEtMVEs5TTMwMDA!/?WCM_GLOBAL_CONTEXT=/wps/
    wcm/connect/ContentLibrary/elenco+siti+tematici/elenco+siti+tematici/area+c.
g. AMAT (2009, 2010, 2010, 2011, 2012).

travel behaviour changes referred to all traffic and in particular to charge-able traffic.

The demand elasticities of car travel in response to a congestion charge are considerably higher than the values in response to fuel costs in literature.[6]

Results and elasticity estimates reported in Table 10.4 show how urban congestion charging, though limited to pioneer experiences, is able to reduce congestion in an effective way.

CONCLUSIONS

In 2008 Milan introduced a cordon pricing scheme called 'Ecopass', with a pollution charge to be paid by most polluting vehicles to access the city centre, proportional to vehicles' PM10 tail emissions. In the first year the system proved very efficient in reducing congestion and car emissions, thanks to both traffic reduction and substitution of older polluting vehicles with new cleaner ones. Then the effect on congestion progressively decreased because of car substitution. Following the results of a public referendum regarding the future of the system, Ecopass was replaced in

2012 by a congestion charge named 'Area C', characterized by a flat charge for all vehicles.

Both schemes have delivered relevant results regarding congestion reduction, public transport speed increase, air quality improvement. Traffic reduction dropped from 20.8 per cent in the first year of Ecopass to −10.8 per cent in 2011, because of car substitution of older charged vehicles with new uncharged vehicles. In 2012 and 2013, Area C substituted Ecopass and traffic decreased by about 38 per cent with respect to base year 2007.

As far as elasticity to charge is concerned, our own measures for Milan indicate an elasticity referred to the Ecopass system varying between −0.46 and −0.66. These values are systematically higher than elasticity to fuel price and even to traditional tolls for roads and bridges.

NOTES

1. See the official website: http://www.comune.milano.it/portale/wps/portal/!ut/p/c1/04_SB 8K8xLLM9MSSzPy8xBz9CP0os_hAc8OgAE8TIwMDJ2MzAyMPIzdfHw8_Y28jQ_1 wkA6zeD9_o1A3E09DQwszV0MDIzMPEyefME8DdxdjiLwBDuBooO_nkZ-bql-QnZ 3m6KioCADL1TNQ/dl2/d1/L2dJQSEvUUt3QS9ZQnB3LzZfQU01UlBJNDIwT1RTM zAySEtMVEs5TTMwMDA!/?WCM_GLOBAL_CONTEXT=/wps/wcm/connect/Cont entLibrary/elenco+siti+tematici/elenco+siti+tematici/area+c (accessed 6 March 2015). See also ICLEI case study: www.iclei.org/casestudies.
2. www.milanosimuove.it a successful wordplay in Italian translatable in English as 'Milan moves on' and 'Milan Yes Moves' suggesting the 'Yes' option at the referenda.
3. This was part of a wider sample interviewed on travel behaviours of commuters, who are responsible for half of the traffic in town.
4. Elasticity is calculated per type of employment and per motivation of entrance in the Ecopass area. Results show that students fall in the high-elasticity class (elasticity level: −1.10) while retired people, housewives and unemployed are medium-elastic (−0.56). Businessmen and entrepreneurs instead, as expected, fall into the low-elasticity class (around −0.25). Similarly travel trips result being much less elastic than pleasure trips, with elasticity of −0.39 and −0.65 respectively.
5. Fonti (2012) provides slightly different values of elasticities: −0.60 for class 3 and −0.41 for class 4 in 2011. She also provides average elasticity values for the whole Ecopass period (2008–2011): −0.44 for class 3, −0.37 for class 4, −0.58 for class 5. Values show stability over time.
6. A charge represents a much larger change in cost than, say, a 10 per cent increase in fuel cost (which is normally considered in literature). For London a charge of £8 is equivalent to a 191 per cent cost increase in fuel cost (TfL, 2008b), considering average trips of 17 km.

BIBLIOGRAPHY

AMAT (2009/2010/2011/2012), Rapporti monitoraggio Ecopass 2008/2009/2010/ 2011.

AMAT (2013/2014), Area C: Sintesi dei risultati 2012/2013.

Börjesson M. et al. (2012), CTS Working Paper 2012:3, in *Transport Policy*, 20: 1–12.

Burris M.W. (2003), The tool-price component of travel demand elasticity. *International Journal of Transport Economics*, 30(1): 45–59.

Burris M.W. et al. (2001), Impact of variable pricing on temporal distribution of travel demand. Transportation Research Record, 1747: 36–43.

CE Delft (2008), *Handbook on Estimation of External Costs in the Transport Sector*. Delft, the Netherlands: CE Delft.

CE Delft (2011), *Infras, Fraunhofer ISI, External Costs of Transport in Europe*. Delft, the Netherlands: CE Delft.

Croci E. (2008), Presentation at the OECD/ITF Global Forum on Sustainable Development: Transport and Environment in a Globalizing World, Guadalajara, 10–12 November 2008.

Erdmenger C. and Frey K. (2010), Urban road charge in European cities: A possible means towards a new culture for urban mobility?, Report of the Joint Expert Group of the EU Commission on Transport and Environment on urban road pricing schemes in European cities.

European Commission (2007), Green Paper, Towards a new culture for urban mobility.

European Commission (2011), White Paper, Roadmap to a single European transportation area – Towards a competitive and resource efficient transport system.

European Commission (2013), Communication, Together towards competitive and resource efficient urban mobility.

Fonti R. (2012), *Urban Road Pricing Schemes: The Case of Milan*. Milan: Bocconi University.

Gifford J.L. and Talkington S.W. (1996), Demand elasticity under time-varying prices: Case study of day-of-week varying tolls on the Golden Gate Bridge. Transportation Research Record, 1558: 55–59.

Goodwin P.B. (1992), A review of new demand elasticities with special reference to short and long run effects of price changes. *Journal of Transport Economics and Policy*, 26(2): 155–169.

Goodwin P.B. et al. (2004), Elasticities of road traffic and fuel consumption with respect to price and income: A review. *Transport Reviews*, 24(3): 275–292.

Harvey G. (1994), Transportation pricing behavior. In: Special Report 242: Curbing Gridlock. Peak-Period Fees To Relieve Traffic Congestion, 2. Washington, DC: Transportation Research Board. National Academy Press: 89–114.

Hirschman I. et al. (1995), Bridge and tunnel toll elasticities in New York: Some recent evidence. *Transportation*, 22: 97–113.

Invernizzi G. et al. (2011), Measurement of black carbon concentration as indicator of air quality benefits of traffic restriction policies within the Ecopass zone in Milan, Italy. *Atmospheric Environment*, 45.

Jones P. and Hervik A. (1992), Restraining car traffic in European cities: An emerging role for road pricing. *Transportation Research A*, 26: 133–145.

Matas A. and Raymond J.L. (2003), The demand elasticity on tolled motorways. *Journal of Transportation and Statistics*, 6(2): 91–108.

Mauchan A. and Bonsall P. (1995), Model predictions of the effects of motorway charging in West Yorkshire. *Traffic, Engineering and Control*, 36: 206–212.

Newbery D.M. (1988), Road damage externalities and road user charges. *Econometrica*, 56(2): 295–316.

Newbery D.M. (1990), Pricing and congestion: Economic principles relevant to pricing roads. *Oxford Review of Economic Policy*, 6(2): 22–38.

Odeck J. and Bråthen S. (2008), Travel demand elasticities and users attitudes: A case study of Norwegian toll projects. *Transportation Research Part A*, 42: 77–94.

OECD, ITF (2010), Implementing congestion charges, Report round table 147.

Pigou A.C. (1920), *The Economics of Welfare*. London: Macmillan.

Transport for London (TfL) (2008a), Congestion charging central London – impacts monitoring. Sixth year report.

Transport for London (TfL) (2008b), Demand elasticities for car trips to central London as revealed by the Central London Congestion Charge.

White P.R. (1984), Man and his transport behaviour Part 4a. User response to price changes: Application of the 'threshold' concept. *Transport Reviews: A Transnational Transdisciplinary Journal*, 4(4): 367–386.

Wuestefeld N.H. and Regan E.J. (1981), Impact of rate increases on toll facilities. *Traffic Quarterly*, 35: 639–655.

11. Motor fuel taxation in Central Europe and international tax competition: simulation of motor fuel tax harmonization

Jan Brůha, Hana Brůhová-Foltýnová and Vítězslav Píša

INTRODUCTION

The final price of goods influences the volume of goods consumed and, therefore, the related environmental effects. This is especially true for motor fuels. Excise duty and VAT comprise a substantial part of the final price of motor fuels. Hence, these taxes represent corrective taxes that allow achievement of a more efficient allocation of resources by incorporating negative externalities into market prices. Furthermore, motor fuel taxation can help to reduce dependence on foreign energy sources, provide a stimulus for private research and innovation for technological progress that involves the use of renewable energy sources and promotion of energy-saving behaviors, greater use of renewable energies and energy-efficient consumption (Brandimarte 2014).

Transport taxes contribute significantly to public revenues because they have broad tax bases and high tax rates which can be justified by the environmental externalities (Sally-Ann 2014). However, there is a trade-off between environmental effectiveness and its fiscal role – the more elastic the demand for fuels, the more the revenues will be eroded by behavioral responses.

The excise duty tax on petroleum products does not overlap with the EU Emission Trading System as CO_2 emissions coming from motor fuel combustion are largely excluded from this regulation (Brandimarte 2014). While there are European Directives setting minimal rates of VAT and excise duty on fuels, the final taxation of fuels differs substantially among European countries (Ward et al. 2013; see also below). The differences might lead to effects such as fuel tourism which deteriorate the fiscal effect of the fuel taxation and, at the same time, they might not bring environmental benefits. Fuel tourism refers to the situation where agents of the country with higher fuel taxes have an incentive to buy motor fuels in the country with lower taxes. This can be relevant especially for households living in the border regions and for haulers. This phenomenon is expected to increase fiscal revenues from fuel taxes in the country with lower taxation and may lead to unwanted fiscal competition among countries.

This chapter deals with motor fuel taxation in the open economies of Central Europe with an emphasis on international tax competition. It introduces an empirical model that is useful for estimating the demand for motor fuels in each of the countries analyzed, taking into account the effect of international tax competition. The model is estimated using Bayesian techniques. Using the model, we estimate impacts of a scenario of motor fuel tax harmonization on fiscal revenues, fuel consumption, and the environment.

The remainder of this chapter is organized as follows. The next section discusses the competition of the motor fuel taxation in Central Europe and summarizes the problem-related literature. Then we describe the development of motor fuel taxation in the Central European countries, before the empirical model is introduced. Simulated scenario and results of the simulation are provided, followed by conclusions and policy implications in the last section.

INTERNATIONAL CONTEXT OF MOTOR FUEL TAXATION

In this section, we review the current situation: first we describe the state of motor fuel taxation in Central Europe, then we overview related literature.

Competition of Motor Fuel Taxation in Central Europe

Taxes on motor fuels (a Pigouvian type of tax) serve as a tool to remedy negative impacts of consumption of 'bads' on the environment. However, there are political barriers to the use of motor fuel taxes as a corrective instrument. The most commonly cited arguments are its regressivity (imposing a heavier burden on low-income households than on their higher-income counterparts) and strong negative impacts on countryside inhabitants with fewer possibilities to decrease consumption of car-related fuels than inhabitants of urban areas (Poterba 1991; McNally and Mabey 1999; Snowdon 2013; Kallbecken et al. 2013). In addition, urban low-income households owning a car will be less able or willing to switch to a more fuel-efficient car (Blobel et al. 2011). Further research contributions suggest careful evaluation of interactions between environmental taxes and other regulations or existing taxes, as they can change the behavioral responses, the optimal level of the taxes and the related costs (Conefrey et al. 2013).

Another argument against increases in motor fuel taxation warns about effects of fuel tourism. It refers to a situation where high domestic motor fuel taxes would increase incentives to buy motor fuels abroad, which leads to a switch that will harm the fiscal revenues but not help the environment. As was shown by Banfi et al. (2005) in the case of Switzerland, people living in the adjacent regions of Italy, France and Germany have had a price incentive to buy gasoline in Switzerland for several years. This phenomenon has increased employment and fiscal revenues from fuel taxes in Switzerland, whereas lower fiscal revenues and a decrease in employment in the gasoline distribution sector were observed in the neighboring countries. Because of this, there has been little room in the border regions for discouraging residential gasoline consumption using tax increases.

This chapter makes the following contributions. It presents an econometric model that can be used to assess the effect of motor fuel taxation and take into account international tax competition. The model is estimated for the following Central European countries: Austria, the Czech Republic, Germany, Hungary, Poland, and Slovakia. Then, the model is applied in order to evaluate a scenario of impacts of harmonization of motor fuel taxes on fuel consumption, tax revenues, and the resulting GHG emissions. As an example, we consider the scenario with the model and simulate impacts of different measures which might be implemented in the respective countries (such as changes to tax rates).

Related Literature

The optimal setting of motor fuel taxation and its impacts are of considerable interest to policymakers and researchers (see, for example, OECD 2000). However, the effects of international tax competition have been analyzed substantially less, even in Europe, which has relatively small countries with differentiated fuel prices.

Rietveld and Woudenberg (2005) show that the level of motor fuel taxation is especially important in European small open economies because they tend to attract a substantial part of consumption (and therefore fiscal revenues) from adjacent countries. Due to this effect, countries may engage in the fiscal and environmental race to the bottom.

Banfi et al. (2005) find behavior is very strongly affected by fuel tourism in border regions of Switzerland, and Rietveld et al. (2001) arrive at the same conclusions for the Netherlands. Both results would support the importance of fuel tourism in small open economies.

Another European study focuses on cross-border fuel shopping in Spanish regions (Leal et al. 2009). The authors find that raising the average price of diesel in neighboring regions has positive and long-term effects on motor fuel sales in the analyzed region.

The problem of the international tax competition in motor fuels is also addressed by the European Commission, which made a proposal for an amendment of Council Directive 2003/96/EC in 2007 (the EC proposal tries to regulate European haulage markets by narrowing differentials of the existing tax on diesel used by trucks).

There has been some interesting research into the international dimension of motor fuel taxation for the Central European countries. For example, Ševčík and Rod (2010) conclude that a decrease in excise duty on diesel would have a positive effect on Czech public revenues, substantially supported by international demand. They supported their analysis by highly price-elastic demand: they suggest a demand elasticity of about −3, but they do not provide empirical evidence for such a high number. Píša (2012) uses a set of econometric models on panel data for the Central European countries and finds a much lower elasticity even if the international price competition is taken into account. Furthermore, Novysedlák and Šrámková (2011) conclude in their ex post empirical analysis that the significant decrease in excise duty rates on diesel had a negative effect on tax revenues in the case of Slovakia. This result is consistent with the elasticities estimated by Píša (2012). However, none of the studies addresses environmental dimension like CO_2 emissions.

MOTOR FUEL TAXATION IN THE CONTEXT OF CENTRAL EUROPE

The situation in taxation on motor fuels in the EU is substantially affected by EU Directives harmonizing the EU indirect tax schemes. Directive 2006/112/EC sets the framework for VAT. Traditional fossil motor fuels have to be taxed by the standard VAT rate. The minimum standard rate is 15 percent and the EU Member States cannot distinguish among products under the standard rate.

Directive 2003/96/EC relates to excise duties and stipulates, among others, the EU minima for gasoline and diesel. The EU minimum excise duty on gasoline is €359/1,000 L and the EU minimum on diesel increased from €302/1,000 L to €330/1,000 L on January 1, 2010.

Table 11.1   Excise duty rates on petrol, diesel and VAT in the analyzed countries

	Petrol Rate		Diesel Rate		VAT
	national currency/1,000 liters	€/1,000 l	national currency/1,000 liters	€/1,000 l	%
AT	482 EUR	482	397 EUR	397	20
CZ	12,840 CZK	464	10,950 CZK	395	21
DE	654.5 EUR	654	470.4 EUR	470.4	19
HU	123,300 HUF	402	113,555 HUF	371	27
PL	1,669 PLN	395	1,459 PLN	345	23
SK	514.5 EUR	514.5	368 EUR	368	20

Note: Recalculated via exchange rates effective November 17, 2014.

Source: European Commission: Excise Duty Tables (2014b).

An overview of the tax rates in the Central European countries is shown in Table 11.1.

The values of the EU minimal excise duty rates show that gasoline has higher taxation than diesel. In fact, none of the EU Member States charges gasoline consumption less than diesel. The next paragraphs describe the development of fuel taxes in the analyzed countries between 2004 and 2014.

Two increases in motor fuel excise tax rates occurred in Austria in the past 10 years: in 2007 and 2011. In 2007, the gasoline rates grew from €417/1,000 L to €442/1,000 L (+6 percent) and the diesel rates increased from €297/1,000 L to €347/1,000 L (+16.8 percent). In 2011, the gasoline rates increased from €442/1,000 L to €482/1,000 L (+9 percent) and the diesel rates from €347/1,000 L to €397/1,000 L (+14.4 percent). Austria did not change its VAT rate (20 percent) in the analyzed period.

The Czech Republic does not belong to the European Monetary Union (EMU). To measure the international tax competitiveness it is therefore crucial not only to take into account the national tax rate but also the exchange rate. When domestic currency appreciates the tax competitiveness worsens and vice versa. The same holds for other countries not belonging to the EMU (Hungary, Poland).

The standard VAT rate changed twice in the considered period, when it increased from 19 percent to 20 percent in 2010 and from 20 percent to 21 percent in 2013 in the Czech Republic. Changes in the excise duty rates on motor fuels happened only once in January 2010, when the excise duty rate on petrol increased by 8.5 percent (quoted in national currency) from

11,840 CZK/1,000 L (€459/1,000 L) to 12,840 CZK/1,000 L (€497/1,000 L) and the excise duty rate on diesel by 10.1 percent from 9,950 CZK/1,000 L (€385/1,000 L) to 10,950 CZK/1,000 L (€424/1,000 L).[1]

Germany is characterized by a relatively high level of indirect taxes. The excise duty imposed on motor fuels did not change in the analyzed period and the country has rates of €654.5/1,000 L for gasoline and €470.4/1,000 L for diesel. The VAT rate that influences the final consumer price changed in 2007 when it increased from 16 percent to 19 percent.

In Hungary, the excise duty rates changed twice, in 2010 and 2012. The changes in 2010 are represented by an increase in the rate on gasoline by 15.9 percent from HUF 103,500/1,000 L (€381/1,000 L) to HUF 120,000/1,000 L (€444/1,000 L) and that on diesel by 14.5 percent from HUF 85,000/1,000 L (€313/1,000 L) to HUF 97,350/1,000 L (€361/1,000 L). In 2012, the rates on gasoline increased by 2.8 percent from HUF 120,000/1,000 L (€420/1,000 L) to HUF 123,300/1,000 L (€416/1,000 L) and on diesel by 16.6 percent from HUF 97,350/1,000 L (€341/1,000 L) to HUF 113,555/1,000 L (€383/1,000 L). In 2011, Hungary introduced a reduced rate on diesel for commercial gas oil as is defined in Article 7(3) of Directive 2003/96/EC. The rate is HUF 96,555/1,000 L (€358/1,000 L).[2] Hungary changed its VAT rates three times. First, in 2005 the VAT rate decreased from 25 percent to 20 percent, in 2007 it increased from 20 percent to 25 percent, and finally in 2012 to 27 percent.

Poland increased its excise duty rates slightly every year. The only exception for gasoline was in 2007, when the rates on gasoline rose by 18 percent from PLN 1395/1,000 L (€355/1,000 L) to PLN 1646/1,000 L (€428/1,000 L) and on diesel in 2010 and 2012, when the rates increased by 11.9 percent from PLN 1146/1,000 L (€280/1,000 L) to PLN 1282/1,000 L (€322/1,000 L), and by 12.3 percent from PLN 1288/1,000 L (€304/1,000 L) to PLN 1446/1,000 L (€340/1,000 L), respectively. Poland increased its standard VAT rate from 22 percent to 23 percent in 2011.

Slovakia changed its VAT rate only once in 2011 (from 19 percent to 20 percent). The gasoline tax did not change and was approximately €514/1,000 L for the whole period (fluctuations of the tax rate in euros happened only due to exchange rate movements before Slovakia had adopted the euro). Nevertheless, the excise tax on diesel decreased sharply in 2010 from €481/1,000 L to €368/1,000 L (that is, by −23.5 percent).

Figure 11.1 reveals that there exist important differences in the final fuel prices among countries. Germany has had the highest gasoline price since 2005, while the lowest price has been in Poland since 2009. After 2010, the final gasoline prices in Austria, Hungary, the Czech Republic and Slovakia have been similar and the differences among them have been influenced mainly by exchange rate movements.

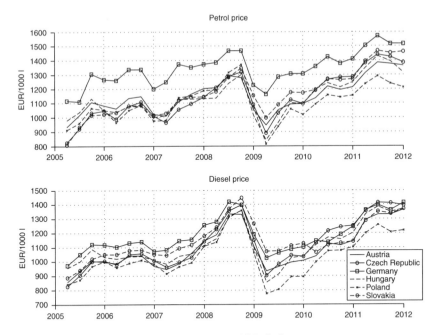

Source: European Commission (2014a): Energy Oil Bulletin.

Figure 11.1 Comparison of final fuel prices in the Central European countries

Since 2009, Poland has also had the lowest diesel price among the six Central European countries analyzed. Unlike in the case of gasoline, there is not one particular country that would exhibit the highest diesel price over the whole period. Nevertheless, it can be said that Germany, the Czech Republic and Slovakia represent three countries with the highest diesel prices.

MODEL FORMULATION AND ESTIMATION

In this section, we introduce an empirical model useful for estimation of the demand for motor fuels in the analyzed countries when taking into account the effect of international tax competition.

Our model is fairly standard (Ajanovic et al. 2012) and is formulated as follows:

$$\log C_{it} = \beta_0 + \beta_y \log y_{it} + \beta_p \log p_{it} + \beta_\beta \log \beta_{it} + \varepsilon_{it}, \quad (11.1)$$

Table 11.2   Estimated elasticities

	Gasoline			Diesel		
	2.5% CI	Posterior mean	97.5% CI	2.5% CI	Posterior mean	97.5% CI
β_0	3.15	3.37	3.57	3.91	4.13	4.34
β_p	−1.18	**−0.99**	−0.84	−1.02	**−0.80**	−0.59
β_y	0.82	0.87	0.93	0.80	0.86	0.92
$\beta_{\hat{p}}$	−0.12	**−0.08**	−0.04	−0.17	**−0.09**	−0.01

Note: 2.5% CI = 2.5% quantile of the credible interval; 97.5% CI = 97.5% quantile of the credible interval.

where C_{it} is the fuel consumption in the country i in the year t, y_{it} is the real GDP, p_{it} is the real fuel price, and $\hat{p}_{it}$ is the relative average price of fuel in neighboring countries defined as follows:

$$\hat{p}_{it} = p_{it} / (\Sigma_j \, w_{ij} \, p_{jt}), \qquad (11.2)$$

where p_{jt} is the fuel price in the region j in the year t and w_{ij} are weights. If this variable is greater than 1 for a particular country, it means that such a country has relatively higher fuel prices than its neighboring countries.

The model has been estimated using Bayesian panel data model methods (Greenberg 2008) on a sample of six Central European countries using quarterly data for the period since 2005. We test for a difference of coefficients across the countries, but the data do not reject the hypothesis that the coefficients are homogenous. The estimation results are provided in Table 11.2: we report the posterior mean and 95 percent Bayesian credible set (this is an interval that contains the true value with a posterior probability of 0.95).

The motor fuel elasticity is the sum of two coefficients: β_p and $\beta_{\hat{p}}$. The first coefficient measures the domestic elasticity only, in other words, the elasticity which would exist if all the countries had the same tax rate. The second coefficient measures the demand response due to the international price differential. Both components are significant and – in line with basic intuition – negative. Consistently with other studies (Pock 2007), we found that diesel is less price-elastic than gasoline.

Although the point estimates are different from those quoted by Píša (2012), the qualitative conclusion is the same: even taking into account the effect of fuel tourism, the demand for motor fuels is not price-elastic enough to support the view that a decrease in the indirect taxes on motor fuels would increase tax revenues.

SIMULATION SCENARIO

The previous section clearly shows that there are differences among the Central European countries regarding taxation of motor fuels. The report by Ward et al. (2013) states that great discrepancy in the tax rates used within and across countries can lead to various economic problems, from inappropriate investments in fuels and technologies, to carbon and economic leakage between countries and, ultimately, overall loss of welfare. Raising or adjusting national taxes on energy and carbon can help to correct these discrepancies while generating useful revenues that can contribute to fiscal re-balancing.

We consider a policy scenario of an increase in the excise duty tax rates on motor fuels in all the Central European countries to the level of Germany. This scenario reflects the need of higher harmonization among excise duty rates and a higher emphasis on the environmentally corrective function of the taxes. The aim of our scenario simulations is not to assess a particular policy proposal,[3] but to discuss the effects of international price differences on fuel consumption and related CO_2 emissions. Although the scenario does not present a particular policy proposal, it is nevertheless utmost important from the European perspective.

Using the scenario defined above, we evaluate its impacts on the following variables of interest: motor fuel consumption, budget revenues, and CO_2 emissions. The change in the variables of interest is given by the specification of the scenario and by the value of parameters of the motor fuel demand equation.

Since the estimates of the motor fuel demand equation are uncertain, we take this uncertainty into account. Hence, when evaluating the scenario, we do not use the point estimate or the posterior mean of unknown parameters only, but we consider the whole posterior distribution. Therefore, we report the mean value (expected change) along with the 2.5 percent and 97.5 percent quantiles of the credible interval of the simulated values. The credible interval is the interval that contains the true outcome with probability 0.95. Table 11.3 shows the results of our simulation.

The simulated scenario is based on an increase in the rates of excise duty tax on motor fuels in all the Central European countries analyzed to the level of Germany. The highest increase of end prices as a result of such a tax rise would occur in Poland (by 22.9 percent for gasoline and by 11.4 percent for diesel) and Hungary (by 22.2 percent and 9.2 percent, respectively). This increase would lead to a substantial decrease in fuel consumption in all countries except Germany, where a slight increase around 1 percent of consumption would take place. The increase in motor fuel consumption in Germany is caused by relaxing the tax competition from

Table 11.3 Simulation results

	Austria						Czech Republic					
	Gasoline			Diesel			Gasoline			Diesel		
	2.5% cred. int.	Posterior mean	97.5% cred. int.	2.5% cred. int.	Posterior mean	97.5% cred. int.	2.5% cred. int.	Posterior mean	97.5% cred. int.	2.5% cred. int.	Posterior mean	97.5% cred. int.
Change in the fuel end price (in %)		14.1%			6.3%			15.0%			5.9%	
Change in fuel consumption (in %)	−17.5%	−14.4%	−12.0%	−6.9%	−5.2%	−3.6%	−18.4%	−15.2%	−12.7%	−6.2%	−4.8%	−3.5%
Change in fuel consumption (mil L)	−381.9	−314.5	−262.8	−620.6	−471.7	−328.7	−424.6	−350.2	−293.3	−287.8	−222.1	−159.3
Change in CO_2 emissions (ths. tons CO_2)	−1008.2	−830.4	−693.8	−1484.4	−1128.3	−786.3	−1121.0	−924.6	−774.3	−688.3	−531.4	−381.0
Change in budget revenues (mil. euro)	126.4	170.5	204.4	372.8	442.8	510.1	151.8	200.5	237.8	193.3	224.2	253.8

	Germany						Hungary					
	Gasoline			Diesel			Gasoline			Diesel		
	2.5% cred. int.	Posterior mean	97.5% cred. int.	2.5% cred. int.	Posterior mean	97.5% cred. int.	2.5% cred. int.	Posterior mean	97.5% cred. int.	2.5% cred. int.	Posterior mean	97.5% cred. int.
Change in the fuel end price (in %)		0.0%			0.0%			22.2%			9.2%	
Change in fuel consumption (in %)	2.1%	1.3%	0.5%	1.3%	0.6%	0.0%	−27.7%	−22.8%	−19.0%	−9.8%	−7.5%	−5.4%
Change in fuel consumption (mil L)	562.5	346.2	138.5	845.8	422.9	4.7	−511.2	−420.0	−349.6	−350.2	−269.4	−191.9
Change in CO$_2$ emissions (ths. tons CO$_2$)	1485.0	913.9	365.5	2023.1	1011.6	11.2	−1349.7	−1108.9	−923.0	−837.7	−644.3	−459.0
Change in budget revenues (mil. euro)	368.2	226.6	90.6	397.9	198.9	2.2	139.7	199.4	245.5	209.3	247.4	283.8

Table 11.3 (continued)

	Poland						Slovakia					
	Gasoline			Diesel			Gasoline			Diesel		
	2.5% cred. int.	Posterior mean	97.5% cred. int.	2.5% cred. int.	Posterior mean	97.5% cred. int.	2.5% cred. int.	Posterior mean	97.5% cred. int.	2.5% cred. int.	Posterior mean	97.5% cred. int.
Change in the fuel end price (in %)		22.9%			11.4%			10.9%			8.6%	
Change in fuel consumption (in %)	−29.0%	−23.8%	−19.7%	−12.9%	−9.7%	−6.6%	−11.7%	−10.0%	−8.8%	−8.7%	−6.8%	−5.0%
Change in fuel consumption (mil L)	−1555.2	−1273.2	−1054.0	−2195.8	−1650.4	−1125.4	−94.0	−80.4	−71.1	−166.2	−129.7	−94.7
Change in CO_2 emissions (ths. tons CO_2)	−4105.8	−3361.3	−2782.5	−5252.3	−3947.6	−2692.0	−248.1	−212.3	−187.7	−397.6	−310.1	−226.6
Change in budget revenues (mil. euro)	338.0	522.6	666.1	1001.5	1258.1	1505.0	51.4	60.2	66.3	116.8	134.0	150.4

the adjacent countries. The final effect on consumption of all countries would be savings of 2 billion liters of gasoline and 2.3 billion liters of diesel and that would lead to 11.1 million tons of CO_2 avoided.

In spite of the decrease of motor fuels consumption in all countries (except Germany), the scenario implies higher public revenues as higher tax rates overweigh the deterioration of the tax base. The scenario would bring in total €3.9 billion of additional public revenues for all countries. The effect of international shifts in demand (fuel tourism) would be alleviated as all countries in the region harmonize their policies.

CONCLUDING REMARKS AND POLICY IMPLICATIONS

This chapter presents an econometric model, which is used for evaluation of motor fuel taxation in six Central European countries (Austria, the Czech Republic, Germany, Hungary, Poland, and Slovakia) with an emphasis on international motor fuel tax competition in this area. The model is used to gauge impacts of changes in motor fuel taxes on fuel consumption, the environment, and public finance.

The scenario analyzed was essentially based on increases in fuel taxation in these countries to the level of Germany. It was chosen to demonstrate various effects of fuel tax harmonization in Central Europe. The literature shows that minimizing discrepancies in energy or carbon tax by adjusting or increasing these taxes can bring useful revenues that can contribute to fiscal re-balancing.

Our results are in concord with those findings. The outputs of our model indicate that an increase in excise tax rates causes a reduction in motor fuel consumption, which depends on the level of taxation in neighboring countries. This implies a significant reduction in CO_2 emissions in the analyzed countries and confirms the conclusions of preceding studies about its substantial importance for good management of climate change.

Furthermore, our results suggest that policymakers should perceive motor fuel taxation more as a tool of environmental policy, not only as a revenue-raising tool. Moreover, further harmonization of the motor fuel taxation (using increases in the fuel taxes) may decrease the fuel tourism in the Central European countries and contribute to a higher predictability of the tax effects on revenues and the environment.

ACKNOWLEDGEMENT

The research has been supported by Czech Science Foundation grant no. 14-22932S. The support is gratefully acknowledged.

NOTES

1. The national tax rates are, for illustration, recalculated to EUR via average exchange rates of the relevant semester. If changes in exchange rates outweigh the changes in the excise tax rate, the tax rates quoted in EUR can decrease despite an increase in excise tax rates. This is, for example, the case of petrol in Hungary in 2012.
2. Recalculated via average exchange rate of the first half of 2011.
3. In fact, for some countries, this scenario would imply a relatively large increase in motor fuel taxes. Although this ambitious scenario need not materialize soon, it is nevertheless useful to consider it in order to illustrate the estimated effects of international tax competition.

REFERENCES

Ajanovic, A., Dahl, C., and L. Schipper (2012), 'Modelling transport (energy) demand and policies – An introduction', *Energy Policy*, 41, iii–xiv.
Banfi, S., Filippini, M., and L.C. Hunt (2005), 'Fuel tourism in border regions: The case of Switzerland', *Energy Economics*, 27, 689–707.
Blobel, D., Gerdes, H., Pollitt, H., Barton, J., Drosdowski, T., Lutz, C., Wolter, M.I., and P. Ekins (2011), 'Implications of ETR in Europe for Household Distribution', in Ekins, P. and S. Speck (eds), *Environmental Tax Reform (ETR) – A Policy for Green Growth*, New York: Oxford University Press, 236–290.
Brandimarte, C. (2014), 'Macroeconomic effects of environmental tax subsidy reform: An evaluation for Italy', in Kreiser, L., Lee, S., Ueta, K., Milne, J.E., and H. Ashiabor (eds), *Environmental Taxation and Green Fiscal Reform. Theory and Impact*, Cheltenham, UK and Northampton, MA, USA: Edward Elgar Publishing, 227–242.
Conefrey, T., Fitz Gerald, J.D., Valeri, L.M., and R.S.J. Tol (2013), 'The impact of a carbon tax on economic growth and carbon dioxide emissions in Ireland', *Journal of Environmental Planning and Management*, 56 (7), 934–952.
Dahl, C. (2012), 'Measuring global gasoline and diesel price and income elasticities', *Energy Policy*, 41, 2–13.
European Commission (2003), Council Directive 2003/96/EC of October 27, 2003 restructuring the Community framework for the taxation of energy products and electricity.
European Commission (2006), Council Directive 2006/112/EC of November 28, 2006 on the common system of value added tax.
Greenberg, E. (2008), *Introduction to Bayesian Econometrics*, Cambridge: Cambridge University Press.
Kallbecken, S., Garcia, J.H., and K. Korneliussen (2013), 'Determinants of public support for transport taxes', *Transportation Research Part A*, 58, 67–78.

Leal, A., López-Laborda, J., and F. Rodrigo (2009), 'Prices, taxes and automotive fuel cross-border shopping', *Energy Economics*, 31, 225–237.

McNally, R.H.G. and N. Mabey (1999), *The Distributional Impacts Of Ecological Tax Reform*, UK: WWF.

Novysedlák, V. and L. Šrámková (2011), *Zníženie spotrebnej dane na naftu neprinieslo slubovaný výsledok*, Inštitút finančnej politiky, Bratislava.

OECD (2000), *Behavioral responses to environmentally-related taxes*, COM/ENV/ EPOC/ DAFFE/CFA(99)111/FINAL. Paris.

Píša, V. (2012), 'The demand for motor fuels in central European region and its impacts on indirect tax revenues', in *20th Annual Conference Proceedings Technical Computing*, Bratislava.

Pock, M. (2007), *Gasoline and Diesel Demand in Europe: New Insights*, Reihe Okonomie Series.

Poterba, J.M. (1991), 'Is the gasoline tax regressive?', *Tax and the Economy*, 5, 145–264.

Rietveld, P., Bruinsma, F.R., and D.J. van Vuuren (2001), 'Spatial graduation of fuel taxes; Consequences for cross-border and domestic fuelling', *Transportation Research Part A*, 35, 433–457.

Rietveld, P. and S. van Woudenberg (2005), 'Why fuel prices differ?', *Energy Economics*, 27, 79–92.

Sally-Ann, J. (2014), 'Environmental taxes – definitional analysis: behavioural change or revenue raising', in Kreiser, L., Lee, S., Ueta, K., Milne, J.E., and H. Ashiabor (eds), *Environmental Taxation and Green Fiscal Reform. Theory and Impact*, Cheltenham, UK and Northampton, MA, USA: Edward Elgar Publishing, 187–201.

Ševčík, M. and A. Rod (2010), *Spotřební daň z pohonných hmot v České republice, když více znamená méně*, Praha, Oeconomica.

Snowdon, C. (2013), *Aggressively regressive. The 'sin taxes' that make the poor poorer*, IEA Current Controversies Paper No. 47.

Ward, J., Smale, R., Krahé, M., and J. Cottrell (2013), 'Less pain, more gain: The potential of carbon pricing to reduce Europe's fiscal deficits', in Kreiser, L., Duff, D., Milne, J.E., and H. Ashiabor (eds), *Market Based Instruments. National Experiences in Environmental Sustainability*, Cheltenham, UK and Northampton, MA, USA: Edward Elgar Publishing, 3–22.

PART III

Analyzing policy choices

12. Climate change law and policymaking: the utility of the Delphi method

Evgeny Guglyuvatyy* and Natalie P. Stoianoff**

THE DELPHI METHOD

A balanced law or policymaking process requires an effective policy assessment approach.[1] However, processes of political decision-making are frequently not rationally based.[2] Many commentators agree that policymaking is strongly influenced by politics and that the choice of available policy options is limited by institutional dependencies and political factors.[3] In achieving their own goals, participants in the policymaking process may have different sets of preferences influencing policy evaluation. These different preferences will inhibit collaboration aimed at ascertaining the most suitable policy option overall.[4] Nonetheless, the principles of rational discussion and balanced problem solving can be employed in policymaking processes.[5]

The history of the evaluation of environmental policy is rather short and the concepts are fragmented, but the interest in evaluations in this field is growing rapidly in many countries.[6] The need for policy evaluation is not only emphasized within environmental research but also policymakers and administrators are more frequently articulating the necessity for environmental policy evaluations. Evaluation of climate change related policies is also recognized as an important stage of policymaking but there are not many examples of climate policy evaluations.[7]

A climate change policy evaluation procedure needs to consider many crucial factors. For example, economics tends to treat economic efficiency as a pivotal concept, while environmental science focuses on pollution, and none of the disciplines combine all concerns.[8] Accordingly, an efficient and effective policy might still be defective if, for instance, it dangerously compromises equity. In a similar vein, hypothetical equity of a policy would not rationalize its lack of efficiency and environmental effectiveness. For this reason, all of the corresponding factors need to be considered simultaneously at the stage of policy evaluation.

This chapter utilizes a policy evaluation study as an example of the utility of the Delphi method in climate change policymaking. In this study the Delphi method assisted in prioritizing the criteria used in the evaluation. The need for policy evaluation is not only emphasized within environmental research but also policymakers and administrators are more frequently articulating the necessity for environmental policy evaluations.[9] This chapter discusses the Delphi method as a useful instrument in environmental policy research. Based on the findings of the Delphi study conducted to facilitate climate change policies assessment in Australia the authors analyze the strengths and limitations of the method.

Defining the Delphi Method

In the 1950s, researchers working at the Rand Corporation developed the Delphi method.[10] This method was designed as a tool for forecasting future events using a series of questionnaires combined with controlled-opinion feedback.[11] The development of this tool has resulted in expanded and more diverse capabilities in academic research, and decision-making by industry and government.[12]

The Delphi method is frequently utilized for the examination of ideas as well as the creation of appropriate information for decision-making.[13] Equipped to handle complex problems or tasks systematically, this method provides a process for collecting knowledge from an identified group of experts by means of a series of questionnaires combined with controlled opinion feedback.[14] These questionnaires facilitate accumulation of personal responses to the problems posed and allow the experts the flexibility to either confirm or vary their responses. The characteristics of the Delphi method are anonymity, controlled feedback, and statistical response,[15] characterized as a 'relatively strongly structured group communication process' where the group is comprised of experts dealing with often incomplete available information.[16] The other important characteristic of the Delphi method is its ability to transfer the implicit and complex knowledge to a simpler plan or proposal.[17] That makes the Delphi method useful for policymaking processes involving a variety of stakeholders.[18]

Some Examples of Use of the Method

The Delphi method has been used in different research contexts. Examples include, analyzing the features of a good offender treatment programme in criminology studies;[19] identifying key words essential for analyzing the international discourse on intellectual property law;[20] and country risk assessment when dealing with export letter of credit transactions.[21]

There are various studies where the Delphi method has been utilized for policy-related issues,[22] such as in the field of taxation policy where Evans has successfully utilized this method.[23] In the environmental policy context, the Delphi method has been applied to natural resource issues such as forest biodiversity, sustainability, heritage tourism, environmental disputes, forecasting, national park selection and aquatic habitat selection.[24] There are also some examples of the Delphi method being applied to climate change policy issues. One of the early examples is the Finnish study by Wilenius and Tirkkonen[25] or the Dutch National Research Programme.[26] The more recent application of the Delphi method in this context is the US Government Accountability Office (GAO) study conducted to identify experts' opinions concerning climate change economic policy options.[27] Another example is a Malaysian study based on the research of Guglyuvatyy and of Mariola.[28] This study was conducted with a group of Malaysian experts and professionals from various fields to identify operative strategies for promoting effective environmental policy in Malaysia.[29]

The Australian example that is discussed in the next section comprises a Delphi study conducted to verify the evaluation criteria for Australian climate change policy and to assess the relative importance of those criteria.[30]

THE AUSTRALIAN CLIMATE CHANGE POLICY CONTEXT

Climate Change Law Making in Australia

With the exception of the current government, both sides of politics in Australia have been committed to establishing an emissions trading scheme (ETS) designed to mitigate climate change.[31] For example, in December 2006, the then Howard government announced that Australia would introduce a domestic ETS by 2012.[32] The succeeding Rudd government announced an Australian Carbon Pollution Reduction Scheme (ACPRS) in 2008 in response to the findings of the Garnaut Report.[33] However, the ACPRS legislation was twice defeated in the Australian Parliament in 2009. The next Australian government, led by Australia's first female Prime Minister, Julia Gillard, established the Multi-Party Climate Change Committee (the Committee)[34] consisting of members of the federal government and senators which proposed a temporary carbon pricing scheme,[35] to be followed by an ETS and incorporating a variety of other complementary measures. This Clean Energy Future scheme, as it was called, came into operation from 1 July 2012. The following briefly considers the process of the Committee in developing this scheme.

The primary task of the Committee was to design a climate change policy framework and specifically to establish a carbon price mechanism. To begin with the Committee issued eleven policy principles that were intended to provide 'a consistent basis for the deliberations on a carbon price'.[36] The principles were as follows:

- Environmental effectiveness
- Economic efficiency
- Budget neutrality
- Competitiveness of Australian industries
- Energy security
- Investment certainty
- Fairness
- Flexibility
- Administrative simplicity
- Clear accountabilities, and
- Supports Australia's international objectives and obligations.[37]

The Committee specified that these 11 principles would facilitate the development of the carbon pricing mechanism.[38]

The implemented carbon price scheme is similar in some respects to the design of the earlier proposed ACPRS.[39] Nevertheless, the Committee's carbon pricing mechanism provided some substantial improvements. For example, a generous industry compensation package was implemented as a temporary measure based on historic emissions levels for the affected industries and the assistance package for households was designed to compensate low and medium income earners rather than high income earners.[40] Additionally, various supporting measures designed to boost energy efficiency and green innovation provided a significant improvement. Meanwhile, the legislation drafted to implement the scheme did not reflect some of the Committee's criteria adequately.[41]

The government announced that the legislation 'is the most cost-effective and economically responsible way of reducing Australia's carbon pollution',[42] indicating that the costs-effectiveness of GHG emissions reduction was favoured over other important criteria. Furthermore, the entire process of the policy design by the Committee is unclear. For instance, there was no information revealed concerning major features of policymaking such as what methods have been employed to prioritize criteria and how policy options were assessed if at all. In addition, the policy was modified in 2012 and once again there was no clarification why the policy had been changed.[43]

Applying the Delphi Method – A Case Study

The Delphi method was used by Guglyuvatyy as one part of a broader research project conducted in 2010.[44] The key question for this study focusses on what would be an optimal policy for climate change mitigation in Australia a carbon tax or an emissions trading scheme. The study assessed carbon tax and emissions trading policy options on the basis of multiple climate change policy criteria and included various research methods. The study demonstrates how the Delphi method can contribute to the policymaking process, in this instance being utilized to assess a set of evaluation criteria.

The Delphi method was designed to obtain experts' opinions concerning the list of criteria relevant to evaluating the two carbon pricing instruments being analyzed and weigh the relative importance of those criteria.[45] The multidisciplinary nature of climate change lends itself to methods, such as Delphi, which bridge the gap between research and practice. It is generally acknowledged that to select an optimal instrument the policies should be first evaluated in accordance with a set of specific criteria.[46] Guglyuvatyy's study selected evaluation criteria on the basis of existing research assessing climate change policies. Moreover, the study tested identified criteria by means of the Delphi method. Thus, to update and verify the list of the criteria, Australian experts were involved in the Delphi study to ensure an Australian perspective was maintained. The criteria presented in Table 12.1 reflect the general principles of rational climate change policy.

The Delphi study was conducted in two rounds targeting a group of experts, who were selected to represent diverse perspectives between the experts from various disciplines related to climate change discourse. In particular, academics, scientists, climate economists and environmental policy consultants were selected for this study. The questionnaire devised for the Delphi study was designed to minimize obscurities. Closed-ended questions and the five points Likert scale[47] were utilized for the first part of the questionnaire and were followed by open-ended questions for the second part.[48] This provided the Delphi study with required quantitative information on criteria weights and qualitative data necessary for in-depth analysis.

Eleven experts participated in the study. They represented internationally recognized Australian specialists bringing a high level of expertise to the study. In the first round, the experts were asked to think of the potential criteria for the climate change policies and then to verify and update

*Table 12.1   Preliminary list of the criteria for climate change policy
            evaluation*

Selected criteria

---

1. Environmental effectiveness
2. Cost-effectiveness
3. Correct price signal
4. Competitiveness issues
5. Administrative costs
6. Compliance costs
7. Predictability/regulatory certainty
8. Effect on technology development
9. Minimize rent-seeking
10. International harmonization
11. Flexibility of the policy
12. Political acceptability
13. Transparency
14. Distribution of benefits and costs across income groups
15. Public acceptability
16. Distribution of benefits and costs across generations

Source: Evgeny Guglyuvatyy, Assessing carbon tax and emissions trading as policy
options for climate change mitigation in Australia. PhD Thesis, The University of New
South Wales, 2011.

the proposed 16 criteria required for policy evaluation in the Australian context. The second question sought participants' views on the importance of those criteria. The experts were asked to weigh each criteria based on a standard rating scale 1–5, where 1 indicating not at all important or considered least necessary criteria and 5 indicating extremely important, and/or most critical criteria. The panel members were also asked to add any other relevant criteria.

In the second round the experts were provided with the opportunity to revise their previous responses. This is a fundamental aspect of the Delphi process. There was a substantial level of agreement among the experts' responses concerning the necessity of evaluation criteria proposed by the Guglyuvatyy study. The average weightings mostly remained the same, thus, a reasonable level of stability had been reached regarding the importance of the criteria.

Additional criteria identified by the experts were listed together and presented for consideration by all of the participants in the second-round questionnaire with the aim of obtaining further weightings and/or comments from the experts. The Delphi study resulted in identification of

Table 12.2   Established evaluation criteria

Criteria	Average weight	Importance value in per cent
Environmental effectiveness	4.63	92.6
Transparency	4.27	85.4
Minimize rent-seeking	4.09	81.8
Correct price signal	4.00	80
Flexibility of the policy	3.90	78
Minimize GHG emissions leakage	3.81	76.2
Public acceptability	3.54	70.8
Political acceptability/feasibility	3.45	69
Predictability/regulatory certainty	3.45	69
Polluter pays principle	3.45	69
Effect on technology development	3.36	67.2
Cost-effectiveness	3.27	65.4
Distribution of benefits and costs across generations	3.27	65.4
Compliance costs	3.09	61.8
Distribution of benefits and costs across income groups	3.00	60
Competitiveness issues	2.45	49
Administrative costs	2.45	49
International harmonization	2.36	47.2

Source: Evgeny Guglyuvatyy, Assessing carbon tax and emissions trading as policy options for climate change mitigation in Australia. PhD Thesis The University of New South Wales, 2011.

two additional imperative criteria namely, to 'minimise GHG emissions leakage' and the 'polluter pays principle' which are included in the list of criteria of this study. The final list of criteria and the importance values of those criteria expressed as a percentage are presented in Table 12.2.

The results of the Delphi method, applied in the Guglyuvatyy study, demonstrate that the main point of agreement was that the criteria identified by this study are valid and essential for climate change policy evaluation in the Australian context. The experts agreed that environmental effectiveness is a principal criterion confirming that GHG reduction is the primary aim for a climate change policy. Overall, the Delphi approach employed by Guglyuvatyy enabled the obtaining of reliable and methodically justified weightings for climate change evaluation criteria.

Current Australian Developments

The results of the study discussed in the previous section deliver the set of criteria which are comparable with the criteria designated by the Multi-Party Climate Change Committee with some important differences. Moreover, the discussed Delphi study confirmed the validity of the proposed criteria and comparative importance of those criteria for climate change policy evaluation. As mentioned in the above section, the Delphi experts agreed that the three principal criteria are non-economic signifying the equity characteristics of a climate change policy. Importantly, the 'transparency' and 'minimising rent-seeking' criteria do not even appear in the list of principles considered by the Multi-Party Climate Change Committee. Conversely, the competitiveness issues, administrative costs and international harmonization criteria while appearing in the 11 principles espoused by the Committee, were assessed as least important in the Guglyuvatyy Delphi study.

The criteria prioritized by the Committee, and as a result the introduced policy, appear to reflect political negotiation rather than an effective and transparent process of policymaking. The result of such a policymaking process is a compromised policy and non-transparent political trade-off. Thus, there is no surprise that the introduced policy has been the subject of significant criticism.

However, the carbon pricing legislation discussed above has been recently repealed by the present Australian government. Instead of the carbon pricing mechanism the Australian government has introduced the Direct Action Plan.[49] Unfortunately, the government did not provide details concerning the development of the Direct Action Plan. It is not clear what the basis for the introduced policy is. Successive Australian governments attempting to introduce climate change related policies were taking into consideration policy developments and proposals of previous governments. However, the policy introduced by the present Abbott government is strikingly different to carbon pricing and/or emissions trading mechanisms favoured by former Australian governments. In the same vein the government neither disclosed what criteria has been used to develop the Direct Action Plan, if any, nor did it explained what criteria or principles were prioritized to establish the proposed legislation.

Nonetheless, the government states that the Direct Action Plan is introduced to 'efficiently and effectively source low cost emissions reductions.'[50] The Direct Action Plan includes as a centerpiece the Emissions Reduction Fund (ERF) which is supposed to provide incentives for GHG reduction activities across the entire Australian economy.[51] Under the ERF the government will pay for projects that will reduce CO_2 emissions at minimal cost.[52] Funding from the ERF will be allocated through reverse auctions.[53] A range of possible projects for CO_2 reduction include: energy efficiency, cleaning up power stations, reforestation and revegetation and/or improvement of soil carbon.[54]

The important feature of the Direct Action Plan is its voluntary nature. Numerous commentators argue that a voluntary carbon mechanism does not provide incentive for businesses to participate and compete for participation in ERF.[55] The Australia Senate inquiry on the Direct Action Plan provides the following comment: 'The committee is persuaded that the government's Direct Action Plan and the proposed Emissions Reduction Fund are fundamentally flawed. They ignore the well-established principle of "polluter pays", and instead propose that the Australian taxpayer should effectively subsidize big polluters.'[56] Overall, the Direct Action Plan has been significantly criticized and it is labelled as a step backwards for Australian climate change policy.[57]

The current Australian government has sought to abolish the Climate Change Authority[58] which was established by the previous government to provide an independent assessment and advice on carbon policy. Should the Authority be abolished, there will be no independent assessment of policy and targets and no requirement for the government to respond to independent review, which would further reduce transparency and accountability of carbon policymaking. In this light, it is difficult to consider the climate change law-making process in Australia as adequate and comprehensive. Thus, the present government's policymaking practice raises even more questions and as one may note the climate change policymaking process in Australia is deteriorating rather than developing.

CRITICALLY EVALUATING THE DELPHI METHOD

The Delphi method has been criticized on the basis of the soundness, reliability and credibility of its application. Some commentators argue that the Delphi method is unscientific, and therefore inherently ambiguous.[59] Nonetheless, some other methods that aimed at consensus such as focus groups and nominal groups also run the same risk. Some other issues which need to be addressed before conducting a Delphi study may include potential administrative complexity and low response rate.[60]

In contrast, there have been numerous studies supporting the utility of the Delphi method. Basu and Schroeder reported that the Delphi studies were 10–15 per cent more accurate than quantitative methods of forecast.[61] Generally, the Delphi method is especially suitable when its results serve as inputs for further investigation.[62] The potential of the Delphi to acknowledge the contribution of each participant and the guaranteed anonymity are some of the major advantages of the method. Furthermore, the experts responses to questions is expected to encourage ideas that are free of influences of others and accordingly more likely to be accurate.[63] The 'collective human intelligence capability' attributable to groups of experts can be used by adopting the Delphi method.[64]

The Delphi study discussed earlier demonstrated the effectiveness of the method as an instrument seeking to clarify ill-defined topics. The Delphi method is a reliable tool providing participants with opportunities to revise their responses through multiple rounds based on feedback received from other members of a panel. The Delphi method with a set of pre-selected options proved to be an effective approach as demonstrated by the Guglyuvatyy study.

The Delphi method may help to improve real-world policymaking. For example, the criteria which are assessed and validated by the multidisciplinary climate change experts in the Guglyuvatyy study could have provided justified and solid determinants that promote joint environmental, economic and equity considerations of a policy. Consideration of these criteria and their importance in policy appraisal would have ensured adequacy of the policy development and selection and provide an essential guide for the law makers. Thus, the application of the Delphi method can provide a foundation for the balanced policymaking model that can be utilized in various fields of environmental policymaking and research.

This chapter advocates a practical method facilitating transparent and comprehensive policymaking procedures. This methodological approach is coherent and simple in that it can be utilized by a single researcher or policymaker/s when considering such a multidimensional policy as climate change. The Delphi method advances the discussion by bringing forward new aspects, ideas and generalizations, enforcing learning processes that can contribute to improving the choices and implementation of policy instruments.

CONCLUSION

The discussion in this chapter illustrates how the Delphi method has and can be applied to climate change policymaking. The examples discussed, including the Delphi study in the Australian Climate Change context, validate both the use of this method in climate policy research and its appropriateness for policymaking. This has strengthened the utility of the technique in theoretical and reform-oriented research, particularly as a method of identifying and ranking key evaluative criteria to be applied in a policy analysis whether of an existing regime or to assist with the choice of a regime from a variety of policy options.

There are criticisms of the Delphi method but the greatest criticism narrates to the way the method is carried out, in particular, how the experts are chosen. It relies upon the skill of the researcher in defining who is an expert in the field being investigated. Conversely, the proponents of the technique hail the flexibility of the Delphi method, its ability to obtain 'equal and balanced participation' with reduced peer-pressure thereby providing for consensus based conclusions, and the ability of the method to clarify complex and ambiguous issues and achieve valid judgements. Whether the Delphi method is utilized in empirical or theoretical research or in policymaking, this chapter has demonstrated the strength of the technique in providing transparent and justified results, which in turn reinforces the utility of the method as a research and/or policymaking tool.

NOTES

*   Evgeny Guglyuvatyy is a Lecturer in the School of Law and Justice at the Southern Cross University.
**   Natalie Stoianoff is a Professor in the Faculty of Law at the University of Technology, Sydney, and the Director of the Intellectual Property Program.
1.   Mickwitz, P. (2006), *Environmental Policy Evaluation: Concepts and Practice*, Tampere, Commentationes Scientiarum Socialium.
2.   Kingdon, J.D. (1995), *Agendas, Alternatives and Public Policy*, New York: HarperCollins; Zahariadis, N. (2003), *Ambiguity and Choice in Public Policy. Political Decision Making in Modern Democracies*, Washington DC: Georgetown University Press.
3.   Becker, G. (1983), 'A Theory of Competition among Pressure Groups for Political Influence', *Quarterly Journal of Economics*, 98, 371–400.
4.   Bernauer, T. and L. Caduff (2004), 'In Whose Interest? Pressure Group Politics, Economic Competition and Environmental Regulation', *Journal of Public Policy*, 24, 99–126, 100.
5.   Sanderson, Ian (2002), 'Evaluation, Policy-learning and Evidence Based Policy Making', *Public Administration*, 80, 1–22, 19.
6.   Hilden, M., J. Lepola, P. Mickwitz, A. Mulders, M. Palosaari, J. Similä, S. Sjöblom and E. Vedung, *Evaluation of Environmental Policy Instruments – a Case Study of the Finnish Pulp & Paper and Chemical Industries*. Monographs of the Boreal Environment Research. Helsinki; Mickwitz above n. 1.
7.   Some examples of climate change related policy evaluations are discussed in the next subsection.
8.   Adger, W.N. (2002), 'Inequality, Environment, and Planning', *Environment and Planning*, 34, 1716–1719.
9.   For example, a policy evaluation requirement is formulated in the 6th Environmental Action Program for the European Union which was adopted in June 2002. Article 10, paragraph C of this document states: '[The objectives shall be pursued by] improvement of the process of policy making through: 1) ex-ante evaluations of the possible impacts, in particular the environmental impacts, of new policies including the alternative of no action and the proposal for legislation and publication of the results; 2) ex-post evaluation of the effectiveness of existing measures in meeting their environmental objectives'.

10. Dalkey, N.C. and O. Helmer (1963), 'An Experimental Application of the Delphi Method to the Use of Experts', *Journal of the Institute of Management Sciences, in: Management Science*, 9, 458–467.

11. It should be noted though, that Dalkey and Helmer were not satisfied with the term Delphi, arguing that the term implied 'something oracular', something signifying a little of the occult rather than a method designed to identify the best possible solutions (Dalkey, N.C. 1968, cited in H. Gunaydin, 'The Delphi Method, Optimization Group' 2006, http://www.iyte.edu.tr/~muratgunaydin/delphi.htm at 9 April 2013).

12. Turoff, M. and H.A. Linstone, 'The Delphi Method: Techniques and Applications', http://is.njit.edu/pubs/delphibook/ at 28 April 2013.

13. Gunaydin, H. (2006), 'The Delphi Method, Optimization Group' http://www.iyte.edu.tr/~muratgunaydin/delphi.htm at June 2013.

14. Ziglio, E. (1996), 'The Delphi Method and Its Contribution to Decision-Making', in Adler, M. and E Ziglio (eds), *Gazing into the Oracle: The Delphi Method and its Application to Social Policy and Public Health*, London: Jessica Kingsley Publishers.

15. Turoff and Linstone, above n. 12.

16. Hader, M. and S. Häder (1995), 'Delphi und Kognitionspsychologie: Ein Zugang zur theoretischen Fundierung der Delphi-Methode', in *ZUMA-Nachrichten*, 37, 12.

17. Gupta, U.G. and R.E. Clarke (1996), 'Theory and Applications of the Delphi Technique: A bibliography (1975–1994)', *Technological Forecasting and Social Change*, 53, 185–211.

18. Eto, H. (2003), 'The Suitability of Technology Forecasting/Foresight Methods for Decision Systems and Strategy. A Japanese View', *Technological Forecasting and Social Change*, 70, 231–249.

19. McCulloch Anna and Mary McMurran (2007), 'The Features of a Good Offender Treatment Programme Manual: A Delphi Survey of Experts', *Psychology, Crime and Law*, 13 (3), 265–274.

20. Ghafele, Roya (2010), 'Of War and Peace: Analysing the International Discourse on Intellectual Property Law', *Intellectual Property Quarterly*, 3, 237–255.

21. Bergami, Roberto (2010), 'A Risk Management Approach for Export Letter of Credit Transactions', *Vindobona Journal of International Commercial Law and Arbitration*, 14, 165.

22. DeLoe, R.C. (1995), 'Exploring Complex Policy Questions Using the Policy Delphi' *Applied Geography*, 15, 53–68; Evans, Chris (2007), 'Unravelling the Mysteries of the Oracle: Using the Delphi Methodology to Inform the Personal Tax Reform Debate in Australia', *eJournal of Tax Research*, 5, 105–135.

23. Evans, above n. 22.

24. Kangas, J.J., M. Alho, O. Kolehmainen and A. Mononen (1998), 'Analysing Consistency of Experts' Judgments – Case of Assessing Forest Biodiversity', *Forest Science*, 44, 610–617; Mendoza G.A. and R. Prabhu (2000), 'Development of a Methodology for Selecting Criteria and Indicators of Sustainable Forest Management: A Case Study of Participatory Assessment', *Environmental Management*, 26, 659–673; Garrod, B. and A. Fyall (2000), 'Managing Heritage Tourism', *Annals of Tourism Research*, 27, 682–708; Miller, A. and W. Cuff (1986), 'The Delphi Approach to the Mediation of Environmental Disputes', *Environmental Management*, 19, 321–330; Ying, L.G. and H. Kung (2000), 'Forecasting up to Year 2000 on Shanghai's Environmental Quality', *Environmental Monitoring and Assessment*, 63, 297–312; Kuo, N.W. and Y.H. Yu (1999), 'Policy and Practice: An Evaluation System for National Park Selection in Taiwan', *Journal of Environmental Planning and Management*, 42, 735–745; Bush, W.D. and S.J. Lary (1996), 'Assessment of Habitat Impairments Impacting the Aquatic Resources of Lake Ontario', *Canadian Journal of Fisheries and Aquatic Life*, 53, 113–120.

25. Wilenius, M. and J. Tirkkonen (1997), 'Climate in the Making. Using Delphi for Finnish Climate Policy', *Futures*, 29 (9), 845–862.

26. Klabbers, J., P. Vellinga, R. Swart, A. Van Ulden and R. Jansson (1996), 'Climate

Change and Climate Policy: Improving Science/Policy Interface', *Mitigation and Adaptation Strategies for Global Change*, 1 (1), 73–93.

27. The group of experts includes respected professionals in the field of climate change economics. GAO. '*Expert Opinion on the Economics of Policy Options to Address Climate Change*'. United States Government Accountability Office. Washington DC 2008.

28. Guglyuvatyy, Evgeny (2011), *Assessing Carbon Tax and Emissions Trading as Policy Options for Climate Change Mitigation in Australia*. PhD Thesis, The University of New South Wales, unsworks.unsw.edu.au/fapi/datastream/unsworks:9300/SOURCE02; Mariola, M.J. (2009), 'Are Markets the Solution to Water Pollution? A Sociological Investigation of Water Quality Trading', The Ohio State University, http://etd.ohiolink.edu/view.cgi?acc_num=osu1250015222 at 5 May 2013.

29. Hong, L.C., D. Lakshmayya and T.L. Cheng (2012), 'Subsidies: Boon or Bane in Promoting Proper Implementation of Good Environmental Public Policy', Research Paper. http://library.wou.edu.my/vertical/vf2012-10.pdf at 5 May 2013.

30. Guglyuvatyy, above n. 28.

31. Wilder, M. and L. Fitz-Gerald (2009), 'Review of Policy and Regulatory Emissions Trading Frameworks in Australia', *Australian Resources and Energy Law Journal*, 27, 1–22.

32. Ibid. Note, however, that in 2005, the Australian State and Territories issued a discussion paper concerning a national emissions trading scheme which would cover the power generation sector.

33. Garnaut, Ross (2008), *The Garnaut Climate Change Review, Final Report*, Cambridge: Cambridge University Press.

34. Multi-Party Climate Change Committee, http://www.climatechange.gov.au/government/initiatives/mpccc.aspx at May 2013.

35. A carbon pricing scheme is often called a 'tax' because during the fixed price period, the liable parties are obliged to purchase fixed price carbon units which is similar to paying tax. However, they cannot trade the units on the market, as under an emissions trading scheme.

36. Multi-Party Climate Change Committee, http://www.climatechange.gov.au/~/media/Files/minister/combet/2011/media/february/mr20110224.pdf at May 2013.

37. It is important to note that the principles are not stated in any order of priority. See Multi-Party Climate Change Committee, http://www.climatechange.gov.au/~/media/Files/minister/combet/2011/media/february/mr20110224.pdf at May 2013.

38. Multi-Party Climate Change Committee, above n. 36.

39. For details see: ACPRS, above n. 33.

40. Clean Energy Future, http://www.cleanenergyfuture.gov.au/wp-content/uploads/2011/06/09-FS-Household-Assistance-Tax-Reform-110708-1234hrs.pdf at December 2014.

41. See for example, Guglyuvatyy, Evgeny (2012), 'Australia's Carbon Policy – a Retreat from Core Principles?' *eJournal of Tax Research*, 10 (3), 552–572.

42. Clean Energy Agreement, http://www.climatechange.gov.au/government/initiatives/mpccc/resources/clean-energy-agreement.aspx at December 2014.

43. On 28 August 2012, the Minister for Climate Change and Energy Efficiency announced that the price floor would no longer be implemented as part of a package agreed with the European Commission to link the European Union Emissions Trading System with Australia's emissions trading scheme. See, Price floor for Australia's carbon pricing mechanism http://www.climatechange.gov.au/government/submissions/closed-consultations/price-floor-carbon-pricing.aspx at December 2014.

44. Guglyuvatyy, Evgeny (2010), 'Identifying Criteria for Climate Change Policy Evaluation in Australia', *Macquarie Journal of Business Law*, 7, 98–130.

45. The weights may be obtained directly from the decision-maker, stakeholders or may be developed by applying appropriate methods. Nonetheless, it is very difficult to obtain objective quantitative weights, as knowledge and the confidence are typically rare. Criteria weighting is sensitive to the expressed preferences of decision-makers or

stakeholders which adds an additional subjectivity to the outcome. Considering this it is necessary to limit the degree of subjectivity in weighting process for this purpose some policy evaluation procedures involve experts. Employing experts instead of decision-makers or stakeholders is expected to bring an element of unprejudiced and objective assessment of the required information. Gough, C. and S. Shackley (2006), 'Towards a Multi-criteria Methodology for Assessment of Geological Carbon Storage Options', *Climatic Change*, 74, 141–174.

46. See for example, Smith, S. and H.B. Vos (1997), *Evaluating Economic Instruments for Environmental Policy*, Paris: OECD, Business and Economics; Dovers, S. (2005), *Environment and Sustainability Policy: Creation, Implementation, Evaluation*, Sydney: The Federation Press; Mickwitz, above n. 1.
47. Carifio, J. and J.P. Rocco (2007), 'Ten Common Misunderstandings, Misconceptions, Persistent Myths and Urban Legends about Likert Scales and Likert Response Formats and their Antidotes', *Journal of Social Sciences*, 3 (3), 106–116.
48. This scale of measurement lists data in rank order but without fixed differences among the entries. The ordinal scale is utilized to weigh the importance of criteria, with values from 1 to 5, where 1 = not at all important; 2 = somewhat important; 3 = moderately important; 4 = quite important; and 5 = extremely important.
49. Australian Government Department of the Environment http://www.environment.gov.au/clean-air at December 2014.
50. Australian Government Department of Environment, http://climatechange.gov.au/reducing-carbon/news-article/repeal-carbon-tax-and-introduction-direct-action-plan at December 2014.
51. Above n. 49.
52. Above n. 49.
53. Above n. 49.
54. Above n. 49.
55. See for example, Australian Government Department of Environment, Emissions Reduction Fund, public submission of Professor David Karoly, Professor Ross Garnaut, WWF-Australia and others, http://www.environment.gov.au/climate-change/emissions-reduction-fund/green-paper at December 2014.
56. The Australian Senate, Environment and Communications References Committee (2014), 'Direct Action: Paying polluters to halt global warming?', 98.
57. Ibid.
58. Climate Change Authority (Abolition) Bill 2013 [No. 2].
59. Sackman, H. (1975), *Delphi Critique: Expert Opinion, Forecasting, and Group Process*, Lexington, MA: Lexington Books.
60. Miller and Cuff, above n. 24.
61. Basu, S. and R.G. Schroeder (1977), 'Incorporating Judgments in Sales Forecasts: Application of the Delphi Method at American Hoist and Derrick', *Interfaces*, 7, 18–27.
62. Gatewood, R.D. and E.J. Gatewood (1983), 'The Use of Expert Data in Human Resource Planning: Guidelines from Strategic Forecasting', *Human Resource Planning*, 5 (1), 83–94.
63. Goodman, C.M. (1987), 'The Delphi Technique: A Critique', *Journal of Advanced Nursing*, 12, 729–734; Snyder-Halpern, R. (2002), 'Indicators of Organizational Readiness for Clinical Information Technology/Systems Innovation: A Delphi Study', *International Journal of Medical Informatics*, 63, 179–204.
64. Linstone, H.A. and M. Turoff (1975), *The Delphi Method Techniques and Applications*, Reading: Addison-Wesley.

13. Motivating environmental tax reform through coalitions of like-minded countries

Sirini Withana and Patrick ten Brink[1]

INTRODUCTION

There is growing use of environmental taxes in Europe and a new momentum behind the environmental tax reform (ETR) agenda. What began as an exercise among a small vanguard of European countries twenty five years ago has gradually expanded to encompass a wider set of countries across the globe. Several plans are underway to introduce new environmental taxes or amend existing systems, either as part of a broader package of fiscal reform or as individual proposals. Some recent initiatives have been in response to fiscal necessities, while others seek to support wider environmental, economic and social objectives. ETR has attracted increasing attention at EU level, for example appearing in policy discussions on climate change; and globally, for example in discussions on reforming incentives harmful to biodiversity (Oosterhuis and ten Brink, 2014).

Environmental taxes are considered a useful and important part of the policy mix. When carefully designed, such instruments can provide incentives to encourage dynamic innovation, change the business case for investment, and inform consumer choice, thus helping to deliver economic (for example, revenue, innovation, employment), social (for example, health, income distribution, affordability) and environmental (for example, resource efficiency, energy security, pollution mitigation) benefits. Impacts depend on several factors including design (such as point of application, breadth of coverage), level (such as rate applied, revisions over time), implementation (such as exemptions granted, associated conditionalities, evolution over time), and use of revenues. Furthermore, impacts need to be seen in the context of the wider policy mix and external factors which drive change (Withana et al., 2013).

Despite efforts to date, the use and application of environmental taxes remains limited. For example, among EU Member States revenues from environmental taxes in 2012 were 2.4 per cent of GDP and 6.1 per cent of total tax revenues, with significant diversity in national experiences (Eurostat, 2014). Moreover, ETR has only led to relatively marginal changes to the tax system and incentives in the economy (with some exceptions – Withana, 2015). There remains scope for the wider application and more effective use of such instruments. For example, a recent study estimated that shifting taxes from labour to pollution in 14 EU Member States could generate up to EUR 111 billion of additional revenue in 2025 (Eunomia, Aarhus University and IEEP, 2015). Despite this potential, progress is often held back by various obstacles including concerns over competitiveness and distribution impacts, public resistance and the political costs of action.

In 2014 the Ministry of Infrastructure and the Environment of the Netherlands (IenM), contracted the Institute for European Environmental Policy (IEEP) to carry out a scoping study to explore where further greening taxation could be appropriate and how to drive this agenda. This chapter presents the final results of the study, in particular the proposal to establish voluntary 'coalitions of like-minded countries'. This chapter will briefly set out different approaches to ETR from the historically favoured unilateral action by countries to potential options for the future which entail increasing degrees of cooperation and harmonization between countries. It goes on to examine the approach of progressing ETR through 'coalitions of like-minded countries', setting out the benefits of cooperation and discussing six potential themes around which such cooperation can be structured. It concludes with an outlook on the future and how to take this agenda forward.

APPROACHES TO ETR IN THE FUTURE

Historically (with due exceptions), countries have progressed the ETR agenda unilaterally according to their own needs, opportunities and political expediencies. In some cases, actions have been inspired by efforts in other countries while sometimes they have been held back or limited by a lack of action in others. For example, in the Netherlands (which has successfully introduced a number of environmental taxes and charges over the last two decades) recent ETR efforts have encountered problems in light of competitiveness concerns. This was the case with the introduction of an air passenger duty in July 2008 which was subsequently phased out after a year due to concerns about passengers diverting to airports in neighbouring Germany and Belgium. Shortly after the Dutch tax was abolished, an air passenger duty was introduced in Germany (from January 2011) and in Austria (from April 2011). More recently, fuel tax increases in the Netherlands have led to cases of fuel tourism, particularly in border areas, and have sparked much political and media attention (Withana et al., 2014).

Such examples highlight some of the limitations to individual action on ETR and how in certain cases some form of cooperation between countries could be helpful. In certain cases progress on ETR has been driven by EU legislation, either explicitly (for example, Energy Tax Directive) or implicitly (for example, cost recovery requirements under the Water Framework Directive); and encouraged through soft processes such as the European Semester. This mix of approaches has led to a significant diversity in practices between countries, which to some extent may be inevitable and appropriate given different national circumstances. However this also has implications for the extent to which there is harmonization and a level playing field in the EU internal market (see Figure 13.1) and could lead to competiveness problems or less effective results in certain areas.

As we look to the future, different approaches to ETR in Europe can be considered (see Figure 13.1). These approaches imply different degrees of cooperation and harmonization, ranging from the currently prevailing unilateral approaches to those which entail some degree of informal cooperation between countries such as 'coalitions of like-minded countries' and benchmarking progress through the open method of coordination (OMC), to a more formal and structured approach of enhanced cooperation and finally to legal approaches at EU level. This chapter focuses on the approach of multi-country cooperation through 'coalitions of like-minded countries'. For a detailed discussion on OMC and enhanced cooperation approaches to ETR see Bassi et al. (2009).

MOTIVATING PROGRESS ON ETR THROUGH COALITIONS OF LIKE-MINDED COUNTRIES

Given that the fiscal unanimity rule often prevents meaningful action on ETR in the EU (Bassi et al., 2010), and that engaging in the formal process of 'enhanced cooperation'[2] on environmental taxes represents a major political challenge, some form of 'enhanced coordination' or 'coalition of like-minded countries' could usefully be explored. Such coalitions would bring together groups of countries (and actors) with similar interests in a particular area to coordinate efforts on ETR. This cooperation would be voluntary and in some cases could lead to more harmonized or synchronized approaches (for example, an agreed minimum level or threshold), while in others it could lead to better information sharing.

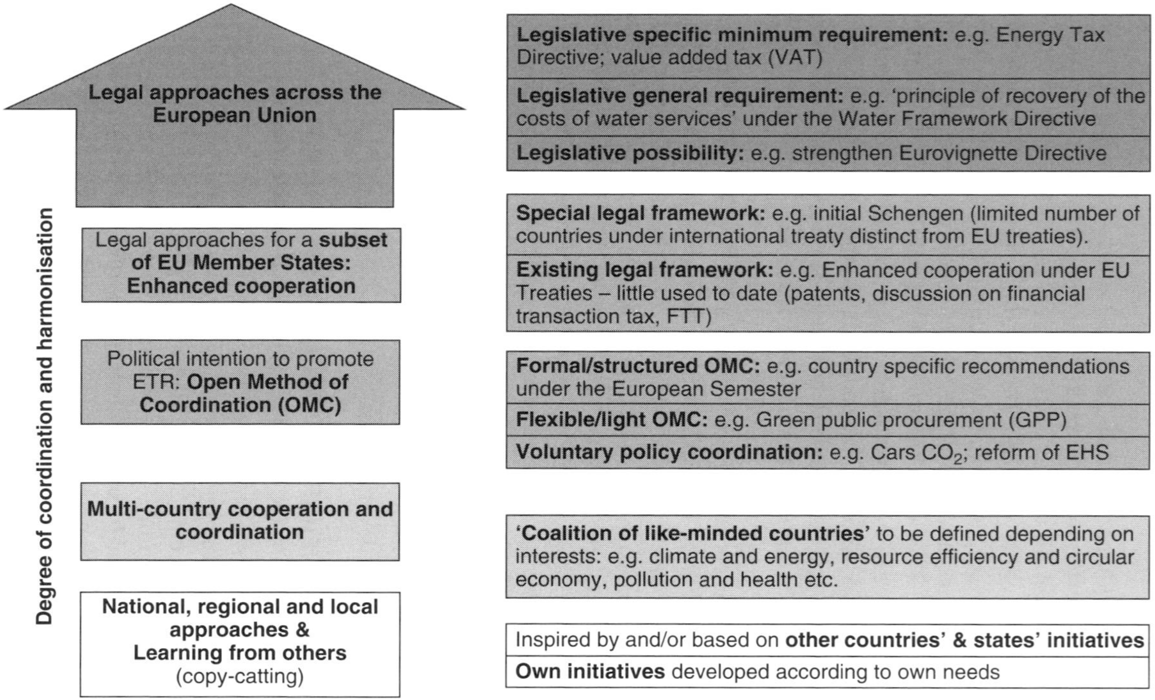

Legislative specific minimum requirement: e.g. Energy Tax Directive; value added tax (VAT)

Legislative general requirement: e.g. 'principle of recovery of the costs of water services' under the Water Framework Directive

Legislative possibility: e.g. strengthen Eurovignette Directive

Special legal framework: e.g. initial Schengen (limited number of countries under international treaty distinct from EU treaties).

Existing legal framework: e.g. Enhanced cooperation under EU Treaties – little used to date (patents, discussion on financial transaction tax, FTT)

Formal/structured OMC: e.g. country specific recommendations under the European Semester

Flexible/light OMC: e.g. Green public procurement (GPP)

Voluntary policy coordination: e.g. Cars CO_2; reform of EHS

'Coalition of like-minded countries' to be defined depending on interests: e.g. climate and energy, resource efficiency and circular economy, pollution and health etc.

Inspired by and/or based on other countries' & states' initiatives

Own initiatives developed according to own needs

Legal approaches across the European Union

Legal approaches for a subset of EU Member States: Enhanced cooperation

Political intention to promote ETR: Open Method of Coordination (OMC)

Multi-country cooperation and coordination

National, regional and local approaches & Learning from others (copy-catting)

Degree of coordination and harmonisation

Source: Adapted from Bassi et al., 2009; 2010.

Figure 13.1   Degree of coordination and harmonization in the EU internal market

Cooperation between countries could help avoid sub-optimal situations, and overcome certain obstacles to progress (for example, competitiveness concerns, EU fiscal unanimity rule on tax issues). Other potential benefits include:

● Facilitating political and public support by overcoming reluctance to be the 'first mover'.
● Contributing to a level playing field.
● Supporting more efficient (for example, compatible road pricing), effective (for example, avoid leakage) and ambitious environmental taxes.
● Enabling informal exchanges of national experiences and plans between countries.
● Facilitating the achievement of targets and objectives.

Such cooperation is likely to be more useful in certain circumstances, in particular depending on the ease with which a given tax or charge could be avoided for instance through trade (for example, waste exports) or movement of consumers (for example, airline tax, fuel tax). It is more difficult to avoid taxes or charges on resources, materials, or products that are generally consumed near the place of purchase (for example, plastic bags). In such situations cooperation is less necessary, although there could still be benefits from information exchanges and political benefits (for example, multiple countries timing the announcement of a tax) which can help reduce public or business opposition.

Different forms of cooperation are likely to be needed for different resources, materials and pollutants. Some issues are more amenable to collaboration between neighbouring countries (for example, to reduce the risk of fuel tourism across borders, the leakage of products or activities), while some may be more suitable to a multi-country regional approach (for example, marine litter in the Baltic Sea). Others could focus on common challenges independent of geography (for example, fiscal consolidation, climate change, energy security, biodiversity). Coalitions could be formed around different themes as discussed below:

Fiscal Consolidation as a New Window of Opportunity for ETR

Environmental taxes (together with consumption and recurrent property taxes) are considered less detrimental to growth than other taxes such as on labour and are increasingly promoted in the context of economic recovery and growth-friendly fiscal consolidation (European Commission, 2013a). Environmental taxes and wider environmental fiscal reform,

including subsidy reform, can be useful tools to contribute to fiscal consolidation through medium-term effects on growth, income, productivity
and tax receipts (European Commission, 2012). Such instruments have
already been used by some countries as part of their response to fiscal consolidation including Denmark, Italy, Ireland and Portugal. In Ireland for
example, the package of measures adopted in response to the 2007–2008
financial and economic crisis included several environmental taxes and
charges such as a carbon tax, changes to the domestic water pricing structure, revisions to the Vehicle Registration Tax (VRT) rate and the Motor
Tax rate (Withana et al., 2014).

Fiscal consolidation can be a useful driver for the ETR agenda among
interested countries as 'the use of green taxes for fiscal consolidation
would be more effective were there to be close coordination across EU
countries' (Barrios et al., 2013) given spill-over effects. Countries could
exchange information to learn from each other's experiences and point at
others' practice to facilitate domestic support. This could build on lessons
from countries where fiscal consolidation concerns have successfully
driven ETR, such as Denmark, Ireland, Italy and Turkey.

Cooperating to Avoid Competitiveness Concerns

Competitiveness impacts are a key concern when introducing ETR
and have often led to the introduction of partial or full exemptions for
certain sectors in the economy (Withana et al., 2013). Such exemptions,
also known as mitigation or compensation measures, reduce the environmental effectiveness of the tax by reducing incentives for investment
and consumption (OECD, 2001). ETR may affect competitiveness with
impacts dependent on design (for example, level of the tax, its point
of application, the existence and level of exemptions, potential to pass
through costs), use of revenues (for example, whether recycled and in
what way, other taxes reduced) and external factors, including wages,
quality of the workforce, infrastructure, regulatory and fiscal framework, trade barriers and exchange rate variations (Ekins and Speck,
2012).

Available literature is not sufficient to clearly claim that ETR either
supports or hinders competitiveness; however there is little evidence of
negative economic impacts (see for example Albrizio et al., 2014). Further
evidence on the competitiveness, innovation and growth impacts of ETR
is needed, looking at both positive and negative impacts. Such evaluations
should distinguish between competitiveness impacts at the national, sector
and firm level (OECD, 2003) as well as between the short- and long-term
as ETR may affect profitability in the short-term; however it can also

---

BOX 13.1   ETR CAN SUPPORT INNOVATION AND
GROWTH – SOME INSIGHTS FROM PRACTICE

As noted by the OECD, 'environmentally related taxes can provide significant incentives for innovation, as firms and consumers seek new, cleaner solutions in response to the price put on pollution' (OECD, 2010a). Some examples of ETR effects on innovation are set out below:

- In Sweden revenues from a NOx tax are recycled back to polluting companies in relation to the amount of energy produced by the specific plant. This has provided a strong incentive for innovation and a reduction in emissions among liable firms. The refund mechanism also made the instrument more acceptable (OECD, 2013).
- The province of British Columbia in Canada (which introduced a CO_2 tax in 2008) attracted green investment at twice the Canadian average and saw a 48 per cent increase in clean technology industry sales from 2008 to 2010 (British Columbia Ministry of the Environment, 2012).

---

catalyze innovation (OECD, 2010a), which in turn improves profit margins in the long-term – see Box 13.1.

It is arguably too early to say whether ETR can drive competitiveness gains, while some modelling results suggest this (see for example Ekins and Speck, 2012); there is still insufficient real world data to provide conclusive evidence in this regard. Nonetheless common concerns about possible negative competitiveness impacts of ETR can be a driver for collaboration between countries. Cooperation could help address such concerns and avoid potential negative impacts (OECD, 2010a). Such cooperation can also support the development of more ambitious efforts as it may be easier to launch an environmental tax (or reform) and garner support if one can show that key competitor countries are working together. Targeted working groups could focus on areas where competitiveness concerns (and opportunities) may merit cooperation, for example, between neighbouring countries on aviation taxes and airport choice, fuel pricing and fuel tourism.

Jobs, Equity, Social Costs and Benefits

Social impacts including on jobs, equity, distribution, consumer prices, and household income levels are sometimes presented as barriers to ETR and thus need careful consideration. Social impacts of ETR vary across applications and over time and strongly depend on a number of factors including consumption patterns across income groups (World Bank,

2014). While carefully designed ETR can support social objectives, such as employment (with gains dependent on the relative labour intensity of affected sectors), there is a need for more evidence on the link between ETR and social objectives. Such assessments could usefully distinguish between implications at the local, national, regional and EU level (where there are likely to be both winners and losers), the nature of the jobs gained and lost, induced structural changes, and distributional impacts of ETR (OECD, 2014).

Given current high unemployment levels and social concerns in many European countries, arguments on the potential of ETR to contribute to such objectives provide a powerful political message that can facilitate support for action. Targeted working groups could focus on specific areas where opportunities to address social objectives are more likely, for example, a landfill tax that encourages recycling and composting can lead to increased employment in these sectors. Some tax reforms can combine both social and environmental objectives, for example, car and airline taxes tend to benefit a certain (usually richer) segment of society and their reform could have environmental and health benefits (OECD, 2010a).

Resource Efficiency and the Circular Economy

Resource efficiency and the circular economy[3] are increasingly important priorities, for policymakers and business. These discussions are linked to wider ambitions to decouple the economy from resource use and impacts, which in turn aim at avoiding resource scarcity, promote green growth and sustainability. The role of environmental taxes in encouraging the more efficient use of resources and supporting the circular economy is recognized, and it is likely that such instruments will play an increasingly important role in this area.

This attention provides a new window of opportunity for action and could be a useful theme around which to establish a coalition. Countries which are frontrunners in this area such as the UK, Germany and the Netherlands could be well-placed to collaborate and support discussions in other countries, for example, France, Belgium, Luxembourg, Denmark and the Czech Republic. Within this coalition, targeted working groups could, for example, focus on waste exports, plastic bags and water pricing as set out in Box 13.2.

Climate Change and Energy

Energy security concerns, particularly in light of recent events in Ukraine, as well as wider discussions on the 2030 EU climate policy framework,

---

BOX 13.2   POTENTIAL AREAS FOR COOPERATION ON RESOURCE EFFICIENCY AND CIRCULAR ECONOMY

- *Waste exports:* Cooperation between countries, in particular front runners (for example, the UK, the Netherlands, Belgium, Norway, Sweden), in setting waste-related taxes and fees could deter the export of waste for which recycling, reuse or prevention is environmentally preferable to the use of such waste as fuel in energy-from-waste plants. Cooperation could ensure the price of waste treatment is higher at the bottom of the waste hierarchy (landfill, incineration without energy recovery and energy recovery) and lower towards the top (recycling, reuse). This would not necessarily mean applying the same tax rate in each country but that rates are set at a level that discourages exports/imports (IEEP et al., 2012).
- *Plastic bags:* Plastic bag taxes or charges are in place in a number of countries (for example, Belgium, Denmark, France, Ireland, Malta, Wales and Northern Ireland). Such instruments have had significant impacts, for example, in Ireland, and are attracting increasing attention (European Commission, 2013b). Further efforts could be encouraged through informal, collaborative approaches where information exchange and sharing of lessons could help other countries considering similar measures (for example, Portugal which recently proposed a plastic bag tax).
- *Water pricing:* Although there is cost recovery of water services in many European countries, the environmental cost of water supply is rarely integrated in pricing systems, with some exceptions for example, Denmark (EEA, 2013). Reforming water pricing systems to provide incentives for more efficient water use could help address water stress and scarcity, however increasing water tariffs is controversial given distributional impacts. Targeted compensatory measures can be put in place for low income groups (for example, discounted tariffs), while higher tariffs are applied to high income groups (OECD, 2010b). Efforts could be encouraged through information exchange and guidelines.

---

international climate negotiations and some countries' decisions to phase out nuclear energy, suggest that climate and energy will remain high on the political agenda. Carbon pricing is a necessary element in the transition to a low carbon economy and ETR will continue to play an important role in the wider policy mix.

Carbon taxes are applied in a number of countries including Denmark, Finland, Ireland, Norway, Slovenia and Sweden (Vivid Economics, 2012), with a number of others considering introducing such taxes (Withana et al., 2013). Cooperation or coordination between countries could be an innovative way to address competitiveness concerns (which have had a strong impact on the design of these taxes) and facilitate reform to make existing instruments more effective. Within this coalition, targeted working

---

BOX 13.3   POTENTIAL AREAS FOR COOPERATION ON CLIMATE AND ENERGY

- *Effective carbon pricing* and how to improve existing carbon and energy taxes, for example, phasing out exemptions, ramping up tax rates, harmonizing carbon price/CO_2 abatement costs across different fuels and users. A coalition could include frontrunners learning lessons from each other, inspire efforts in other countries discussing proposals for CO_2 taxes (for example, Portugal, Italy) and those contemplating how to achieve national choices to phase out nuclear energy (for example, Germany, Switzerland).
- *Phasing out reduced VAT rates on energy.* A number of countries apply lower VAT rates on electricity, natural gas and district heating (for example, Belgium, France, UK – see European Commission, 2013a). This is allowed under EU VAT legislation; however such practices reduce incentives for efficient consumption and can be considered an environmentally harmful subsidy (Withana et al., 2012). Phasing out such subsidies will be challenging, inter alia given arguments on social protection, however such concerns can be addressed through careful design and targeted support (for example, to vulnerable households) and there are lessons to be learnt from experiences in other countries.

---

groups could, for example, focus on effective carbon pricing and on phasing out reduced VAT rates on energy as set out in Box 13.3.

Transport and Mobility

Addressing growing emissions from the transport sector and improving the mobility of citizens remains a challenge for several European countries. While a number of environmental taxes and charges are already applied in this area, primarily in relation to road transport, there remains significant potential for further ETR efforts including on fuel taxes. Within this coalition, targeted working groups could, for example, focus on fuel taxation; vehicle taxes; infrastructure charging; air passenger taxes; and kerosene tax exemptions as set out in Box 13.4.

Pollution and Pressures on the Environment, Biodiversity and Health

Traditionally, environmental taxes and charges have focused on certain aspects of pollution including a (growing) subset of products and in a few cases on sustainable use of natural resources. There is increasing interest in incentive measures relating to biological resources (such as fisheries, forestry) and wider biodiversity which reflects inter alia the adoption of commitments such as the Strategic Plan for Biodiversity for 2011–2020

BOX 13.4   POTENTIAL AREAS FOR COOPERATION ON
TRANSPORT AND MOBILITY

- *Taxation of transport fuels:* Excise duties on diesel are generally lower than on petrol in European countries (with some exceptions, for example, the UK, Switzerland, Turkey), despite evidence of the harmful impacts of diesel on human health of diesel (Cottrell, 2014). There is potential to raise significant revenues from equal tax treatment of petrol and diesel (Eunomia and Aarhus University, 2014); however there remains significant opposition to such reforms. This underlines the importance of collaboration, particularly between neighbouring countries, for example, Belgium, France, Germany, Luxembourg and the Netherlands, to avoid issues of fuel tourism (European Commission, 2013a).
- CO_2-*related vehicle taxation:* In a number of countries, vehicle registration taxes have been designed to promote the purchase of low-carbon vehicles (for example, the Netherlands, Spain, Ireland) and have had positive environmental effects (Green Fiscal Commission, 2010). Countries with such approaches could consider cooperating to further strengthen efforts and/or inspire progress in others, for example, Estonia, Slovakia, Czech Republic, Lithuania, Bulgaria and Poland (European Commission, 2013a).
- *Kerosene used in aviation, shipping/fishing and agriculture sector:* Exemptions from kerosene taxes are provided in the aviation, shipping/fishing and agriculture sectors in several European countries. Such provisions are guided (or limited) by international treaties and EU legislation (Council Directive 2003/96/EC). Thus, some form of EU or international cooperation (for example, OECD) is required to address such issues and there is scope to learn from others.
- *Air passenger taxes:* The lack of cooperation, particularly between neighbouring countries could lead to sub-optimal situations as in the Netherlands (see above). These experiences highlight the case for a coordinated approach especially among neighbouring countries to avoid concerns about passengers diverting to airports in countries which do not apply such taxes/duties.

---

under the Convention on Biological Diversity (CBD) which contains a target to reform incentives harmful to biodiversity (Oosterhuis and ten Brink, 2014).

Given multiple pollution sources and pressures on the environment, biodiversity and health, as well as numerous legislative requirements and commitments, it is likely that there will be increasing interest in the use of environmental taxes and incentive measures in this area. Such instruments have the potential to play a role in reducing local, national and in some cases international pressures alongside other supporting instruments. Within this coalition, targeted working groups could, for example, focus on marine litter and pesticides as elaborated in Box 13.5.

BOX 13.5   POTENTIAL AREAS FOR COOPERATION ON
            POLLUTION AND PRESSURES ON THE
            ENVIRONMENT, BIODIVERSITY AND HEALTH

- *Marine litter* is a growing problem with costly environmental and socio-economic impacts, for example, municipalities in the UK spend approximately EUR 18 million each year removing beach litter (Mouat et al., 2010). This can be addressed through various tools including instruments to address land-based litter such as deposit-refund schemes (for example, Denmark, Germany, Malta) and plastic bag charges (for example, Ireland) (ten Brink et al., 2009; Newman et al., 2015). A regional approach could be considered, for example, within the framework of the OSPAR Convention or Regional Action Plans under the Marine Strategy Framework Directive in the Baltic, North or Mediterranean Seas.
- *Sustainable use of pesticides:* Pesticides taxes are in place in some European countries, for example, Denmark and Norway, and the use of such market-based instruments is encouraged by the Sustainable Use Directive on Pesticide (Directive 2009/128/EC). Cooperation between countries could include frontrunners learning lessons from each other and inspiring efforts in others considering introducing such taxes. A related issue is the application of low VAT rates on pesticides (and fertilizers) which could also merit reform.

FUTURE OUTLOOK

As we look to the future, different approaches to ETR can be considered. This can range from the currently prevailing unilateral approaches, to informal cooperation between regions and countries, to more formal legal approaches. Coalitions of like-minded countries, as set out in this chapter, would complement existing approaches and would be an innovative way to overcome certain obstacles to progress. Such cooperation is likely to be more useful in certain circumstances, in particular depending on the ease with which a given tax or charge could be avoided. Different forms of cooperation are likely to be needed in relation to different resources, materials, pollutants. Some issues are more amenable to collaboration between neighbouring countries; some may be more suitable for a multi-country or regional focus, while others could focus on common challenges independent of geography.

The coverage of coalitions would need to be carefully considered to ensure the process is manageable and ideally kept open to allow development over time in terms of reach and scope. Further analysis is needed to identify particular issues on which such coalitions could focus on and specific actors to engage, including potential drivers of coalitions which could be individual countries (for example, early vanguard countries such as the Netherlands, Denmark, Sweden, Finland and Norway, or new vanguard countries such as Ireland, Portugal and Italy) or regions (for example, progressive regions in Spain or Belgium), groups of countries (for example, Nordic Countries, Green Growth Group) and/or other actors (for example, European Commission, OECD, EEA, UNEP, IMF). It is important that these coalitions engage policymakers from different areas, including finance, economics and tax departments as well as wider stake-holders such as the scientific community, business and civil society. They could be supported by parallel coalitions of like-minded civil society and make use of existing platforms such as the EU Forum for market-based instruments (MBI Forum) and the OECD Environmental Tax Group.

Such collaboration should be coordinated with wider policy processes and build on relevant windows of opportunity. At national level this includes budget announcements, legislative proposals, meetings of national fiscal commissions/committees, elections and relevant stakeholder reports. At the regional (multi-country) level, this could include institutions and processes around regional multilateral agreements, such as HELCOM and the Baltic Seas. At European level, this includes the European Semester, processes and reviews of relevant pieces of EU legislation such as the Energy Tax Directive, Eurovignette Directive, Water Framework Directive, the Regulation on Accounts, waste legislation and so on, as well as parallel initiatives and commitments on Environmentally Harmful Subsidies (EHS) reform which includes tax reform. At the international level this includes relevant Conferences of the Parties (COPs) to the CBD and UNFCCC, G-20 and APEC meetings, events organized by NGOs, academics and other actors.

There could also be lessons to be learnt from experiences with establishing coalitions in other parts of the world. For example collaboration between states and provinces in North America such as the Regional Greenhouse Gas Initiative (RGGI) and the Western Climate Initiative (WCI) have had different degrees of success which reflect a number of factors including the flexibility of the schemes and their ability to build support among affected groups (Rabe, 2015).

To support the above process, further research into specific areas which may merit multi-country or multi-region cooperation would be helpful. This could include work to quantify the potential benefits and added value of cooperation, how to best structure such cooperation and what policy processes and stakeholder engagement would be needed to realize it. In addition, further ex-post assessments of experiences with ETRs can be useful to show the impacts of such reforms and identify where cooperation could have led to further progress. Such insights can inform the design and implementation of future ETRs and help build wide political and public support for such efforts (Withana, 2015).

This would offer an evidence base on the benefits of cooperative approaches to ETR and encourage long-term commitment to such efforts. This would complement existing arguments, interests and needs for such collaboration and support efforts to champion ETR in the coming years.

NOTES

1. This chapter is based on a study by the Institute for European Environmental Policy (IEEP) (Withana et al., 2014).
2. Enhanced cooperation on environmental taxes is in principle possible within the EU. The principles for enhanced cooperation are laid down in Article 20 of the Treaty on the European Union and detailed procedures for its application are given in Articles 326–334 in the Treaty on the Functioning of the European Union. A minimum of nine countries must be involved to initiate enhanced cooperation, but others can join later. Enhanced cooperation can only be undertaken as a last resort after the Council has established that the objectives of the proposed cooperation cannot be attained within a reasonable period of time (EU, 2012).
3. In contrast to the existing 'take–make–use–dispose' linear economy, a circular economy is one where production chains and consumption patterns are transformed to keep materials circulating in the economy for longer, where re-use, remanufacture, repair and recycling is the norm, waste is eliminated and virgin resource extraction is reduced. This requires systemic change and innovation within and across value chains, new business models and substantial changes in consumer behaviour (European Commission, 2014).

REFERENCES

Albrizio, S., Botta, E., Koźluk, T. and Zipperer, V. (2014), 'Do environmental policies matter for productivity growth? Insights from new cross-country measures of environmental policy', OECD Economic Department Working Papers No. 1176, Paris: OECD.

Barrios, S., Pycroft, J. and Saveyn, B. (2013), 'The marginal cost of public funds in the EU: The case of labour versus green taxes', DG TAXUD Taxation Papers, Working Paper No. 35 – 2013, Luxembourg: Publications Office of the European Union.

Bassi, S., Pallemaerts, M. and ten Brink, P. (2010), 'Exploring the potential of harmonizing environmental tax reform efforts in the European Union', in C. Dias Soares, J.E. Milne, H. Ashiabor, L. Kreiser and K. Deketelaere (eds), *Critical Issues in Environmental Taxation – International and Comparative Perspectives Volume VIII*, New York: Oxford University Press, 89–107.

Bassi, S., ten Brink, P., Pallemaerts, M. and von Homeyer, I. (2009), 'Feasibility of implementing a radical ETR and its acceptance', Report for *Study on Tax Reform in Europe over the Next Decades: Implication for the Environment, for Eco-Innovation and for Household Distribution* for the European Environment Agency, Brussels/London, IEEP, http://www.ieep.eu/assets/636/Final_

part_c_radical_ETR_december_2_2009_FINAL.pdf, accessed 20 November 2014.

British Columbia Ministry of the Environment (2012), 'Making progress on BC's Climate Action Plan', http://www.env.gov.bc.ca/cas/pdfs/2012-Progress-to-Targets.pdf, accessed 4 March 2013.

Cottrell, J. (2014), 'Reforming EHS in Europe: Success stories, failures and agenda setting', in F. Oosterhuis and P. ten Brink (eds), *Paying the Polluter. Environmentally Harmful Subsidies and their Reform*, Cheltenham, UK and Northampton, MA, USA: Edward Elgar Publishing, 205–235.

Council Directive 2003/96/EC of 27 October 2003 restructuring the Community framework for the taxation of energy products and electricity.

Directive 2009/128/EC of the European Parliament and of the Council of 21 October 2009 establishing a framework for Community action to achieve the sustainable use of pesticides.

EEA (2013), Assessment of cost recovery through water pricing, EEA Technical Report No 16/2013, Copenhagen: European Environment Agency.

Ekins P. and Speck, S. (2012), 'Impact on competitiveness: what do we know from modelling?', in Milne, J. and Skou Andersen, M. (eds), *Handbook of Research on Environmental Tax Reform*, Cheltenham, UK and Northampton, MA, USA: Edward Elgar Publishing, 377–396.

Eunomia and Aarhus University (2014), 'Study on environmental fiscal reform potential in 12 EU Member States – Final Report to DG Environment of the European Commission', 28 February 2014, http://ec.europa.eu/environment/integration/green_semester/pdf/EFR-Final%20Report.pdf, accessed 10 April 2015.

Eunomia, Aarhus University and IEEP (2015), 'Study on environmental fiscal reform potential in 14 EU Member States – Final Report to DG Environment of the European Commission'.

European Commission (2012), 'Growth-friendly tax policies in Member States and better tax coordination in the EU', COM(2011)815, 5/5, Annex IV to Commission Communication on the Annual Growth Survey 2012.

European Commission (EC) (2013a), 'Tax reforms in EU Member States 2013 – Tax policy challenges for economic growth and fiscal sustainability', European Economy 5|2013, Directorate-General for Economic and Financial Affairs, Brussels: European Commission.

European Commission (EC) (2013b), Proposal for a Directive of the European Parliament and of the Council amending Directive 94/62/EC on packaging and packaging waste to reduce the consumption of lightweight plastic carrier bags, COM(2013)761, Brussels: European Commission.

European Commission (EC) (2014), 'Towards a circular economy: A zero waste programme for Europe, Communication from the Commission to the European Parliament, the Council, the European Economic and Social Committee, the Committee of the Regions', COM(2014)398, Brussels: European Commission.

European Union (EU) (2012), Consolidated version of the Treaty of the European Union, *Official Journal of the European Union*, C 326/13, 26 October.

Eurostat (2013), Taxation trends in the European Union – Data for the EU Member States, Iceland and Norway, 2013 edition, Taxation and Customs Union, Luxembourg: European Commission.

Eurostat (2014), 'Environmental tax statistics Data from February and March 2014', http://epp.eurostat.ec.europa.eu/statistics_explained/index.php/Environmental_tax_statistics, accessed 13 August 2014.

Green Fiscal Commission (2010), 'Reducing carbon emissions through transport taxation', Briefing Paper 6, March 2010, p. 4.

IEEP, Eunomia, BIO IS, Umweltbundesamt, Ecologic and Arcadis (2012), 'Economic instruments to improve waste management', Final report to DG Environment of the European Commission, http://www.ieep.eu/publications/2012/04/economic-instruments-to-improve-waste-management, accessed 19 November 2014.

Mouat, J., Lozano, R.L. and Bateson, H. (2010), 'Economic impacts of marine litter', Report of Kimo international, http://www.kimointernational.org/Home.aspx, accessed 8 August 2013.

Newman, S., Watkins, E., Farmer, A., ten Brink, P. and Schweitzer, J-P. (2015), 'The economics of marine litter', in Bergmann, M., Gutow, L. and Klages, M. (eds), *Marine Anthropogenic Litter*, Berlin: Springer.

OECD (2001), 'Environmentally related taxes in OECD countries: Issues and strategies', Paris: Organisation for Economic Co-operation and Development.

OECD (2003), 'Environmental taxes and competitiveness: An overview of issues, policy options and research needs', Paris: Organisation for Economic Co-operation and Development.

OECD (2010a), 'Taxation, innovation and the environment', Paris: Organisation for Economic Co-operation and Development.

OECD (2010b), 'Pricing water resources and water and sanitation services', Paris: Organisation for Economic Co-operation and Development.

OECD (2013), 'The Swedish tax on nitrogen oxide emissions: Lessons in environmental policy reform', OECD Environment Policy Paper No. 2, December 2013, Paris: Organisation for Economic Co-operation and Development.

OECD (2014), 'Addressing social implications of green growth – Energy sector reform and its impact on households', Issue note prepared for Session 1 of the Green Growth and Sustainable Development Forum, 13–14 November 2014, Paris: Organisation for Economic Co-operation and Development.

Oosterhuis, F. and ten Brink, P. (eds) (2014), *Paying the Polluter. Environmentally Harmful Subsidies and their Reform*, Cheltenham, UK and Northampton, MA, USA: Edward Elgar Publishing.

Rabe, B. (2015), 'The durability of carbon cap and trade policy', *Governance: An International Journal of Policy, Administration, and Institutions*, 28, *forthcoming*.

ten Brink, P., Lutchman, I., Bassi, S., Speck S., Sheavly, S., Register, K. and Woolaway, C. (2009), *Guidelines on the Use of Market-based Instruments to Address the Problem of Marine Litter*, Brussels: Institute for European Environmental Policy (IEEP), and Virginia Beach, Virginia, USA: Sheavly Consultants.

Vivid Economics (2012), *Carbon Taxation and Fiscal Consolidation: The Potential of Carbon Pricing to Reduce Europe's Fiscal Deficits*, Report prepared for the European Climate Foundation and Green Budget Europe, May 2012, 19.

Withana, S. (2015), 'Overcoming Obstacles to Green Fiscal Reforms', Paper commissioned by the UNEP Green Growth Knowledge Platform (GGKP).

Withana, S., ten Brink, P., Franckx, L., Hirschnitz-Garbers, M., Mayeres, I., Oosterhuis, F. and Porsch, L. (2012), *Study Supporting the Phasing out of Environmentally Harmful Subsidies*. A report by the Institute for European Environmental Policy (IEEP), Institute for Environmental Studies – Vrije

Universiteit (IVM), Ecologic Institute and VITO for the European Commission – DG Environment, Final Report, Brussels: IEEP.

Withana, S., ten Brink, P., Illes, A., Nanni, S. and Watkins, E. (2014), *Environmental Tax Reform in Europe: Opportunities for the Future*. A report by the Institute for European Environmental Policy (IEEP) for the Netherlands Ministry of Infrastructure and the Environment, Final Report, Brussels: IEEP. http://www.ieep.eu/work-areas/environmental-economics/market-based-instruments/2014/06/environmental-tax-reform-in-europe-opportunities-for-the-future accessed 16 January 2015.

Withana, S., ten Brink, P., Kretschmer, B., Mazza, L., Hjerp, P. and Sauter, R. (2013), *Evaluation of Environmental Tax Reforms: International Experiences*. A report by the Institute for European Environmental Policy (IEEP) for the State Secretariat for Economic Affairs (SECO) and the Federal Finance Administration (FFA) of Switzerland, Final Report, Brussels: IEEP.

World Bank (2014), Transitional policies to assist the poor while phasing out inefficient fossil fuel subsidies that encourage wasteful consumption, Contribution by the World Bank to G20 Finance Ministers and Central Bank Governors, 18–20 September 2014.

14. Developments and opportunities for an ecological tax reform in Spain

Ignasi Puig Ventosa, Eike Meyer, Marta Jofra Sora and Maria Calaf Forn

INTRODUCTION

Spain is facing serious economic challenges. The public debt in 2013 reached 92.10 per cent of GDP and the unemployment rate in December 2013 was at 25.8 per cent. In this context, there is an urgency to develop fiscal strategies that have the least impact on the real economy and that will affect employment positively, in a way that the welfare of the population is guaranteed, assuring the best possible impact on the financial sustainability of the State.

At the same time, reducing the environmental impact, tackling climate change and reducing inequality are the main challenges in reaching a sustainable economic development. In addition, moving towards an energy efficient and low carbon economic development gives the opportunity to improve competiveness in the future.

Spain is failing to meet the objectives established by the Kyoto protocol with domestic measures adopted within Spain, in comparison with other European countries and the OECD. Greenhouse gas emissions have fallen since 2008,[1] but this decrease is largely as a result of the reduction in the economic activity which has been particularly notable in Spain. The Spanish industry still has not made sufficient advances in terms of energy efficiency and decarbonization of the economy, and the exterior dependency on primary energy sources continues to be very high (about 75 per cent in 2012[2]).

Various studies show that taxes in energy and carbon have a lower impact on the economic system and on unemployment than other approaches to fiscal consolidation, such as an increase in VAT or a reduction in social spending.[3]

ENVIRONMENTAL AND ENERGY TAXES IN SPAIN, WITHIN THE EUROPEAN CONTEXT

In comparison with other Member States of the European Union, the revenue from environmental taxes in general is low. In 2012, energy taxes generated 13.64 billion EUR of revenue. This is equivalent of 4.82 per cent of overall tax revenue or 1.57 per cent of GDP. In all of the 27 Member States together, environmental taxes in 2012 accounted for 6.09 per cent of overall tax revenue and 2.40 per cent of GDP. The share of environmental taxes in overall tax revenue in Spain in 2012 was the second lowest among the EU Member States (only in France it was lower with 4.08 per cent). The ratio of environmental tax revenue to GDP was lowest in Spain among all EU Member States.

On the EU level, energy taxes are regulated by the EU energy taxation directive (ETD) (Directive 2003/96/EC of 27 October 2003 restructuring the Community framework for the taxation of energy products and electricity). This directive was designed to avoid competitive distortions in the energy sector within the EU internal market. It sets out common rules on what should be taxed, when and what exemptions are allowed. Minimum rates, based mainly on the volume of energy consumed, are laid down for products used in heating, electricity and motor fuels. Above these minimum rates, Member States are free to set their own national rates as they see fit.

In April 2011, the European Commission presented a proposal to revise the ETD. The proposed new rules were aiming at restructuring the way energy products are taxed, now taking into account both their CO_2 emissions and energy content. Existing energy taxes would have been split into two components: energy and carbon content of energy products. That, taken together, would determine the overall rate at which a product is taxed. However, after more than three years of unsuccessful negotiations in the Council, the European Commission is now likely to withdraw its proposal. In Spain the implementation of the proposal would have made necessary increases of the rates of energy taxes for heavy fuel oils, natural gas and solid fuels.[4]

Another policy process on European Union level, which has become increasingly relevant for members states' fiscal policy in general, and which has created some momentum for increasing energy taxation is the so called 'European semester' process. The European Semester is an annual cycle of macroeconomic, budgetary and structural policy coordination which is conceived to combine monitoring of Member States' progress on accomplishing the Europe 2020 targets, as well as their compliance with both the stability and growth pact and the macroeconomic imbalance

procedure. Throughout annual cycles, Member States' policy performances are monitored and country specific recommendations are prepared
by the European Commission and adopted by the Council. In this context,
the European Council issued country specific recommendations urging the
Spanish government to reform its taxation structure shifting the burden
of taxation away from labour towards consumption and environmental
taxation in 2013 and 2014 (recommendation number 2, p. 7 in 2013,[5] and
recommendation number 1, p. 8 in 2014[6]).

TOWARD AN ECOLOGICAL TAX REFORM IN SPAIN

Adopting an ecological economic reform would allow budgets to be
targeted towards the objectives of environmental sustainability. Besides
reaching environmental objectives, a well-designed environmental tax
reform could increase the global efficiency of the economy, creating
employment and improving national competiveness in the medium and
long term.

Usually this is achieved by giving most weight to environmental taxes
and simultaneously reducing the tax burden on other areas (work, consumption, and so on). While generally the ecological tax reforms are
based on being globally neutral in terms of revenue, recently with the need
of resources by public administrations, that neutrality has come to be
understood that the increase in environmental taxes allowed not having to
increase other taxes that could be more distortive of the economic activity.

Thus, an ecological tax reform would:

- *Create the price signal necessary to reduce the emission of greenhouse
  gases and reach the environmental objectives*
  The international, European and national climate objectives require
  reducing the greenhouses gases in an efficient manner, that is to say,
  at the lowest cost. Taxation and the auctioning of emission permits
  are the main instruments for creating economic signals that contribute to this. The answer to an increase in the price of carbon favours
  the change towards less carbon intense fuels, improving energy efficiency or renewable energy investment.
- *Correct market failures and increase the efficiency of the economy*
  The excessive consumption of resources and pollution create economic costs as a result of the impact that is produced in health and
  well-being, in the reduction of agricultural production, reduction of
  tourism in the affected areas or the impact of extreme climatic events
  as a consequence of climate change. These costs, in general, are not

included in the price of these activities, generating externalities and economic inefficiencies. Applying taxes to reflect (at least in part) the external costs will create initiatives so that the economic activities change behaviour and reduce the associated pollution.

● *Create incentives for sustainable economic development and improvement of national competitiveness in the medium and long term*
The ecological fiscal reform has the potential to stimulate innovation and economic development, helping to position the economy on the path to a greener development. The development of a low carbon economy connects with the European roadmap in this regard, and would create green jobs and boost ecoinnovation.[7]

TAXES ON ENERGY IN SPAIN

The Spanish regulatory framework distributes the powers of taxation on energy between the state, the autonomous communities and local governments.

State Taxes

Amongst the energy taxes that are applied at a state level, the main ones are:

● *Fuel tax*, levied on the consumption of petrol, gas, natural gas and other products. This is regulated by the excise duties law (Ley 38/1992, de 28 de diciembre, de impuestos especiales) (art. 46–55), and subsequent amendments. This tax creates strong incentives to save energy; however, in Spain its effectiveness is conditioned by the numerous tax benefits (that are concentrated on agriculture, fishing, professional transport and airports, and that in 2011 reached more than 5000 million EUR[8]) and for its lower tax rates in comparison with the average of EU countries.
  By far, this is the tax on energy that reaches the highest revenue; however, this revenue has decreased significantly in recent years (12.8 per cent in 2012 compared with 2009) due to a reduction in consumption caused by the economic crisis.[9]

● *Tax on electricity*, which is applied on the production or importation of electricity. This is regulated by the excise duties law (Ley 38/1992, de 28 de diciembre, de impuestos especiales) (art. 64), and subsequent amendments. This tax is potentially very effective in encouraging the efficient use of electricity; however, its low tax rate limits its effectiveness. Its design could be much improved, since the tax base is the price of electricity instead of electricity consumed.

- *Tax on carbon*, which is levied on the consumption of hard coal, anthracite, lignite, coke, tar, bitumen, asphalt and bituminous materials, amongst others by the excise duties law (Ley 38/1992, de 28 de diciembre, de impuestos especiales) (art. 75–88), and subsequent amendments. The applied tax rates and revenues are relatively low compared with other energy taxes.

- *Tax on certain means of transport* (more commonly known as vehicle registration tax), which is applied to the registration of vehicles, vessels and aircraft and regulated by the excise duties law (Ley 38/1992, de 28 de diciembre, de impuestos especiales) (art. 65–74), and subsequent amendments. In the case of vehicles, the tax rate depends on the respective CO_2 emissions (for example cars under 120 gCO_2/km pay a zero tax rate and from this limit tax rates increase for different categories as the emissions increase). The revenue from this tax has dropped significantly in recent years (56 per cent between 2008 and 2011[10]).

Table 14.1 shows the revenue raised by these taxes and their relative weight in 2013:

Table 14.1   Revenue from state energy taxes in absolute terms and relative to total energy taxes and total state tax, 2013 (provisional data)

Tax	Revenue (million EUR)	% of energy taxes	% of total taxes
Excise duty on fuels	9,933	84.17%	5.88%
Excise duty on electricity	1,445	12.24%	0.86%
Excise duty on certain means of transport	275	2.33%	0.16%
Excise duty on carbon	148	1.25%	0.09%
TOTAL	11,801	100.00%	6.99%

Source: Based on Agencia Tributaria (www.agenciatributaria.es).

Finally, there are another three taxes created by the law on tax measures for energy sustainability (Ley 15/2012, de 27 de diciembre, de medidas fiscales para la sostenibilidad energética), and for which there is not yet enough information on their results:

- *The tax on value of production of electrical energy*, created in 2012 and implemented from 2013, whose tax base, unlike the electricity tax is the value of the electricity fed into the grid, measured in the power stations. In 2013 the revenue was 1257 million EUR.[11]

- *The tax on the production of spent nuclear fuel and radioactive waste*, which is applied to the production of spent fuel and the storage of it and other radioactive waste in nuclear plants. It is estimated that in 2014 the revenue of this tax will be 270 million EUR.[12]

- *The tax on storage of spent nuclear fuel and radioactive waste in centralized facilities*, which unlike the above applies to spent fuel and radioactive waste which is stored in centralized facilities (not in power plants). It is estimated that in 2014 the revenue from this tax will be 19 million.[13]

- *The tariff for the use of inland waters for the production of electricity*, which applies to the value of hydro produced. The revenue of this tax in 2013 was 298 million EUR.[14]

Regional Taxes

Some state taxes on energy are transferred to the regional governments, which mean that they receive the revenue in part or completely. This is the case of the fuel tax, which is ceded 58 per cent, and excise taxes on electricity and on certain means of transport (vehicle registration tax), which are 100 per cent ceded. In most cases, the autonomous communities have no regulatory power over taxation transferred. Two exceptions are the excise duty on certain means of transport and excise duty on fuels, of which the autonomous communities can set tax rates within the state set margins. In the first case, the autonomous communities can set tax rates to values up to 15 per cent higher than the default values defined at state level. In the case of excise duties on mineral oils, the maximum tax rates to be charged by regional governments in addition to the state tax rates are shown in Table 14.2.

Table 14.2   Maximum tax rates of regional section of excise duties on mineral oils

Energy product	Tax rate
Petrol (€/1000 l)	0–48
Oil for general use (€/1000 l)	0–48
Oil for specific use and heating (€/1000 l)	0–12
Fuel (€/t)	0–2
Kerosene for general use (€/1000 l)	0–48
Kerosene for heating (€/1000 l)	–

Moreover, the autonomous communities have the power to create and implement their own taxes. The limited scope of energy taxation at the state level has indeed been identified by the autonomous communities as an opportunity to establish their own taxes.

It is worth noting the large disparity between regions own taxes and the clear lack of harmonization between them, as far as energy taxes are concerned. In 2013, nine autonomous communities had introduced some form of energy taxation; among the most common are taxes on the transport of electricity, for the environmental impact of its infrastructure; second, on the production of energy (thermonuclear or hydraulic source), on wind energy facilities or on radioactive waste deposits. Also five autonomous regions have introduced taxes on air emissions, which amongst others affect power plant facilities.

Normally, the revenue of such taxes is generically allocated to environmental programs or measures. Only in some cases are specific funds allocated or more specific purposes set. According to Labandeira et al. (2009) and Labandeira and Linares (2013), energy taxes introduced by the autonomous communities, despite its alleged environmental nature, in practice in some cases they are purely tax collection figures with little environmental impact.[15]

Moreover, the weight of energy taxes on total tax revenues of the regions is still generally very low (between 0.03 and 5 per cent[16]).

Municipal Taxes

The operating capacity of local authorities in tax and economic issues are regulated by royal legislative decree 2/2004, of 5 March, approving the consolidated text of the law regulating local treasuries (Real decreto legislativo 2/2004, de 5 de marzo, por el que se aprueba el texto refundido de la ley reguladora de las haciendas locales) (LHL). Only the municipalities (and not the other local authorities) have a role worth noting on taxation of energy. According to LHL, municipalities must charge, compulsorily, the following taxes:

- The *property tax* (impuesto sobre bienes inmuebles) (IBI). This tax applies to owners of real estates, and the amount depends on their value. For urban estates the tax rate should be set between 0.4 and 1.10 per cent, and for rural properties between 0.3 and 0.9 per cent. The LHL (art. 74.5) allows municipalities to apply bonuses of up to 50 per cent to buildings that have systems for thermal or electrical conversion of solar energy.
- The *tax on economic activities* (impuesto sobre actividades económicas) (IAE). This tax is levied on the owners of economic activities

which have an annual turnover of over one million euros. The tax rate depends on the type of activity. The LHL (art. 88) provides that municipalities can apply discounts of up to 50 per cent in tax on economic activities that 'use or produce energy from facilities using renewable energy sources or cogeneration systems' and for those that 'establish a transportation plan for its employees which aims to reduce energy consumption and emissions caused by commuting to the workplace and encouraging the use of more efficient means of transport such as public or shared transport'.

- The *vehicles circulation tax* (impuesto sobre vehículos de tracción mecánica) (IVTM). This tax applies to owners of vehicles registered in the municipality, depending on the type of vehicle and its power. The LHL provides (art. 95.4) that municipalities can apply a coefficient of between 1 and 2 on basic quotas established by law. In addition, municipalities can apply discounts of up to 75 per cent of the tax depending on the type of fuel used by the vehicle, the environmental impact of the fuel, and the engine characteristics and its environmental impact (art. 95.6).

In addition, municipalities can voluntarily apply the following taxes:

- The *tax on construction, installations and works* (impuesto sobre construcciones, instalaciones y obras) (ICIO). This tax applies to the types of works requiring municipal license (minor works are exempt). The LHL provides for a maximum tax rate of 4 per cent on the cost of the work and provides that municipalities can apply discounts of up to 95 per cent to the works of installation of solar thermal or photovoltaic systems (art. 103.2.b).
- The *tax on the increase in value on urban land* (impuesto sobre el incremento del valor de los terrenos de naturaleza urbana) (IIVTNT). This tax applies to the transfer of property when an increase in the value of the property occurs, and does not provide any tax benefit related to energy.

Thus, energy tax policy by municipalities on their taxes is limited, directly, to the tax credits that they can potentially articulate in relation to: IBI, IAE, IVTM and ICIO, and, indirectly, to the intensity with which the IVTM is applied.

In addition to these taxes, municipalities may impose voluntarily charges for the private use of the public domain, for providing services or for performing administrative activities involving a specific benefit to a person or activity. One of the cases in which the LHL allows local authorities to impose charges is the private use of the local public domain by 'lines, pipes and conduits galleries for power' (art. 20.3.k).

On the other hand LHL prevents from establishing charges on some services, such as street lighting (art. 21.1.b of LHL). While the leeway of municipalities to introduce environmental criteria in municipal taxes is greater than the tax, the potential impact of municipalities through taxes on energy is relatively low.

Currently there are no studies on the current status of the introduction of environmental criteria in the taxes and charges of Spanish municipalities.

PROPOSALS

Environmental taxation, and more specifically energy taxation, should be designed primarily to reduce the environmental impact of production and consumption of energy, promoting efficiency and penalizing wastage, and applying the 'polluter pays' principle. Reforms in this area should be directed to these objectives without losing sight that they should also help alleviate public deficit and ensure social protection.

The margin that the government has on environmental taxation is broad, given that environmental taxation in Spain is low compared with the European average, as discussed above. It would be advisable to be placed at least at the average level of the European Union and that environmental taxes represent at least 6 per cent of the GDP. However, to minimize the negative effects on the domestic economies, compensatory measures should be enabled (for example, to prevent fuel poverty), always ensuring the maintenance of energy efficiency incentives created by the tax.

In February 2014, the commission of experts for the reform of the Spanish tax system presented a report commissioned by the Spanish government.[17] This report contains an entire section (chapter VI) dedicated to excise duties and environmental taxes.

The authors of this article considered the proposals of the committee of experts and also other proposals and, in the framework of the CEPRiE project – Carbon and energy pricing reform in Europe[18] – prepared a series of proposals that were formulated as concrete articulated proposals and presented to the different political parties in the Spanish parliament as suggested amendments[19] to various taxation bills that the government of Spain sent to parliament.[20] These bills did not include any relevant proposal on environmental taxation; not even those suggestions included in the report by the committee of experts.

Thus, the developed proposals suggest reforming the taxes on oil and coal, increasing them and reducing some of the existing tax benefits, such as those that apply to fuel used on domestic flights. It is also suggested that the tax rates depends both on the energy content of the product and the carbon dioxide emitted, in line with European discussions regarding possible amendments to the Directive 2003/96/EC restructuring the Community framework for the taxation of energy products and electricity. This would be achieved by taxing CO_2 from sectors currently outside the European emission trading scheme. Since this tax affects many sectors of the economy, some of them in a difficult economic situation, the reform should be accompanied by transitional measures and if necessary temporary compensatory measures. However, the reform should ensure that the incentives created by the tax are maintained. It should also ensure that there is no double taxation when oil or coal are consumed by facilities subject to the emissions trading scheme, although being part of the scheme should not imply a lower contribution, either. Finally, it is recommended to move towards a convergence between the tax rates on petrol and diesel (currently petrol tax rates are about 33 per cent higher than those for diesel).

Furthermore it is proposed to amend the electricity tax replacing the tax base (€) (*ad valorem*) for kWh to increase the incentive of efficiency, with a possible differentiation between contracted power and actual consumption. This would not only transform the tax into an environmental tax, but it would make it clearer that currently the tax is much cheaper per kWh for large consumers, since they benefit from cheaper electricity prices. The proposal includes four different types of users: households, SMEs, some metallurgic and chemical processes for which electricity represents more than 50 per cent of the cost of the product, and rest of consumers. Each category would have its respective tax rate, being initially lower for large consumers, to facilitate the transition from the current situation, but with the idea that the taxes rates would be gradually converging.

Moreover, tax rates could eventually consider air pollution in terms of SOx, NOx, particles and others, unless this question was specifically addressed by a new tax on polluting air emissions.

In relation to transport, it is recommended that the vehicle registration tax (Impuesto especial sobre determinados medios de transporte) extends its reach to consider other emissions from the vehicle as well as CO_2. A more modest proposal consists of lowering the limit from which cars face a zero tax rate, reducing it from 120 to 100 gCO_2/km, and similarly for motorcycles.

Regarding the regional taxes, it is not considered advisable to apply a harmonization for all existing taxes, as some of them have very satisfactory results or respond to specific circumstances of the autonomous communities. However, some taxes could be regulated at the state level, leaving room for the regional governments to set tax rates within a range. This, for example, could be the case for the existing taxes on air pollution. In addition, we propose to eliminate some taxes without environmental purposes, such as taxes on wind energy.

At a local level, in the context of a more comprehensive reform, it would make sense that the greatest of the municipal taxes (the property tax) depended on part on the energy certification of the property. As a specific reform it has been proposed that the vehicle circulation tax should have rates dependent on CO_2 emissions (and even other environmental criteria), rather than dependent on vehicle power (as it now occurs). This change would align this tax with the national vehicle registration tax, which is already dependent on CO_2 emissions. Moreover, municipalities could be allowed to introduce new congestion charges, which could make sense in selected cities, with the aim of favouring public transportation.

All these proposals could contribute to implementing an ecological fiscal reform in Spain, as well as bring about an increase in revenue. Substantial increases in energy and environmental taxation would not only reduce the public deficit but also eventually reduce the tax burden on work or consumption, thereby fostering job creation and improving the welfare of citizens.

NOTES

1. http://www.eea.europa.eu/media/newsreleases/eu-greenhouse-gas-emissions-more (accessed 17 November 2014).
2. http://epp.eurostat.ec.europa.eu/portal/page/portal/product_details/dataset?p_product_code=TSDCC310 (accessed 17 November 2014).
3. For example: Vivid Economics (2012), *Carbon taxation and fiscal consolidation: the potential of carbon pricing to reduce Europe's fiscal deficits*, Report prepared for the European Climate Foundation and Green Budget Europe, May 2012. http://www.vivideconomics.com/index.php/publications/fiscal-consolidation-and-carbon-fiscal-measures (accessed 17 November 2014); or Andersen, M.S., Barker, T., Christie, E., Ekins, P., Gerald, J.F., Jilkova, J., Junankar, S., Landesmann, M., Pollitt, H., Salmons, R., Scott, S. and Speck, S. (eds) (2007), *Competitiveness Effects of Environmental Tax Reforms (COMETR). Final report to the European Commission*. National Environmental Research institute, University of Aarhus, 543 pp. http://www.dmu.dk/Pub/COMETR_Final_Report.pdf (accessed 17 November 2014).
4. European Commission (2011), *Impact Assessment accompanying the Proposal for a Council Directive amending Directive 2003/96/EC restructuring the Community framework for the taxation of energy products and electricity (SEC(2011) 410)* http://ec.europa.eu/taxation_customs/resources/documents/taxation/sec_2011_409_impact_assesment_part2_en.pdf (accessed 17 November 2014).
5. Council of the European Union. *Recommendation for a Council Recommendation on Spain's 2013 national reform programme and delivering a Council opinion on*

Spain's stability programme for 2012–2016 {SWD(2013) 359 final} http://ec.europa.eu/europe2020/pdf/nd/csr2013_spain_en.pdf (accessed 17 November 2014).

6. Council of the European Union (2014), *Recommendation for a Council Recommendation on Spain's 2014 national reform programme and delivering a Council opinion on Spain's 2014 stability programme for 2012–2016* {SWD(2014) 410 final} http://ec.europa.eu/europe2020/pdf/csr2014/csr2014_spain_en.pdf (accessed 17 November 2014).

7. COM (2011) 112: *A roadmap for moving to a competitive low carbon economy in 2050* (8 March 2011) http://eur-lex.europa.eu/resource.html?uri=cellar:5db26ecc-ba4e-4de2-ae08-dba649109d18.0002.03/DOC_2&format=PDF (accessed 17 November 2014).

8. Agencia Tributaria (2012), *Impuesto sobre hidrocarburos 2011. Estudio relativo al año 2011* (Tax on fuels 2011 report) Madrid. http://www.agenciatributaria.es/AEAT.internet/Inicio_es_ES/La_Agencia_Tributaria/Memorias_y_estadisticas_tributarias/Estadisticas/Estadisticas_por_impuesto/Impuestos_especiales/Estudio_relativo_al_ano_2011/Estudio_relativo_al_ano_2011.shtml (accessed 17 November 2014).

9. Agencia Tributaria (2014), *Impuestos Especiales: Consumos e Ingresos* http://www.agenciatributaria.es (accessed 17 November 2014).

10. Agencia Tributaria (2010), *Impuesto Especial sobre determinados Medios de Transporte* http://www.agenciatributaria.es/static_files/AEAT/Aduanas/Contenidos_Privados/Impuestos_especiales/Estudio_relativo_2010/7_MEDIOS_TRANSPORTE.docx (accessed 17 November 2014).

11. Larrea Basterra, M., Puig Ventosa, I., Álvarez Pelegry, E., Calaf Forn, M., Jofra Sora, M. and Orena Domínguez, A. (2014), *Revisión de los impuestos energéticos en España.* CEPRiE Project. Fundación Deusto, Fundació ENT, Universidad del País Vasco, Green Budget Europe http://fundacioent.cat/images/stories/ENT/pdf/revisin%20impuestos%20energticos%20espaa.pdf (accessed 17 November 2014).

12. Idem.

13. Idem.

14. Idem.

15. Labandeira, X., López-Otero, X. and Picos, F. (2009), *La fiscalidad energético-ambiental como espacio fiscal para las Comunidades Autónomas*, in Lago-Peñas, S., Martínez-Vázquez, J. (eds), *La Asignación de Impuestos a las Comunidades Autónomas: Desafíos y Oportunidades.* Instituto de Estudios Fiscales, Madrid, pp. 237–268.
Labandeira, X. and Linares, P. (2013), *Impuestos energético-ambientales en España. Informe 2013.* Economics for Energy http://eforenergy.org/docpublicaciones/informes/Informe_Completo_EfE_2013.pdf (accessed 17 November 2014).

16. Labandeira, X. and Linares, P. (2013), *Impuestos energético-ambientales en España. Informe 2013.* Economics for Energy http://eforenergy.org/docpublicaciones/informes/Informe_Completo_EfE_2013.pdf (accessed 17 November 2014).

17. Lagares, M. et al. (2014), *Informe: Comisión de expertos para la reforma del sistema tributario español.* Madrid http://www.minhap.gob.es/es-ES/Prensa/En%20Portada/2014/Documents/Informe%20expertos.pdf (accessed 17 November 2014).

18. http://www.foes.de/internationales/green-budget-europe/gbe-projekte/ceprie/?lang=en (accessed 17 November 2014).

19. *Propuestas de enmiendas con finalidad ambiental a diferentes Proyectos de Ley y respuesta de los Grupos Parlamentarios.* Green Budget Europe and Fundació ENT http://fundacioent.cat/images/stories/ENT/pdf/enmiendas%20a%20los%20proyectos%20de%20ley%20sobre%20fiscalidad.pdf (accessed 17 November 2014).

20. The three bills sent to the Spanish Parliament and for which the amendments were prepared were:
Proyecto de Ley por la que se modifican la Ley 35/2006, de 28 de noviembre, del Impuesto sobre la Renta de las Personas Físicas, el texto refundido de la Ley del Impuesto sobre la Renta de no Residentes, aprobado por el Real Decreto Legislativo 5/2004, de 5 de marzo, y otras normas tributarias.
Proyecto de Ley por la que se modifica la Ley del Impuesto de Sociedades.

Proyecto de Ley por la que se modifican la Ley 37/1992, de 28 de diciembre, del Impuesto sobre el Valor Añadido, la Ley 20/1991, de 7 de junio, de modificación de los aspectos fiscales del régimen económico fiscal de Canarias, la Ley 38/1992, de 28 de diciembre, de Impuestos Especiales, y la Ley 16/2013, de 29 de octubre, por la que se establecen determinadas medidas en materia de fiscalidad medioambiental y se adoptan otras medidas tributarias y financieras.

Index

developing countries (and) 100–105
  common but differentiated
    responsibility 100–101
  the Enabling Clause 102
  flexibility of commitments, action
    and use of policy instruments
    103
  least developed (LDC) 100 *see also*
    United Nations (UN)
  problems with special and
    differential treatment provisions
    104–5
  provisions aimed at increasing trade
    opportunities of 102–3
  provisions relating to least-developed
    countries 104
  provisions for safeguarding interests
    of 103
  special and differential treatment
    provisions 102
  technical assistance 103–4
  transitional time periods 103
developments and opportunities for an
  ecological tax reform in Spain *see*
  Spain
Distelkamp, M. 120
*Dominican Republic – Measures
  Affecting the Importation and
  International Sale of Cigarettes* 98
Durban Platform 77

Economic Co-operation and
  Development, Organisation for
  (OECD) 5, 18, 208
  countries 112
    constraints on coal use in 134
    Environmental Tax Group 203
    and indirect consumption taxes 112
Edenhofer, O. 76
Ekins, P. 13, 112, 196–7
Elgie, S. 6
Elsworth, R. 64
emission reduction units (ERUs) 70
Environmental Protection Agencies 39
environmental tax reform (ETR)
  191–9, 202–4 *see also* Germany
  and Japan(ese)
  agenda 191–2
  and different approaches to be
    considered 202

future approaches to 192–3
  motivating progress on 193–202
environmentally harmful substances
  (EHS) reform 203
Erdmenger, C. 142, 152
Estonia 117
EU emission trading scheme: first
  evidence on Phase 3 63–75
  development of EU ETS framework
    (phases 1, 2 and 3) 63–6
    and Joint Implementation (JI)
    64
  empirical evidence 66–9
    database 66–7
    free allocation and emissions 67
    price development in the EU ETS
    67–9
  structural surplus of allowances in
    the EU ETS 69–71
EU emission trading schemes/system
  32–6, 38–9, 95, 159
  New Entrants Reserve (in Phase 3)
    71
EU ETS *see* EU emission trading
  schemes/system
Europe 2020 targets 209
European Allowances (EUAs) 70
European Aviation Allowances
  (EUAAs) 66
European Commission 203
  environmental levies 37
  Europe 2020 strategy 127
  European 20-20-20 targets 127
  Member States' NAPs 67
  National Allocation Plans (NAPs)
    64, 67, 69
  NER 300 program 71
  proposal for EU ETS Phase 4 71–2
*European Communities – Measures
  Affecting Asbestos and Asbestos-
  Combining Products* 98
European Environment Agency (EEA)
  203
European Monetary Union (EMU)
  163
European Parliament 116
European Semester 193, 203
European Union 32–3, 37–40 *see also*
  legislation (EU)
  agreement on 2030 climate and